Texts in Computer Science

Series Editors

David Gries, Department of Computer Science, Cornell University, Ithaca, NY, USA

Orit Hazzan⬥, Faculty of Education in Technology and Science, Technion—Israel Institute of Technology, Haifa, Israel

More information about this series at https://link.springer.com/bookseries/3191

Zhe Hou

Fundamentals of Logic and Computation

With Practical Automated Reasoning and Verification

 Springer

Zhe Hou ⓘ
Griffith University
Brisbane, Australia

ISSN 1868-0941   ISSN 1868-095X (electronic)
Texts in Computer Science
ISBN 978-3-030-87884-9   ISBN 978-3-030-87882-5   (eBook)
https://doi.org/10.1007/978-3-030-87882-5

This Springer imprint is published by the registered company Springer Nature Switzerland AG
The registered company address is: Gewerbestrasse 11, 6330 Cham, Switzerland

To all my past, present, and future students.

Preface

It is no coincidence that some universities, such as the University of Pennsylvania and the Australian National University, have a "Logic and Computation" research group, and many offer courses under the same name. The fields of logic and computation are intrinsically related to each other, although the connection has only been made explicit since 1980.

Despite that there are plenty of excellent courses and material about logic and computation around the world, most of them treat the two topics separately. My personal favourites are John Harrison's "Handbook of Practical Logic and Automated Reasoning" and Hopcroft, Motwani and Ullman's "Introduction to Automata Theory, Languages, and Computation", both of which heavily inspire this book. It is also difficult to find a single course that delivers theories of the two topics with practical exercises in modern tools. This book aims to address the two problems by compressing and unifying important concepts of the two areas and providing exercises in widely-used software applications. We give a transition from logic to computation via linear temporal logic and state machines.

The first half of the course is accompanied by exercises in Isabelle/HOL, which is a popular and user-friendly theorem prover. The second half of the course involves modelling and verification in Process Analysis Toolkit (PAT), a feature-rich model checker based on Hoare's Communicating Sequential Processes. This book also provides entry-level tutorials for Isabelle/HOL and PAT. The hybrid skill set of practical theorem proving and model checking should be helpful for the future of readers should they pursue a research career or engineering in formal methods.

This course has 21 hours of lectures and 20 hours of tutorials/labs—every section corresponds to 1 hour of lecture and 1 hour of lab. The final chapter serves as the conclusion of the book and has no exercises. Sections in Part II of this book are noticeably longer than those in Part I, so they may require more hours. In reality, the user can allocate 6 hours of lectures for each of Chaps. 4, 5, and 2 hours for Chap. 6, thus totalling 26 hours of lectures. The user can easily add more hours by giving more examples or providing a review lecture at the end of the term. For exercises, there are many examples of Isabelle/HOL theories in the Archive of Formal Proofs (https://www.isa-afp.org), and many examples of PAT models built into the software, should the user decide to extend the hours of labs. I also recommend devising large group projects on formal verification tasks during the course.

The road map of this book is illustrated below.

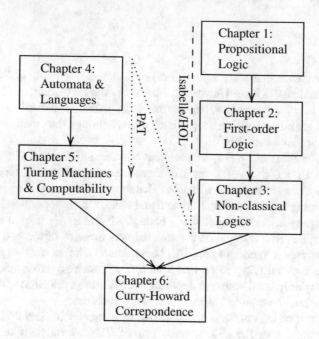

This book is written for two sets of audiences. Undergraduate students who are getting a Bachelor's degree in computer science should at least *pass* this course. Higher degree research (HDR) students who *excel* at this course should have the foundation to pursue a Ph.D. degree in computer science.

Brisbane, Australia   Zhe Hou
August 2021   z.hou@griffith.edu.au

Acknowledgements I would like to thank Rajeev Goré, who guided me with extraordinary patience and gave valuable comments on this book. I also want to thank Paulo de Souza and Jin Song Dong for their incredible support on this textbook project. I want to thank my family most of all because none of the wonderful things would happen without you.

Contents

Part I
Logic

Introduction to Logic

Logic, in the broad sense, is the study of valid reasoning. It is a cross-disciplinary subject involving philosophy, mathematics, computer science, and artificial intelligence. Logical reasoning takes many forms. Historically, humans have been reasoning in informal natural languages.

> All men are mortal.
> Socrates is a man.
> Therefore, Socrates is mortal.

An evolution of the above reasoning is focused on the form of the sentence rather than the content. Aristotle (384BC–322BC)'s syllogistic arguments are often in the above three-line form of a major premise, a minor premise, and a conclusion. Abstracting the meaning away and looking at the pattern of objects, we can express the above reasoning in a more symbolic form:

> All X are Y.
> a is an X.
> Therefore, a is Y.

And we know that every inference of the above form is valid.

Leibniz (1646–1716) pushed the notion of symbolism further by attempting to find a universal language that abstracts everything and a calculus of reasoning with some mechanisation to decide the truth of assertions in the language. Two hundred years later, Hilbert's program targeted a related task of capturing mathematics in consistent and complete theories. Later in the 1930s, Gödel and Turing et al. showed that Leibniz and Hilbert were far too ambitious. However, the idea of formalising reasoning using abstract symbols laid the foundation of *automated reasoning*. After all, machines are best at pattern matching and symbolic manipulations.

© The Author(s), under exclusive license to Springer Nature Switzerland AG 2021
Z. Hou, *Fundamentals of Logic and Computation*, Texts in Computer Science,
https://doi.org/10.1007/978-3-030-87882-5_1

In Part I of this book, we will look at *symbolic logics*, which are formal languages of reasoning, and we will study them in the following aspects: syntax, semantics, and proof theory.

In the context of logic, the formal language is made up of a set of logical *formulae*. The *syntax* of a language defines the rules for generating well-formed formulae. We say a formula is *in the language* if it can be generated by the syntax; otherwise, it is not in the language. The *semantics* of a language gives the meaning of well-formed formulae. The semantics of a logic defines when a formula is true under what assumptions. The *proof theory* of a logic is a calculus of reasoning—it is often in the form of axioms and inference rules from which a logical derivation can be produced. We will revisit these concepts with concrete examples in the following chapters.

Goré argues that only two of the above components are essential for *defining* a logic—syntax and semantics, or syntax and proof theory. Either pair can determine which formulae are permitted in the language and which ones are logically valid.

$$\text{Logic} = \begin{cases} \text{syntax} + \text{semantics, or} \\ \text{syntax} + \text{proof theory.} \end{cases}$$

1.1 Boolean Algebra and Truth Tables

Let us begin with a simple example: Boolean algebra [1]. Boole's algebra concerns only two values: *true* and *false*. These values are often represented by $\top$ (pronounced "top") and $\bot$ (pronounced "bottom"), or 1 and 0, respectively, and they are *constants*. In contrast to constants, there are also *variables*, which we denote by $x, y, \cdots$.

Expressions (also called terms) in Boolean algebra are composed of variables and subexpressions (note the recursion) which are connected by *logical connectives* (also called logical operators). We will often use the Backus-Naur form (BNF) to define the syntax of languages. In the case of Boolean algebra, expressions are defined as follows:

Definition 1.1 (*Syntax of Boolean Expressions*)

$$E ::= 1 \mid 0 \mid x \mid \neg E \mid E \wedge E \mid E \vee E.$$

The above definition means that an expression can be a constant (1, 0), a variable $(x, y, \cdots)$, and other expressions (defined recursively) connected by $\neg$ (negation), $\wedge$ (conjunction) and $\vee$ (disjunction). Note that the symbol x in the above definition stands for an *arbitrary* variable, and E stands for an *arbitrary* expression. For instance, the two Es in $E \wedge E$ may refer to two different expressions, and $x \wedge y$ is an instance of this schema.

We call $\wedge$ and $\vee$ *binary* connectives because they take two operands, and $\neg$ an *unary* connective because it only takes one operand. We pronounce $x \wedge y$ as "x and y", $x \vee y$ as "x or y", and $\neg x$ as "not x".

The first three cases of the syntax, i.e., $1, 0$, and x, generate *atomic* expressions—those that cannot be broken down into smaller expressions. The last three cases, i.e., $\neg E$, $E \wedge E$ and $E \vee E$, generate *compound* expressions. Given a compound expression, say $E_1 \wedge E_2$, the *main/principal connective* is $\wedge$, and E_1 and E_2 are *subexpressions*.

Example 1.1

1. The expression x has no subexpressions.
2. The expression $(x \wedge (\neg z)) \vee y$ is a compound expression; its main connective is $\vee$, and $x \wedge (\neg z)$ and y are its subexpressions.
3. The expression $\neg(x \wedge y)$ is also a compound expression; its main connective is $\neg$, and $x \wedge y$ is its subexpression.

The term "subexpression" is transitive. For example, $A \wedge (\neg B)$ is a subexpression of $(A \wedge (\neg B)) \vee C$, and $\neg B$ is a subexpression of $A \wedge (\neg B)$, and $\neg B$ is also a subexpression of $(A \wedge (\neg B)) \vee C$. In this case, we say $\neg B$ is an *immediate subexpression* of $A \wedge (\neg B)$ but is *not* an immediate subexpression of $(A \wedge (\neg B)) \vee C$ as it is nested inside another subexpression.

The notion of expression is purely syntactical—it only describes what format is correct and what is not; it does not tell us what an expression *means*. We give the semantics of Boolean expressions below to understand their truth values.

Definition 1.2 (*Semantics of Boolean Expressions*) The semantics of $\wedge$, $\vee$, and $\neg$ is defined as follows, where E, E_1, and E_2 are Boolean expressions:

$$E_1 \wedge E_2 = \begin{cases} 1 & \text{if } E_1 = 1 \text{ and } E_2 = 1 \\ 0 & \text{otherwise} \end{cases}$$

$$E_1 \vee E_2 = \begin{cases} 0 & \text{if } E_1 = 0 \text{ and } E_2 = 0 \\ 1 & \text{otherwise} \end{cases}$$

$$\neg E = \begin{cases} 1 & \text{if } E = 0 \\ 0 & \text{otherwise} \end{cases}$$

Intuitively, when we say "E_1 and E_2" is true, we usually mean that *both* of the expressions are true. Formally, $E_1 \wedge E_2 = 1$ when both $E_1 = 1$ and $E_2 = 1$, and $E_1 \wedge E_2 = 0$ otherwise.

In English, the word "or" is ambiguous: E_1 or E_2 can be interpreted inclusively (E_1 or E_2 or both) or exclusively (E_1 or E_2 but not both), although the latter is often implied in daily usage. The now-standard sense in formal logic, on the other hand, takes the inclusive interpretation. A joke from "The IT Crowd" does follow the logical semantics:

-Roy: "···, was it Julie or Judy?"
-Moss: "Yes, one of those."

Formally, $E_1 \vee E_2 = 0$ when both $E_1 = 0$ and $E_2 = 0$, and $E_1 \vee E_2 = 1$ otherwise. The semantics of $\vee$ is equivalent to saying $E_1 \vee E_2 = 1$ when $E_1 = 1$ *or* $E_2 = 1$.

Negation naturally returns the opposite truth value of the negated expression. That is, $\neg E = 1$ when $E = 0$ and $\neg E = 0$ when $E = 1$.

Besides the above logical connectives, which are often called basic operations, there are also *secondary operations*: $\rightarrow$ (implication), $\oplus$ (exclusive or), and $\equiv$ (equivalence). They are secondary because they can be derived from the basic operations, as shown below.

Definition 1.3 The Boolean operators $\rightarrow$, $\oplus$, and $\equiv$ are defined as follows:

$$x \rightarrow y = (\neg x) \vee y$$
$$x \oplus y = (x \wedge (\neg y)) \vee ((\neg x) \wedge y)$$
$$x \equiv y = (x \wedge y) \vee ((\neg x) \wedge (\neg y)).$$

The implication in logic is also called *material implication*. It is only false when the left-hand side is true, and the right-hand side is false. This interpretation may cause some confusion when mixed with the daily usage of English. For example, the sentence

'The earth is flat' implies 'the movie Titanic doesn't exist.'

is logically true because the left-hand side is false.

Example 1.2 Consider the expression $E = (x \vee y) \rightarrow (x \wedge y)$.

- Under the variable assignment $x = 0$ and $y = 0$, the subexpression $x \vee y$ evaluates to 0, and the subexpression $x \wedge y$ also evaluates to 0. We convert this implication to $(\neg(x \vee y)) \vee (x \wedge y)$. The subexpression $\neg(x \vee y)$ is then 1. Finally, by the semantics of $\vee$, $1 \vee 0 = 1$, thus $E = 1$ under this assignment. When the implication is satisfied because the left-hand side is 0/false, we say the implication *vacuously holds*.
- If we assign 1 to x and 0 to y, then $x \vee y = 1$ and $\neg(x \vee y) = 0$. Also, $x \wedge y = 0$. Since $0 \vee 0 = 0$, we have $E = 0$ in this case.
- If both x and y are 1, then $x \vee y = x \wedge y = 1$. We do not need to check the truth value of $\neg(x \vee y)$ in this case because "anything or 1" gives 1, so $E = 1$ under this truth assignment.

Implication ($\rightarrow$) is a common operator in logic, and exclusive or (XOR, $\oplus$) is widely used in digital circuits. Definition 1.3 also introduces the equivalence operator, which at first glance may be confused with equality in mathematics. We distinguish them by giving their formal definitions below.

Equivalence is often denoted by $\equiv$, and equality is often denoted by $=$. By convention, $x \equiv y$ is pronounced "x is equal to y", and $x = y$ is pronounced "x equals y". Logically, $x \equiv y$ can be alternatively defined as $(x \to y) \wedge (y \to x)$. In the remainder of this book, we shall shorten "if and only if" as "iff", which is the equivalence relation in logic.

From an algebraic point of view, an equivalence relation is defined as follows.

Definition 1.4 (*Binary Relation*) A binary relation R between two sets X and Y is a subset of all possible pairs (x, y) such that $x \in X$ and $y \in Y$.[1] We say x is related to y by the relation R if and only if $(x, y) \in R$.

A binary relation over a set S is a special case of the above where $X = Y = S$. We often write a binary relation infix. For example, the "less than" relation $<$ over two integers x, y is written as $x < y$.

Definition 1.5 (*Equivalence Relation*) A binary relation $\sim$ over a set S is an equivalence relation if it satisfies the following properties for any $x, y, z \in S$:

reflexivity: $x \sim x$;
symmetry: if $x \sim y$ then $y \sim x$;
transitivity: if $x \sim y$ and $y \sim z$ then $x \sim z$.

Definition 1.6 (*Equality Relation*) A binary relation $\sim$ over a set S is an equality relation if it is an equivalence relation and additionally satisfies the following for any $x, y \in S$:

antisymmetry: if $x \sim y$ and $y \sim x$ then x and y are the same item in S (or in a slightly relaxed sense, they designate the same item).

The reader can see that equality is a special case of equivalence. Equality is quite unique in the sense that it is regarded as the *only* relation on a set that satisfies all the above four properties.

Example 1.3 To see an example of an equivalence relation which is not equality, consider the relation "has the same birthday as". Clearly, a person x has the same birthday as himself/herself, which means this relation obeys reflexivity. If x has the same birthday as y then vice versa, which means this relation is symmetric. If additionally y has the same birthday as z, then we deduce that x has the same birthday as z, which means this relation is transitive. So this relation satisfies reflexivity, symmetry, and transitivity. But x and y in the above example may not be the same person, so this is not an equality relation.

---

[1] Formally, "all possible pairs" of X and Y are given by the *Cartesian product* $X \times Y$ defined as $X \times Y = \{(x, y) \mid x \in X \text{ and } y \in Y\}$.

To reduce clutter, we shall assume that unary operators *bind tighter* than binary operators. For example, $\neg x \wedge y$ should be read as $(\neg x) \wedge y$ rather than $\neg(x \wedge y)$. Moreover, $\wedge$ and $\vee$ bind tighter than $\rightarrow$, which in turn binds tighter than $\equiv$ and $=$. For example, $x \wedge y \rightarrow y \vee z$ should be read as $(x \wedge y) \rightarrow (y \vee z)$.

Laws of Boolean algebra. As an alternative to semantics, Boolean algebra can be defined by a set of laws in the form of equations. Such equations can be used to simplify expressions or convert expressions to a specific format, both of which are useful when evaluating the truth value of expressions. A common set of laws is given below, where x, y, and z are arbitrary Boolean variables. These equations also hold when we globally substitute variables with Boolean expressions.

Associativity of $\vee$: $x \vee (y \vee z) = (x \vee y) \vee z$.
Associativity of $\wedge$: $x \wedge (x \wedge z) = (x \wedge y) \wedge z$.
Commutativity of $\vee$: $x \vee y = y \vee x$.
Commutativity of $\wedge$: $x \wedge y = y \wedge x$.
Distributivity of $\wedge$ over $\vee$: $x \wedge (y \vee z) = (x \wedge y) \vee (x \wedge z)$.
Identity for $\vee$: $x \vee 0 = x$.
Identity for $\wedge$: $x \wedge 1 = x$.
Annihilator for $\wedge$: $x \wedge 0 = 0$.
Annihilator for $\vee$: $x \vee 1 = 1$.
Idempotence of $\vee$: $x \vee x = x$.
Idempotence of $\wedge$: $x \wedge x = x$.
Absorption 1: $x \wedge (x \vee y) = x$.
Absorption 2: $x \vee (x \wedge y) = x$.
Distributivity of $\vee$ over $\wedge$: $x \vee (y \wedge z) = (x \vee y) \wedge (x \vee z)$.
Complementation 1: $x \wedge \neg x = 0$.
Complementation 2: $x \vee \neg x = 1$.
Double negation: $\neg(\neg x) = x$.
De Morgan 1: $\neg(x \vee y) = \neg x \wedge \neg y$.
De Morgan 2: $\neg(x \wedge y) = \neg x \vee \neg y$.

Example 1.4 If we interpret $\vee$ as $+$ and $\wedge$ as $\times$, the first 8 laws hold in ordinary algebra as well. For instance, identity for $\vee$ becomes

$$x + 0 = x,$$

and identity for $\wedge$ says

$$x \times 1 = x.$$

Annihilator for $\wedge$ is interpreted as

$$x \times 0 = 0.$$

On the other hand, the other laws of Boolean algebra may not hold in ordinary algebra. For instance,

$$x + 1 \neq 1,$$

for $x = 1$. And in general,

$$x \times x \neq x.$$

The above set of laws is *complete* in the sense that they entail all other equations in Boolean algebra. In fact, the subset of the first 16 laws is already complete. The study of the minimal complete set of laws eventually led to a single law that can derive all other equations in Boolean algebra:

$$\neg(\neg(\neg(x \vee y) \vee z) \vee \neg(x \vee \neg(\neg z \vee \neg(z \vee u)))) = z.$$

Example 1.5 Let E be the expression $((x \rightarrow y) \wedge (x \vee 1)) \rightarrow (y \wedge (z \wedge 1))$. We simplify E as follows:

1. By annihilator for $\vee$, $x \vee 1 = 1$, thus the expression is simplified to $((x \rightarrow y) \wedge 1) \rightarrow (y \wedge (z \wedge 1))$.
2. By identity for $\wedge$, $(x \rightarrow y) \wedge 1 = x \rightarrow y$, so the expression is now $(x \rightarrow y) \rightarrow (y \wedge (z \wedge 1))$.
3. Similarly, $z \wedge 1 = z$, so we have $(x \rightarrow y) \rightarrow (y \wedge z)$.
4. By the definition of $\rightarrow$, the above expression is equivalent to $\neg(\neg x \vee y) \vee (y \wedge z)$.
5. By De Morgan 1, we have $E = (x \wedge \neg y) \vee (y \wedge z)$.

One can still apply laws such as commutativity, but they do not remove logical operators any further.

As another example, let us prove that the single law is a correct equation.

Lemma 1.1 $\neg(\neg(\neg(x \vee y) \vee z) \vee \neg(x \vee \neg(\neg z \vee \neg(z \vee u)))) = z$

Proof The left-hand side of the single law can be simplified as follows:

$$\neg(\neg(\neg(x \vee y) \vee z) \vee \neg(x \vee \neg(\neg z \vee \neg(z \vee u))))$$

$= (\neg(x \vee y) \vee z) \wedge (x \vee \neg(\neg z \vee \neg(z \vee u)))$	(De Morgan 1)
$= ((\neg x \wedge \neg y) \vee z) \wedge (x \vee \neg(\neg z \vee \neg(z \vee u)))$	(De Morgan 1)
$= ((\neg x \wedge \neg y) \vee z) \wedge (x \vee \neg(\neg z \vee (\neg z \wedge \neg u)))$	(De Morgan 1)
$= ((\neg x \wedge \neg y) \vee z) \wedge (x \vee (z \wedge \neg(\neg z \wedge \neg u)))$	(De Morgan 1)
$= ((\neg x \wedge \neg y) \vee z) \wedge (x \vee (z \wedge (z \vee u)))$	(De Morgan 2)
$= ((\neg x \wedge \neg y) \vee z) \wedge (x \vee z)$	(Absorption 1)
$= (z \vee (\neg x \wedge \neg y)) \wedge (x \vee z)$	(Commutativity of $\vee$)
$= (z \vee (\neg x \wedge \neg y)) \wedge (z \vee x)$	(Commutativity of $\vee$)
$= z \vee ((\neg x \wedge \neg y) \wedge x)$	(Distributivity of $\vee$ over $\wedge$)
$= z \vee ((\neg y \wedge \neg x) \wedge x)$	(Commutativity of $\wedge$)
$= z \vee (\neg y \wedge (\neg x \wedge x))$	(Associativity of $\wedge$)
$= z \vee (\neg y \wedge (x \wedge \neg x))$	(Commutativity of $\wedge$)
$= z \vee (\neg y \wedge 0)$	(Complementation 1)
$= z \vee 0$	(Annihilator for $\wedge$)
$= z$	(Identity for $\vee$).

So the left-hand side equals the right-hand side.   □

Table 1.1 The truth table for logical operations

x	y	$\neg x$	$x \wedge y$	$x \vee y$	$x \rightarrow y$	$x \oplus y$	$x \equiv y$
0	0	1	0	0	1	0	1
0	1	1	0	1	1	1	0
1	0	0	0	1	0	1	0
1	1	0	1	1	1	0	1

Truth tables are a common means to determine the truth value of Boolean expressions. We give the truth table for usual logical operations in Table 1.1.

Table 1.1 has a header row, which contains Boolean expressions where the first two columns contain only the atomic expressions x and y, and the other columns, after the double vertical lines, contain various compound expressions that can be built up from x and y. Each row then begins with one possible combination of the truth values 0 and 1, which can be assigned to x and y. Each subsequent column then shows the truth value of the compound expression in the header for this particular combination of truth values for x and y. For example, the first row captures the case when both x and y take the value 0, and the third column tells us that, in this case, the compound expression $\neg x$ takes the value 1 while the fourth row tells us that, in this case, the compound expression $x \wedge y$ takes the value 0.

To make a truth table for an expression, we recursively break the expression down into subexpressions and eventually decompose it to constants and variables. We write each constant, variable, and subexpression as an item in the header row in an order that puts the smallest item in the leftmost place, and we write the target expression as the last item. That is, if E is a subexpression of E', then E is placed to the left of E'.

The truth values of constants are quite straightforward: the column for 0 has all 0s, and the column for 1 has all 1s. For variables, we simply list all the possible assignments. This means that if there are n variables in the largest expression, then there should be 2^n rows of truth values.

Finally, we compute the truth values of an expression based on the truth values of its subexpressions using Table 1.1 by looking up the column for the main connective.

Given an expression, the truth values in the corresponding column have the following three cases:

- If all the values in the column are 1s, then the expression is *valid*, i.e., it is true under *all* assignments. A valid formula is true under all interpretations, variable assignments, and assumptions. Such an expression is often called a *tautology*. For instance, the expression $x \vee \neg x$ is a tautology because it is true regardless of the value of x.
- If *some* of the values in the column are 1s, then the expression is *satisfiable*, i.e., it is true under *some* assignments. For example, the expression $x \wedge y$ is satisfiable with the truth assignment of $x = 1$ and $y = 1$.

- If all the values in the column are 0s, then the expression is *unsatisfiable*, i.e., it is *false* under all assignments. Such an expression is often called a "contradiction". For example, $x \wedge \neg x$ is unsatisfiable because it is false under all assignments of x.

Clearly, a valid expression is satisfiable. If an expression is not valid, we say it is *invalid*, in which case it may be either satisfiable or unsatisfiable. For example, none of the expressions in Table 1.1 is valid, but they can all be satisfied by some variable assignments.

Example 1.6 Consider the expression $(1 \wedge x) \to (x \vee y)$. We build the truth table below to check the validity of the expression.

1	x	y	$1 \wedge x$	$x \vee y$	$(1 \wedge x) \to (x \vee y)$
1	0	0	0	0	1
1	0	1	0	1	1
1	1	0	1	1	1
1	1	1	1	1	1

For instance, assuming the first 5 columns have been filled, we fill the column of the last expression row by row. In the first row, both the subexpressions $1 \wedge x$ and $x \vee y$ are 0s. Using the implication column of Table 1.1, we know that when both sides of the implication are 0s, the result is 1, which is the truth value of the first row of our final expression.

The expression $(1 \wedge x) \to (x \vee y)$ is valid because its column has all 1s. On the other hand, the subexpression $x \vee y$ is invalid but satisfiable.

Example 1.7 We give the truth table for the expression $x \to (x \wedge y)$ as follows:

x	y	$x \wedge y$	$x \to (x \wedge y)$
0	0	0	1
0	1	0	1
1	0	0	0
1	1	1	1

This expression is satisfiable, and it is satisfied by the variable assignments of row 1, 2, and 4.

Example 1.8 We give the truth table for the expression $x \wedge \neg x$ as follows:

x	$\neg x$	$x \wedge \neg x$
0	1	0
1	0	0

This expression is unsatisfiable as it has a 0 in every row.

Example 1.9 If we take any of the laws of Boolean algebra and change the equal sign $=$ to $\equiv$, then the resultant Boolean expression is valid. The reader can check this by building truth tables for such expressions.

Exercises

1.1 Which of the following are well-formed Boolean expressions?

1. $x \neg y$
2. $\neg 1$
3. $\neg x \rightarrow y$
4. $\neg \neg x \rightarrow y$
5. $\wedge \neg x \vee y$
6. $(x \wedge \neg x) \vee 0$

1.2 For each of the following Boolean expressions, give a real-life example which you think is a true statement:

1. $x \rightarrow y$
2. $x \vee y$
3. $x \oplus y$

1.3 Compute the truth tables for the following Boolean expressions:

1. $\neg \neg x \rightarrow x$
2. $x \wedge y \rightarrow x \wedge z$
3. $x \wedge (y \vee z) \rightarrow (x \wedge y) \vee (x \wedge z)$
4. $x \wedge \neg x$
5. $x \vee \neg x$
6. $\neg (x \wedge y) \rightarrow \neg x \vee \neg y$

1.4 In the above question, which expressions are valid? Which ones are satisfiable? Which ones are unsatisfiable? Which ones are invalid?

1.2 Propositional Logic

There are many propositional logics. The one we study here is arguably the most common. Still, sometimes to distinguish it from the others, we explicitly call it *classical propositional logic*.[2] It involves logical formulae called propositions which

---

[2] It is also called zeroth-order logic.

can be either true or false. As in Boolean algebra, there are logical constants, i.e., truth ($\top$) and falsity ($\bot$). *Atomic formulae* are those without a logical connective and often denoted by $p, q, r, \cdots$. *Compound formulae* are built from constants and atomic formulae using logical connectives. We denote a formula by $F, A, B, \cdots$.

Definition 1.7 (*Syntax of Propositional Logic*) The syntax of propositional logic is given below, where F stands for an arbitrary formula and p is an arbitrary atomic formula.

$$F ::= \top \mid p \mid \neg F \mid F \wedge F.$$

Definition 1.8 (*Semantics of Propositional Logic*) The semantics of propositional logic is given as follows:

$\top$ is true
$\neg A$ is true iff A is false
$A \wedge B$ is true iff A is true and B is true

The reader may notice that we have only presented a subset of the syntax of Boolean algebra, though the semantics for those operations is consistent in the two formalisms. The reason is that the above syntax and semantics are sufficient to derive the other ones in the logic. For example, we can obtain the following "derived" constant and connectives, where we write $:: =$ for "is defined as":

$$\bot :: = \neg \top$$
$$A \vee B :: = \neg(\neg A \wedge \neg B)$$
$$A \to B :: = \neg(A \wedge \neg B).$$

The semantics for the above syntax is defined as follows:

$\bot$ is false
$A \vee B$ is true iff A is true or B is true
$A \to B$ is true iff A is false or B is true

As a re-cap, the equivalence connective $A \leftrightarrow B$ (pronounced "A iff B" in the context of logic) can be defined as $(A \to B) \wedge (B \to A)$.

Historically people have used many different symbols to represent common logical operations. An incomplete summary of common notations is given in Table 1.2.

It can be observed that Boolean algebra and classical propositional logic have identical syntax and semantics. Some scholars deem the latter a modern version of the former [2], while others view Boolean algebra as a purely algebraic system characterised by a set of algebraic laws. Some may argue that classical propositional logic is one of many mathematical structures that satisfy the laws of Boolean algebra.

Table 1.2 Common notations for the syntax of propositional logic

In this book	Other notations in the literature
$\top$	$1, T, True, true$
$\bot$	$0, F, False, false$
$\neg A$	$-A, \sim A, \overline{A}, !A$
$A \wedge B$	$A \times B, A \cdot B, A \cap B, A \& B, A \&\& B$
$A \vee B$	$A + B, A \cup B, A \mid B, A \parallel B$
$A \rightarrow B$	$A \Rightarrow B, A \supset B$
$A \leftrightarrow B$	$A \equiv B, A \sim B$

For example, operations on a set also form a Boolean algebra under the interpretation that $\neg$ is set complement, $\wedge$ is intersection ($\cap$), $\vee$ is union ($\cup$), and $\rightarrow$ is the superset relation ($\supset$). Such an interpretation that maps elements of a system to those in another system in a *one-to-one* manner, meanwhile preserving the structure of the two systems, is called an *isomorphism*. This book does not distinguish Boolean algebra and classical propositional logic; we just consider them as isomorphic formalisms.

Given a propositional logic formula, we can assign a truth value to each atomic proposition and obtain a truth value for the formula. Such an assignment can be viewed as a function, often called *truth assignment* or *valuation*, that maps propositions to either true or false.

Definition 1.9 (*Formula Validity*)   A propositional logic formula is valid if *every* truth assignment makes it true.

Definition 1.10 (*Formula Satisfiability*)   A propositional logic formula is satisfiable if *some* truth assignment makes it true.

In the context of logic, *axioms* are a set of formulae that are assumed valid. Axioms are often used as starting points of a proof. Such a formula is often in the form of $A \rightarrow B$, which says that if we can find anything that matches the form of A, then we can derive a formula of form B. We can apply axioms to derive other formulae by globally substituting each symbol in the axiom with another formula.

Example 1.10   If $A \rightarrow A$ is an axiom, then we can globally replace every A into another formula, such as $B \wedge C$, and derive $(B \wedge C) \rightarrow (B \wedge C)$.

In addition to axioms, we may sometimes also use *inference rules* in derivations. An inference rule often consists of a number of *premises* written above a line and a *conclusion* written below a line. For example, the famous *Modus Ponens* (MP) rule can be written as follows.

Definition 1.11 (*Modus Ponens*)

$$\frac{A \qquad A \to B}{B} \, _{MP}$$

This rule has two premises: A and $A \to B$. It requires finding two formulae that match the form of the two premises, respectively, and then we can derive a formula of the form B. The space above the line can be read as a "conjunction", i.e., both premises are needed to derive the conclusion. Since conjunction is commutative, the order of premises does not matter. We can apply rules to derive formulae via global substitutions.

Example 1.11 If we have already derived $B \wedge C$ and $(B \wedge C) \to D$, then we can globally replace every A by $B \wedge C$ and every B by D in the MP rule to derive D. This application of MP is given as follows:

$$\frac{B \wedge C \qquad B \wedge C \to D}{D} \, _{MP}$$

A finite set of axioms and inference rules is often referred to as a *proof theory* or a *proof calculus*. A proof theory is said to be *complete* for a logic if it can derive *all* the valid formulae in the logic. It is *sound* if it cannot derive contradictions. There can be many sound and complete proof theories for a logic.

Definition 1.12 (*Hilbert's Calculus*) Hilbert's axiomatic system for classical propositional logic consists of the MP rule and the axioms given below.

$$A \to (B \to A)$$
$$(A \to (B \to C)) \to (B \to (A \to C))$$
$$(B \to C) \to ((A \to B) \to (A \to C))$$
$$A \to (\neg A \to B)$$
$$(A \to B) \to ((\neg A \to B) \to B).$$

Hilbert is often regarded as the pioneer of modern proof theory, and proof theory of the above form of axioms are often called *Hilbert(-style) calculi*. The above axioms are found to be equivalent to the following three, which are due to Łukasiewicz and are also sound and complete when combined with MP.

Definition 1.13 (*Łukasiewicz's Axioms*)

$$A \to (B \to A)$$
$$(A \to (B \to C)) \to ((A \to B) \to (A \to C))$$
$$(\neg A \to \neg B) \to (B \to A).$$

A *proof* is a series of axiom or rule applications. The process of finding proofs is called *proof search*. A formula that can be proved in a proof theory is a *theorem* of the proof theory. If a proof theory is sound, then every theorem of the proof theory is valid; if the proof theory is additionally complete, then the set of theorems is exactly the set of valid formulae. The activity of proving theorems is called *theorem proving*. Let us see an example of proving $A \to A$ using Łukasiewicz's axioms.

Lemma 1.2 $A \to A$ *is valid in classical propositional logic.*[3]

Proof We begin by choosing the second axiom of Łukasiewicz:

$$(A \to (B \to C)) \to ((A \to B) \to (A \to C))$$

and substitute each B with $B \to A$, and substitute each C with A. We then obtain Fact 1.

Fact 1: $(A \to ((B \to A) \to A)) \to ((A \to (B \to A)) \to (A \to A))$.

Next, we choose the first axiom:

$$A \to (B \to A)$$

and replace each B by $B \to A$, then we get Fact 2.

Fact 2: $A \to ((B \to A) \to A)$.

Note that the above formula matches the left-hand side of Fact 1. By the Modus Ponens rule, we can derive Fact 3.

Fact 3: $(A \to (B \to A)) \to (A \to A)$.

Now, the left-hand side of Fact 3 is exactly the first axiom. Using these two and the Modus Ponens rule again, we obtain

$$A \to A,$$

which is what we need to prove.   □

We can also derive deduction rules by having assumptions. For example, the rule for transitivity of implication is written as follows:

$$\frac{A \to B \qquad B \to C}{A \to C} \; trans$$

Lemma 1.3 *The rule* trans *can be derived from Łukasiewicz's calculus.*

---

[3] In writing, we usually only refer to very important and significant findings as theorems and refer to less important ones or intermediate steps as lemmas.

Proof We prove that this deduction rule is correct by assuming that the premises are true and using them to prove the conclusion. We abbreviate "Assumption" as "Assum" given below.

$$\text{Assum 1: } A \to B$$
$$\text{Assum 2: } B \to C.$$

We take the first axiom of Łukasiewicz and substitute every A with $B \to C$ and every B with A, and obtain the fact given below.

$$\text{Fact 1: } (B \to C) \to (A \to (B \to C))$$

Applying the MP rule on Assum 2 and Fact 1, we have the fact as follows:

$$\text{Fact 2: } A \to (B \to C)$$

Applying the MP rule again but on Fact 2 and the second axiom of Łukasiewicz, we obtain another fact.

$$\text{Fact 3: } (A \to B) \to (A \to C)$$

Finally, we apply the MP rule on Assum 1 and Fact 3, then have

$$A \to C,$$

which is the conclusion of the deduction rule. ◻

The reader can see that proof search is essentially a process of pattern matching and substitution, and the key to success is to know *when* to apply *which* axiom or rule. Unfortunately, even for a trivial formula such as $A \to A$, finding a proof using Hilbert-style calculi requires some skills and familiarity with the calculi. If we choose a different axiom in a step, we may not be able to finish the proof. These difficulties prompt an investigation of other proof theories that support easier proof search in the following senses:

- it should be easy to know which rule to use in each step;
- if multiple rules are applicable, any choice should not lead to unsuccessful proofs unless the formula is not provable;
- the proof should be as short (in terms of the number of steps) as possible.

The above points are essential for devising a *systematic* proof search strategy towards *automated reasoning*.

Exercises

1.5 Prove using truth tables that the definitions of derived constant and connectives ($\bot$, $\vee$, $\to$) are correct.

Instruction. For a definition $A :: = B$, you will need to prove that $A \to B$ and $B \to A$, or alternatively, $A \leftrightarrow B$ (i.e., $A \equiv B$).

1.6 Can you simplify the syntax of propositional logic defined on Page 13 even further? Prove that your simplification is correct.

Instruction. You can define the logical connective "nand" ($\uparrow$) as $A \uparrow B :: = \neg(A \wedge B)$, and use it to express all other connectives. For example, $\neg A$ can be expressed as $A \uparrow A$, and $A \wedge B$ can be expressed as $(A \uparrow B) \uparrow (A \uparrow B)$. Try to do the same for $\top$, $\bot$, $\vee$ and $\rightarrow$.

Alternatively, we can define the logical connective "nor" ($\downarrow$) as $A \downarrow B :: = \neg(A \vee B)$, and use it to express all other connectives.

1.7 Prove $A \rightarrow A$ using Hilbert's axiom system.

1.8 Prove $A \rightarrow (\neg A \rightarrow B)$ using Łukasiewicz's axiom system.

1.9 Do the above proofs in Isabelle/HOL.[4]

Instruction. Once you have downloaded Isabelle/HOL, put it in your preferred directory and run the application. It will initialise some libraries when it runs for the first time. Then you will be presented with a text editor. Copy the following into the editor and save the file as *file_name.thy*. Note that the name of the file must match the name of the theory. You can obviously replace file_name with your preferred name.

```
1  theory file_name
2  imports Main
3  begin
4
5  end
```

Then you can write your own code between "begin" and "end".

The table below shows how to type some basic symbols in Isabelle/HOL. You may need to select symbols from a drop-down menu which will be activated as you type. See more information in tutorials such as "prog-prove" and "main" in the documentation directory located at the left border of the editor.

---

[4] Download from https://isabelle.in.tum.de.

Symbols	Meaning	In Isabelle/HOL
⊤	true	True
⊥	false	False
¬	not	~ or \not
∧	and	/\
∨	or	\/
→	implies	-->
↔	iff	<-->
↑	to be defined	\up
↓	to be defined	\down

For instance, to prove the formula $\bot \rightarrow \neg\top$, type the following:

```
1 lemma "False --> \not True"
```

Note that after typing \not, you can select ¬ in the drop-down menu. The keyword "lemma" creates a proof state for the formula (called "goal"). You can monitor the proof state in the output panel by ticking the box for "Proof state". You need to close the proof state by giving a valid proof before you can write another lemma; otherwise, you will see errors. Formulae as simple as the above example can be proved via the proof tactic "simp". To use the tactic, write "apply simp". You should see that the proof state says "No subgoals!" after you apply "simp". To finish the proof, write "done". The complete Isabelle/HOL proof for the above lemma is given as follows.

```
1 lemma "False --> \not True"
2 apply simp
3 done
```

We often abbreviate the last tactic application as "by xxx", which is equivalent to "apply xxx done". Thus, the above code can be shortened as follows.

```
1 lemma "False --> \not True"
2 by simp
```

The ↑ operator can be defined with the following code:

```
1 definition nand{:}{:} "bool => bool => bool" (infixr "\up" 35)
2 where "A \up B \equiv \not (A /\ B)"
```

This definition defines an operator (or a non-recursive function) called "nand". The "bool => bool => bool" part gives the type signature of the function: it takes two input arguments of type "bool" and "bool", respectively, and returns an output of type "bool". The "(infixr"\up" 35)" part specifies that this operator can be written as an infix operator, i.e., written between the two input arguments, and it associates to the right-hand side. The number 35 specifies the level of binding for the operator. For example, the level of binding for → is 25 in Isabelle/HOL, so ↑ binds tighter than →. The last part "A \up B \equiv \not (A /\B)" gives the actual definition, where "\equiv" (≡) is *not* the ↔ logical connective but a special symbol in Isabelle/HOL for giving definitions, much like the :: = we used previously.

When proving formulae with user-defined symbols such as ↑, you may need to unfold the definition to let Isabelle/HOL know what the symbol means. To unfold a definition "xxx", we can write "unfolding xxx_def". For example, the formula $\neg A \leftrightarrow A \uparrow A$ can be proved as follows.

```
1  lemma "\not A <--> A \up A"
2  unfolding nand_def by simp
```

Continue and finish the other proofs.

1.3   Natural Deduction for Propositional Logic

Truth tables are the first method of evaluating logical formulae we introduced in this book. Its construction is quite systematic, but the number of rows grows exponentially with the number of variables (i.e., atomic propositions) in the formula, which makes this method inefficient in complex tasks. On the other hand, while Hilbert's axiomatic proof calculus may yield shorter proofs, it is non-trivial to obtain a systematic proof search procedure. Despite the important role of Hilbert's axioms in mathematical reasoning in the early twentieth century, Łukasiewicz advocated a more natural treatment of logic in 1926. In 1934, Gentzen developed another proof calculus that aimed to mimic humans' natural way of reasoning. The term "natürliches Schließen", which translates to "natural deduction", is coined in his dissertation [3]. This proof calculus is often referred to as NK.[5]

The natural deduction system has two flavours of inference rules: the introduction rules and the elimination rules. We present them in a similar fashion as the Modus Ponens rule on Page 14: we write the premises above a horizontal line and the conclusion below the line. We write the name of the rule on the right side of the line. An *introduction* rule combines the facts of the premises and introduces a logical connective in the conclusion. On the contrary, an *elimination* rule looks at a logical connective in the premises and removes it in the conclusion.

The rule for ⊤. We do not need any premise to derive ⊤, as it is just true. Therefore, the simplest introduction rule is to introduce ⊤ from nothing.

$$\frac{}{\top} \ {\scriptstyle TI}$$

This rule is often called "unit" or $\top I$. Since it has no premises, it is considered as an axiom, i.e., we can use it to initiate a proof.

In a proof, we can introduce assumptions and reason under them. However, we need to ensure that all the assumptions are *discharged* before we complete the proof.

---

[5] Stands for "Natürliche Kalkül". The NK system includes rules for classical first-order logic. We only present the subset for classical propositional logic in this section.

We will be explicit when we discharge an assumption in a rule. To facilitate a clean presentation, every time we introduce an assumption, we give it a different name $(a_1, a_2, \cdots)$ and put the assumption in square brackets, e.g., $[a_1 : A]$. We do not need any premise to introduce an assumption, so this can be written as follows:

$$\overline{[a_1 : A]}$$

Thus, we can also start a proof by introducing assumptions. This and the $\top I$ rule are the only two ways to start a proof in NK.

The rules for $\bot$. Falsity does not hold. Recall that the semantics of implication $A \rightarrow B$ means that if A is false, then $A \rightarrow B$ is vacuously true. Similarly, $\bot \rightarrow A$ holds for any A. Thus, if we assume that $\bot$ holds, then we can derive anything, even if it is absurd. This is expressed in the $\bot$ elimination rule below, where A is an *arbitrary* formula.

$$\frac{\bot}{A} \, {\scriptstyle \bot E}$$

Another interesting rule related to $\bot$ is called *reductio ad absurdum* (RAA). It says that if we assume that $\neg A$ is true and we deduce $\bot$, then we know that the assumption must be false, and therefore, A must be true.

$$[a : \neg A]$$
$$\vdots$$
$$\frac{\bot}{A} \, {\scriptstyle RAA, \, \text{discharge } a}$$

Once we obtain the conclusion of the rule RAA, we can *discharge* the assumption—this is written explicitly next to the name of the rule. The rule RAA is essentially "proof by contradiction".

The rules for $\neg$. In the literature, $\neg A$ is often considered an abbreviation of $A \rightarrow \bot$, thus the rules for $\neg$ bears some resemblance with the rules for $\bot$. To deduce $\neg A$ (i.e., introduce $\neg$ in the conclusion), we can assume that A is true and try to derive $\bot$. If the derivation is successful, we can conclude that $\neg A$ holds and *discharge* the assumption. This is expressed in the $\neg I$ rule as follows

$$[a : A]$$
$$\vdots$$
$$\frac{\bot}{\neg A} \, {\scriptstyle \neg I, \, \text{discharge } a}$$

The $\neg I$ rule is sometimes presented in the following form:

$$[a : A]$$

$$\vdots$$

$$\frac{p}{\neg A} \ \neg I', \text{discharge } a$$

where p is an arbitrary proposition. The reasoning is similar to the $\bot E$ rule: if we can derive *anything* from the assumption, then the assumption must be false, so we can deduce the opposite of the assumption. Note the discharge of the assumption similarly to the $\neg I$ form.

The $\neg E$ rule also comes in two forms in the literature. One way to eliminate $\neg$ is simply to convert it to the implication form, as shown below.

$$\frac{\neg A}{A \to \bot} \ \neg E$$

Another way to eliminate $\neg A$ is to also derive A, and then conclude that there is a contradiction, from which we can derive anything. This is expressed in the alternative rule $\neg E'$ below, where B is an arbitrary formula.

$$\frac{\neg A \quad A}{B} \ \neg E'$$

In the above rule, there are two premises: $\neg A$ and A.

Although the rules for $\neg$ have many forms, technically, only one form is needed for the completeness of the proof theory. The reader can choose any one form for each rule and stick with it.

The rules for $\to$. It is straightforward to introduce an implication: if we can assume that A is true and deduce B, then we can conclude that $A \to B$ is true and *discharge* the assumption. This reasoning is written in the $\to I$ rule as follows:

$$[a : A]$$

$$\vdots$$

$$\frac{B}{A \to B} \ \to I, \text{discharge } a$$

Do not confuse this rule with the $\neg I'$ rule, in which p is arbitrary. In the $\to I$ rule, B is a formula specific to the derivation. In other words, every occurrence of B in the $\to I$ rule application must designate the same formula.

The elimination of an implication takes the form of Modus Ponens: if we know that A is true, and we know that $A \to B$ is true, then we can conclude that B is true. This is given in the rule as follows:

$$\frac{A \quad A \to B}{B} \ \to E$$

Naturally, people often call this rule MP.

The rules for $\vee$. To introduce $\vee$, we only need to derive one of the disjuncts. In other words, if we know that A is true, then we can conclude $A \vee B$. Similarly, if we know that B is true, we can also conclude $A \vee B$. These are given in the two rules below to introduce $\vee$ from the left and right sides, respectively.

$$\frac{A}{A \vee B}\ {\vee}I_l \qquad\qquad \frac{B}{A \vee B}\ {\vee}I_r$$

The elimination of a $\vee$ is essentially a proof by cases. We know that $A \vee B$ is true, and we see what we can derive in each case. If assuming A is true, we can derive C, and assuming B is true, we can also derive C, then we know that C must be true in any case because at least one of A and B is true. Thus, we conclude with C and *discharge* both assumptions. This rule is given as follows:

$$\frac{A \vee B \qquad \begin{array}{c}[a_1 : A] \\ \vdots \\ C\end{array} \qquad \begin{array}{c}[a_2 : B] \\ \vdots \\ C\end{array}}{C}\ {\vee}E,\,\text{discharge } a_1 \text{ and } a_2$$

The reader may notice that the sub-proof by cases matches the derivation in the $\rightarrow I$ rule. Thus, sometimes the $\vee E$ rule is presented in the following form by applying the $\rightarrow I$ rule on the last two branches:

$$\frac{A \vee B \qquad A \rightarrow C \qquad B \rightarrow C}{C}\ {\vee}E'$$

The rules for $\wedge$. To introduce $\wedge$, we need to obtain both conjuncts. This is given in the rule as follows:

$$\frac{A \qquad B}{A \wedge B}\ {\wedge}I$$

On the other hand, if we know that $A \wedge B$ is true, we can eliminate the conjunction and obtain either of the conjuncts.

$$\frac{A \wedge B}{A}\ {\wedge}E_l \qquad\qquad \frac{A \wedge B}{B}\ {\wedge}E_r$$

We put together the deduction rules for propositional logic in Fig. 1.1.

The above subset of rules in Gentzen's natural deduction system NK is sound and complete for classical propositional logic. We will give the following theorems without proofs:

$$\frac{}{\top}\ \top I \qquad \frac{\bot}{A}\ \bot E \qquad \begin{array}{c} [a:\neg A] \\ \vdots \\ \dfrac{\bot}{A}\ RAA, \text{ discharge } a \end{array}$$

$$\begin{array}{c} [a:A] \\ \vdots \\ \dfrac{\bot}{\neg A}\ \neg I, \text{ discharge } a \end{array} \qquad \frac{\neg A}{A \to \bot}\ \neg E \qquad \begin{array}{c} [a:A] \\ \vdots \\ \dfrac{B}{A \to B}\ \to I, \text{ discharge } a \end{array} \qquad \frac{A \qquad A \to B}{B}\ \to E$$

$$\frac{A}{A \vee B}\ \vee I_l \qquad \frac{B}{A \vee B}\ \vee I_r \qquad \begin{array}{ccc} & [a_1:A] & [a_2:B] \\ & \vdots & \vdots \\ \dfrac{A \vee B \qquad C \qquad C}{C}\ \vee E, \text{ discharge } a_1 \text{ and } a_2 \end{array}$$

$$\frac{A \qquad B}{A \wedge B}\ \wedge I \qquad \frac{A \wedge B}{A}\ \wedge E_l \qquad \frac{A \wedge B}{B}\ \wedge E_r$$

Fig. 1.1 The subset of the natural deduction system NK for propositional logic

Theorem 1.1 (Soundness of NK) *If a formula can be proved in NK,[6] then it is valid in classical propositional logic.*

Theorem 1.2 (Completeness of NK) *If a formula is valid in classical propositional logic, then it can be proved in NK.*

Let us see how to use the above rules in some example proofs. We begin by proving the transitivity of implication.

Lemma 1.4 $(A \to B) \wedge (B \to C) \to (A \to C)$ *is valid in classical propositional logic.*

Proof First, note that $\wedge$ binds tighter than $\to$, so the above formula should be read as $((A \to B) \wedge (B \to C)) \to (A \to C)$. Thus, we can view this formula as $D \to E$ where D is $(A \to B) \wedge (B \to C)$ and E is $A \to C$. We call D and E the "sub-formulae" of the formula. We can always view formula in such a way that logical connectives in sub-formulae are "hidden", and only one logical connective is visible at a time—we call this connective the *main* (or principal) connective of the formula. These concepts are analogous to subexpressions in Boolean algebra. We can guess which rule to use based on the main connective of the formula we are trying to prove.

---

[6] The NK in this section refers to the subset of rules for propositional logic.

In this example, the main connective of the above formula is $\to$, which means that we will likely need to use the $\to I$ rule to introduce $\to$ into the target formula. To do so, we need to assume the left-hand side $(A \to B) \land (B \to C)$ and derive the right-hand side $A \to C$. This partial proof is shown as follows:

$$
\cfrac{\cfrac{\overline{[a_1 : (A \to B) \land (B \to C)]}}{\vdots \quad A \to C}}{(A \to B) \land (B \to C) \to (A \to C)} \ {\scriptstyle \to I,\, \text{discharge } a_1}
$$

We only need to fill in the $\vdots$ part. Again, this sub-proof aims to derive $A \to C$, whose main connective is $\to$. Thus, we will use the $\to I$ rule again to introduce $\to$ into $A \to C$. This rule application requires us to assume A and derive C. We can now add another part of the proof as follows:

$$
\cfrac{\cfrac{\overline{[a_1 : (A \to B) \land (B \to C)]} \qquad \overline{[a_2 : A]}}{\vdots \qquad\qquad \vdots}{\cfrac{C}{A \to C} \ {\scriptstyle \to I,\, \text{discharge } a_2}}}{(A \to B) \land (B \to C) \to (A \to C)} \ {\scriptstyle \to I,\, \text{discharge } a_1}
$$

Now we need to derive C, which does not involve any logical connective for us to work with. Instead of looking at what we need to prove and reason backwards, we can also look at the assumptions or facts we currently have and try to figure out what we can derive forward. This sort of forward reasoning often involves using elimination rules. We cannot do much with assumption a_2 since it does not contain any logical connective, either. But a_1's main connective is $\land$, and we can use the $\land E$ rule to obtain both conjuncts $A \to B$ and $B \to C$. We can copy a_1 to another branch of the proof and apply $\land E_l$ and $\land E_r$, respectively, on those branches. This inference is shown as follows:

$$
\cfrac{\cfrac{\overline{[a_1 : (A \to B) \land (B \to C)]}}{A \to B} {\scriptstyle \land E_l} \qquad \overline{[a_2 : A]} \qquad \cfrac{\overline{[a_1 : (A \to B) \land (B \to C)]}}{B \to C} {\scriptstyle \land E_r}}{\cfrac{\begin{array}{ccc} \vdots & \vdots & \vdots \end{array}}{\cfrac{\cfrac{C}{A \to C} \ {\scriptstyle \to I,\, \text{discharge } a_2}}{(A \to B) \land (B \to C) \to (A \to C)} \ {\scriptstyle \to I,\, \text{discharge } a_1}}}
$$

On the left branch, it becomes clear that we can use the $\to E$ rule, i.e., Modus Ponens, to eliminate $\to$ from $A \to B$ and derive B. On the other hand, the assumption a_2 is not really useful on the right branch, so we can reorganise the presentation as follows:

$$\cfrac{[a_2 : A] \qquad \cfrac{\cfrac{[a_1 : (A \to B) \land (B \to C)]}{A \to B} \wedge E_l}{} }{\cfrac{B}{\vdots}} \to E \qquad \cfrac{[a_1 : (A \to B) \land (B \to C)]}{B \to C} \wedge E_r$$

$$\cfrac{\cfrac{\cfrac{C}{A \to C} \to I, \text{discharge } a_2}{(A \to B) \land (B \to C) \to (A \to C)} \to I, \text{discharge } a_1}{}$$

We can use $\to E$ rule again on B and $B \to C$ and obtain C to complete the proof, which is shown as follows:

$$\cfrac{[a_2 : A] \quad \cfrac{\cfrac{[a_1 : (A \to B) \land (B \to C)]}{A \to B} \wedge E_l}{B} \to E \quad \cfrac{\cfrac{[a_1 : (A \to B) \land (B \to C)]}{B \to C} \wedge E_r}{} }{\cfrac{\cfrac{C}{A \to C} \to I, \text{discharge } a_2}{(A \to B) \land (B \to C) \to (A \to C)} \to I, \text{discharge } a_1} \to E$$

Now all the assumptions have been discharged, and the proof is finished.   □

The above example involves rules for $\to$ and $\land$. Let us see another example with $\top$, $\bot$, and $\lor$.

Lemma 1.5 $A \lor \bot \to A \land \top$ *is valid in classical propositional logic.*

Proof From the main connective $\to$, we know that we will use $\to I$ in the last step of the proof.

$$\cfrac{\cfrac{\overline{[a_1 : A \lor \bot]}}{\vdots}}{\cfrac{A \land \top}{A \lor \bot \to A \land \top}} \to I, \text{discharge } a_1$$

To derive $A \land \top$ in the second last step, we need to use the $\land I$ rule, which requires two branches. We can copy assumption a_1 to both branches, but we immediately see that the right branch only requires deriving $\top$, which can be obtained by the rule $\top I$ and it does not need any premise.

$$\cfrac{\cfrac{\cfrac{\overline{[a_1 : A \lor \bot]}}{\vdots}}{A} \qquad \cfrac{}{\top} \top I}{\cfrac{A \land \top}{A \lor \bot \to A \land \top} \to I, \text{discharge } a_1} \wedge I$$

Working forward from assumption a_1, we will need to use the rule $\vee E$, for which we introduce two assumptions A and $\bot$, and we aim to derive A from both new assumptions.

$$\cfrac{[a_1 : A \vee \bot] \qquad \cfrac{\overline{[a_2 : A]} \quad \overline{[a_3 : \bot]}}{\begin{array}{cc} \vdots & \vdots \\ A & A \end{array}} \vee E, \text{discharge } a_2 \,\&\, a_3 \qquad \cfrac{}{\top} \top I}{\cfrac{A \wedge \top}{A \vee \bot \to A \wedge \top} \to I, \text{discharge } a_1} \wedge I$$

The branch with a_2 can be simplified—the assumption is already the goal. The branch with a_3 only requires an application of the $\bot E$ rule. These are shown as follows:

$$\cfrac{\overline{[a_1 : A \vee \bot]} \quad \overline{[a_2 : A]} \quad \cfrac{\overline{[a_3 : \bot]}}{A} \bot E}{\cfrac{A}{A \vee \bot \to A \wedge \top} \to I, \text{discharge } a_1} \vee E, \text{discharge } a_2 \,\&\, a_3 \quad \cfrac{}{\top} \top I$$

The above derivation is the complete proof.   □

In mathematics, we say $e \in S$ is an *identity* of the operation $\circ$ on the set S if $e \circ a = a \circ e = a$ for *any* item $a \in S$. For example, 0 is the identity of $+$ on the set of integers, and 1 is the identity of $\times$ on the set of integers. The above lemma is an example that $\top$ is the identity of $\wedge$ and $\bot$ is the identity of $\vee$, which are reflected in the laws of Boolean algebra (cf. Page 8).

Example 1.12 Let us see an example of a failed proof. Consider the formula $A \to A \wedge B$. To prove this implication, we assume A and try to derive $A \wedge B$. However, there is nothing we can use to derive B, so we can only obtain the following partial derivation:

$$\cfrac{\cfrac{\overline{[a : A]} \quad B}{A \wedge B} \wedge I}{A \to A \wedge B} \to I, \text{discharge } a$$

As there is no obvious way to derive B, we have an *open* branch in the derivation, denoted by B without a horizontal bar on top of it; such a derivation is *not* a successful proof of the bottom formula.

One may argue that we can always assume that B is true, and assumptions can be used to close a branch, as shown below.

$$\frac{\dfrac{[a:A] \qquad [b:B]}{A \wedge B} \wedge I}{A \to A \wedge B} \to I, \text{discharge } a$$

However, the above derivation has an undischarged assumption b, so it is *not* a successful derivation of the bottom formula, either.

To summarise, a successful derivation should apply all the inference rules correctly, close all branches and discharge all assumptions. The reader can check that there is no way to derive the said formula in NK.

Finally, let us see a slightly more involved example which contains $\neg$.

Lemma 1.6 $\neg A \wedge \neg B \to \neg(A \vee B)$ *is valid in classical propositional logic.*

Proof A derivation in natural deduction is given below, where Π is a *sub-derivation* which is shown separately for formatting reasons.

$$\frac{\dfrac{\dfrac{\dfrac{\dfrac{[a_1 : \neg A \wedge \neg B]}{\neg A} \wedge E_l}{A \to \bot} \neg E \qquad [a_3 : A]}{\bot} \to E \qquad \Pi}{\dfrac{\bot}{\neg(A \vee B)} \neg I, \text{discharge } a_2}}{\neg A \wedge \neg B \to \neg(A \vee B)} \to I, \text{discharge } a_1$$

with $[a_2 : A \vee B]$ and $\vee E$, discharge a_3 & a_4.

The sub-derivation Π is analogous to the second branch from the left. For completeness, we show it as follows:

$$\frac{\dfrac{\dfrac{[a_1 : \neg A \wedge \neg B]}{\neg B} \wedge E_r}{B \to \bot} \neg E \qquad [a_4 : B]}{\bot} \to E$$

We do not give the rationale behind each step for this example. The reader is invited to reproduce this proof step by step. $\square$

Reasoning in natural deduction is often bi-directional: sometimes we perform backward reasoning via introduction rules. Sometimes we perform forward reasoning via elimination rules. It is hard to come up with a systematic approach to deciding when to switch between the two. The lack of a purely forward or a purely backward proof search method makes it unsuitable for fully automated reasoning. Nonetheless, natural deduction produces arguably shorter and more explainable proofs than Hilbert's system, and it has become the foundation of interactive proof assistants such as Isabelle/HOL and Coq.

Exercises

1.10 Prove $A \rightarrow A$ using natural deduction.

1.11 Prove $A \rightarrow (\neg A \rightarrow B)$ using natural deduction.

1.12 Prove $(A \rightarrow B) \rightarrow (\neg B \rightarrow \neg A)$ using natural deduction.

1.13 Prove $A \wedge (B \vee C) \rightarrow (A \wedge B) \vee (A \wedge C)$ using natural deduction.

1.14 Do the above proofs in Isar proof style in Isabelle/HOL.

Instruction. The "apply" style proofs shown in the previous section are concise but sometimes obscure, especially when the proofs are complex and lengthy. Isabelle offers another way to write human-readable proofs, called the Isar style, which is based on natural deduction. See isar-ref in the Isabelle/HOL documentation for a comprehensive tutorial.

In the Isar style, a proof state can be proved via the following block of code (in contrast to "apply xxx"):

```
proof
...
qed
```

Within the proof block, we can make an assumption A by

```
assume "A"
```

For convenience, we can give the assumption a name so we can refer to it later. For instance, we can call it a_0.

```
assume a0: "A"
```

If we want to derive a sub-goal B and call it f_0, we can write

```
have f0: "B"
```

which creates a sub-proof state required to be proved. If it is straightforward to prove the sub-goal, we can always mix the "apply" style proofs within Isar, such as the following:

```
have "B" by simp
```

It is recommended to only use "apply" and "by" when the sub-proof is simple. If a sub-goal C is the final goal of the proof state, instead of writing "have C", we write

```
show "C"
```

Just like "lemma" and "have", "show" also creates a proof state. The user should be mindful about entering into proof states.

We can chain the proof steps so that we can use previously proved sub-goals as facts. For example, if we have previously proved sub-goals named f_1 and f_2, and we want to use them in the current step to prove a formula A, we can write

```
from f1 f2 have "A"
```

Alternatively, we can write

```
have "A" using f1 f2
```

If we want to use the last step to prove the current step, we can use the "then" keyword.

```
then have "A"
```

Isabelle/HOL has built-in basic tactics based on natural deduction. To use such tactics, simply write "..". You can consider it as a weaker version of "by simp". For example, if A is simple enough to be proved by the basic tactics, we can write

```
have "A" ..
```

Natural deduction rule templates in Isabelle/HOL. We provide the following "templates" in Isar style for natural deduction rules. We write "sorry" as a placeholder for a proof block to be replaced with actual proofs. You can think of "sorry" as the vertical dots in the proof rules. The $\top I$ rule is simply the following line:

```
have "True" ..
```

The rule $\bot E$ says that if we can prove $\bot$, then we can prove anything, including an arbitrary formula A.

```
have "False" sorry
then have "A" ..
```

The $\neg I$ rule says that to prove $\neg A$, we can assume A and prove $\bot$. This is shown as follows:

```
have "\not A"
proof
    assume "A"
    show "False" sorry
qed
```

The $\neg E$ rule says that if we have $\neg A$, then we have derived $A \to \bot$. This form of $\neg E$ is not the default reasoning rule in Isabelle/HOL, so we cannot derive it using "..". Instead, we will use "by simp" here.

```
have f1: "\not A" sorry
then have "A --> False" by simp
```

The alternative rule $\neg E'$ can be derived by "..", where B can be an arbitrary formula. However, this tactic is quite strict—if you change the third line to "from f2 f1 have B ..", the proof will not work.

```
1 have f1: "\not A" sorry
2 have f2: "A" sorry
3 from f1 f2 have "B" ..
```

The $\rightarrow I$ rule requires assuming A and then proving B. We give the template as follows:

```
1 have "A --> B"
2 proof
3     assume "A"
4     show "B" sorry
5 qed
```

The $\rightarrow E$ rule requires two sub-proofs for A and $A \rightarrow B$, respectively, and then we can derive B.

```
1 have f1: "A" sorry
2 have f2: "A --> B" sorry
3 from f1 f2 have "B" by simp
```

The $\lor I_l$ rule requires a sub-proof for A, from which we obtain $A \lor B$.

```
1 have "A" sorry
2 then have "A \/ B" ..
```

The $\lor I_r$ rule is similar.

```
1 have "B" sorry
2 then have "A \/ B" ..
```

The $\lor E$ rule requires a sub-proof for $A \lor B$, a sub-proof for $A \rightarrow C$ and a sub-proof for $B \rightarrow C$. We can then derive C. This is encoded as follows:

```
1 have f1: "A \/ B" sorry
2 have f2: "A --> C"
3 proof
4     assume a1: "A"
5     show "C" sorry
6 qed
7 have f3: "B --> C"
8 proof
9     assume a2: "B"
10    show "C" sorry
11 qed
12 from f1 f2 f3 have "C" by auto
```

The $\land I$ rule requires a sub-proof for A and a sub-proof for B, from which we deduce $A \land B$.

```
1 have f1: "A" sorry
2 have f2: "B" sorry
3 from f1 f2 have "A /\ B" ..
```

The $\wedge E_l$ rule requires a sub-proof for $A \wedge B$, then we obtain A.

```
1 have "A /\ B" sorry
2 then have "A" ..
```

The $\wedge E_r$ rule is similar but derives B instead.

```
1 have "A /\ B" sorry
2 then have "B" ..
```

With the above templates for natural deduction rules, you should be able to prove the previous exercises by substituting "sorry" for sub-proofs.

1.4   Sequent Calculus for Propositional Logic

In a natural deduction proof, we may assume that A is true and prove B, and then we can introduce $A \rightarrow B$ and discharge the assumption A.

$$[a : A]$$

$$\vdots$$

$$\frac{B}{A \rightarrow B} \rightarrow I, \text{discharge } a$$

If we later discover that A is indeed true, then we can derive B by eliminating the implication.

$$[a : A]$$

$$\vdots$$

$$\frac{A \quad \dfrac{B}{A \rightarrow B} \rightarrow I, \text{discharge } a}{B} \rightarrow E$$

While the above rule applications are correct, they form a "detour" in the proof—we introduce the implication only to eliminate it later, and formula $A \rightarrow B$ may not be a part of our goal at all. Ideally, we would like to remove such introduction-elimination pairs and convert a proof into a "normal form" which does not have "detours".

Definition 1.14 (*Normal Deduction*) A natural deduction proof is in *normal form* if, for every principal connective, its introduction rule follows its elimination rule.

The conversion of a proof to normal deduction is referred to as "normalisation". Moreover, we would prefer to construct a proof without ever using a formula that does not appear in our goal. In other words, when we prove A, we should only use sub-formulae of A in the proof.

Unfortunately, Gentzen could not prove a normalisation theorem for natural deduction. He therefore invented another proof calculus called *sequenzenkalkul,* or *sequent calculus,*[7] also known as LK,[8] in order to achieve normalised proofs. Ironically, this means that Gentzen used a roundabout proof to prove the absence of roundabout proofs.

Definition 1.15 (*Sequent*) A *sequent* is of the form

$$A_1, \cdots, A_n \vdash B_1, \cdots, B_m$$

where $A_1, \cdots, A_n$ and $B_1, \cdots, B_m$ are *sequences* of formulae.

The symbol $\vdash$ (called the "turnstile") is a meta-level[9] symbol which can be understood as "implies" or "entails". The left-hand side of $\vdash$ is called the *antecedent*, and the right-hand side is the *succedent*. The comma is also a meta-level symbol—it means "and" in the antecedent, and it means "or" in the succedent. Therefore, the above sequent is semantically equivalent to the following formula:

$$A_1 \wedge \cdots \wedge A_n \rightarrow B_1 \vee \cdots \vee B_m$$

We shall use uppercase Greek letters such as Γ, Δ for arbitrary *structures*, i.e., comma-separated formulae.

Definition 1.16 (*Inference Rule*) An inference rule r is of the form

$$\frac{\rho_1 \quad \cdots \quad \rho_n}{\alpha} \, r$$

where the sequents $\rho_1, \cdots, \rho_n$ are *premises* and the sequent α is the *conclusion*.

A rule with no premises is called a *zero-premise rule*. A rule is *unary* (resp. *binary*) if it has one premise (resp. two premises). The subset of inference rules in LK [5] for propositional logic are given in Fig. 1.2.[10]

---

[7] Sequenzenkalkul literally translates to "calculus of sequences". The word "sequent" was coined by the American mathematician Stephen Kleene in Introduction to Metamathematics [4]. He argued that the word "sequence" was already used for any succession of objects, corresponding to "folge" in German.

[8] Stands for **k**lassische Prädikatenlogik (some say "Logistiche Kalkül"). The LK calculus includes the rules for classical first-order logic. We only present the subset for classical propositional logic in this section.

[9] We say a symbol is on the meta-level when it is *not* in the formal language of our concern. In this example, $\vdash$ is not in the language of propositional logic.

[10] The rules $\vee L$ and $\wedge R$ copy all the context upwards, while the rule $\rightarrow L$ splits the context in the conclusion. These are Gentzen's original rules in LK.

Identity and Cut:

$$\dfrac{}{A \vdash A}\; id \qquad\qquad \dfrac{\Gamma \vdash \Delta, A \qquad A, \Gamma' \vdash \Delta'}{\Gamma, \Gamma' \vdash \Delta, \Delta'}\; cut$$

Logical Rules:

$$\dfrac{\Gamma, A \vdash \Delta}{\Gamma, A \wedge B \vdash \Delta}\; {\wedge}L_1 \qquad\qquad \dfrac{\Gamma, B \vdash \Delta}{\Gamma, A \wedge B \vdash \Delta}\; {\wedge}L_2$$

$$\dfrac{\Gamma \vdash A, \Delta}{\Gamma \vdash A \vee B, \Delta}\; {\vee}R_1 \qquad\qquad \dfrac{\Gamma \vdash B, \Delta}{\Gamma \vdash A \vee B, \Delta}\; {\vee}R_2$$

$$\dfrac{\Gamma, A \vdash \Delta \qquad \Gamma, B \vdash \Delta}{\Gamma, A \vee B \vdash \Delta}\; {\vee}L \qquad\qquad \dfrac{\Gamma \vdash A, \Delta \qquad \Gamma \vdash B, \Delta}{\Gamma \vdash A \wedge B, \Delta}\; {\wedge}R$$

$$\dfrac{\Gamma \vdash A, \Delta \qquad B, \Gamma' \vdash \Delta'}{\Gamma, \Gamma', A \rightarrow B \vdash \Delta, \Delta'}\; {\rightarrow}L \qquad\qquad \dfrac{\Gamma, A \vdash B, \Delta}{\Gamma \vdash A \rightarrow B, \Delta}\; {\rightarrow}R$$

$$\dfrac{\Gamma \vdash A, \Delta}{\Gamma, \neg A \vdash \Delta}\; {\neg}L \qquad\qquad \dfrac{\Gamma, A \vdash \Delta}{\Gamma \vdash \neg A, \Delta}\; {\neg}R$$

Structural Rules:

$$\dfrac{\Gamma \vdash \Delta}{\Gamma, A \vdash \Delta}\; WL \qquad \dfrac{\Gamma \vdash \Delta}{\Gamma \vdash A, \Delta}\; WR \qquad \dfrac{\Gamma, A, A \vdash \Delta}{\Gamma, A \vdash \Delta}\; CL \qquad \dfrac{\Gamma \vdash A, A, \Delta}{\Gamma \vdash A, \Delta}\; CR$$

$$\dfrac{\Gamma, A, B, \Gamma' \vdash \Delta}{\Gamma, B, A, \Gamma' \vdash \Delta}\; EL \qquad\qquad \dfrac{\Gamma \vdash \Delta, A, B, \Delta'}{\Gamma \vdash \Delta, B, A, \Delta'}\; ER$$

Fig. 1.2 The subset of sequent calculus LK for classical propositional logic

Inference rules in LK can be categorised into two groups: *logical rules*, which introduce a new logical connective in the conclusion, and *structural rules*, which manipulate the structure of sequents. There are two exceptions: the identity rule (also called the axiom) and the cut rule.

We can read each rule from top to bottom. The identity rule id states that without any premise, we can derive the sequent $A \vdash A$, which means $A \rightarrow A$.

The cut rule is quite special. It has two premises: one derives A, and the other assumes A. The rule "cuts" the occurrence of A and combines the two sequents into one. Intuitively, it means that if we can assume Γ and derive Δ *or* A, and we can assume A *and* Γ' and derive Δ', then we can remove A and assume Γ and Γ' and derive Δ or Δ'.

The $\wedge L_1$ rule says "if we can derive $\Gamma, A \vdash \Delta$, then we can derive $\Gamma, A \wedge B \vdash \Delta$". More specifically, "if we can assume Γ and A and derive Δ, then we can also assume Γ and $A \wedge B$ and derive Δ". That is, adding the extra assumption B does not invalidate the proof.

In the $\wedge R$ rule, we have two premises: one from Γ derives A or Δ, the other from Γ derives B or Δ. We can then conclude that from Γ, we can derive $A \wedge B$ or Δ. If we abuse the notation and allow connecting formulae with structures, then we can understand this rule as follows: we can derive both $A \vee \Delta$ and $B \vee \Delta$; thus we can derive $(A \vee \Delta) \wedge (B \vee \Delta)$. By applying the distribution law of $\vee$ over $\wedge$ backwards, we obtain $(A \wedge B) \vee \Delta$.

The reading of $\vee$ rules is symmetric. In the $\vee L$ rule, we have two premises: one has A in the antecedent, and the other has B in the antecedent. We conclude that if we have $A \vee B$ in the antecedent with Γ then we can derive Δ. This is analogous to the $\vee E$ rule in natural deduction. In the $\vee R_1$ rule, the premise is that we can derive A or Δ. We then conclude that we can derive $A \vee B$ or Δ. The $\vee R_2$ rule is similar.

The rules for $\neg$ are really simple: if we have A in the antecedent, we are allowed to move it to the succedent by negating it. Likewise, if we have A in the succedent, we can move it to the antecedent by negating it. The reasoning is as follows: for $\neg L$, if we can assume Γ and derive A or Δ, then when we assume Γ and $\neg A$, we must be able to derive Δ. The premise of $\neg R$ says that we can assume Γ and A and prove Δ. Then we can assume Γ and prove $\neg A$ or Δ, i.e., "$A \rightarrow \Delta$".

The rules for $\rightarrow$ is easy to understand—we can interpret $A \rightarrow B$ as $\neg A \vee B$ and use other rules to derive $\rightarrow L$ and $\rightarrow R$. For example, we can turn the A in the rule $\vee L$ into $\neg A$, and obtain the following rule application:

$$\frac{\Gamma, \neg A \vdash \Delta \qquad \Gamma, B \vdash \Delta}{\Gamma, \neg A \vee B \vdash \Delta} \vee L$$

Then, we use $\neg L$ backwards to obtain the following derivation:

$$\frac{\dfrac{\Gamma \vdash A, \Delta}{\Gamma, \neg A \vdash \Delta} \neg L \qquad \Gamma, B \vdash \Delta}{\Gamma, \neg A \vee B \vdash \Delta} \vee L$$

The above derivation results in an alternative $\rightarrow L'$ rule given as follows:

$$\frac{\Gamma \vdash A, \Delta \qquad \Gamma, B \vdash \Delta}{\Gamma, A \rightarrow B \vdash \Delta} \rightarrow L'$$

Unlike the original $\rightarrow L$ rule given by Gentzen, the above rule does not split the context of the conclusion but copies Γ and Δ to both premises. It is sometimes preferred for simplicity.

Structural rules in LK has three main kinds: the *weakening rules*[11] WL and WR add a formula A in the conclusion. They are called weakening because the conclusion of WL and WR has a weaker antecedent and succedent, respectively. In the WL rule, we know that from Γ we can derive Δ, then we can also assume Γ and A and derive Δ—but the latter assumption is weaker because we assume more (than we need). In the conclusion of the WR rule, we assume Γ and derive A or Δ, which is weaker because what we deduce is less certain. The *contraction rules* CL and CR remove duplicate occurrences of a formula in the premise. The CL rule is sound because $A \wedge A$ is equivalent to A. The CL rule is sound because $A \vee A$ is also equivalent to A. Lastly, the *exchange rules* EL and ER encode the commutativity of $\wedge$ and $\vee$, respectively.

With the help of structural rules, we can derive the $\to R$ as follows:

$$\cfrac{\cfrac{\cfrac{\cfrac{\Gamma, A \vdash B, \Delta}{\Gamma \vdash \neg A, B, \Delta}\ ^{\neg R}}{\Gamma \vdash \neg A, \neg A \vee B, \Delta}\ ^{\vee R_2}}{\Gamma \vdash \neg A \vee B, \neg A \vee B, \Delta}\ ^{\vee R_1}}{\Gamma \vdash \neg A \vee B, \Delta}\ ^{CR}$$

The original LK system does not include rules for logical constants $\top$ and $\bot$, which can be encoded as $P \to P$ and $P \wedge \neg P$, respectively. We give the derived rules for $\top$ and $\bot$ as follows:

$$\cfrac{\Gamma \vdash \Delta}{\Gamma, \top \vdash \Delta}\ ^{TL} \qquad \cfrac{}{\Gamma \vdash \top, \Delta}\ ^{TR} \qquad \cfrac{}{\Gamma, \bot \vdash \Delta}\ ^{\bot L} \qquad \cfrac{\Gamma \vdash \Delta}{\Gamma \vdash \bot, \Delta}\ ^{\bot R}$$

Definition 1.17 (*Provability*) A propositional logic formula A is *provable* or *derivable* if we can build a derivation using the inference rules in Fig. 1.2 such that $\vdash A$ is the bottom sequent of the derivation, and each top sequent in the derivation is the empty sequent, i.e., the top of a zero-premise rule.

Although we read the rules in a top-down fashion previously, we often perform proofs bottom-up, i.e., start from $\vdash A$ and apply the rules *backwards*. The applications of rules form a *derivation tree*. When we apply a zero-premise rule on a sequent upwards, we say the corresponding branch is *closed*. The formula is proved when every branch in the derivation tree is closed. This proof process is called *backward proof search*.

When we perform a backward proof search using logical rules, we often focus on a formula and decide which rule to use based on the main connective of the formula and whether the formula is in the antecedent or the succedent. This formula is called the *main/principal formula* of the rule application. However, structural rules do not depend on logical constants and connectives, so their applications are less systematic.

We give an example derivation of $A \to (B \to (A \wedge B))$ in LK as follows

---

[11] Called "thinning" in the original LK.

Lemma 1.7 $A \to (B \to (A \land B))$ *is derivable in* LK.[12]

Proof Starting from $\vdash A \to (B \to (A \land B))$, the main connective of the only formula in this sequent is the $\to$ in the succedent, so we naturally apply the $\to R$ rule backwards (bottom-up) and obtain

$$\frac{A \vdash B \to (A \land B)}{\vdash A \to (B \to (A \land B))} \to R$$

It is then clear that we need to apply the $\to R$ rule again on the top sequent.

$$\frac{\dfrac{A, B \vdash A \land B}{A \vdash B \to (A \land B)} \to R}{\vdash A \to (B \to (A \land B))} \to R$$

Now the only logical connective in the top sequent is the $\land$ in the succedent; thus, we apply the $\land R$ rule, which splits the derivation into two branches.

$$\frac{\dfrac{\dfrac{A, B \vdash A \qquad A, B \vdash B}{A, B \vdash A \land B} \land R}{A \vdash B \to (A \land B)} \to R}{\vdash A \to (B \to (A \land B))} \to R$$

The remainder of the proof is quite straightforward. We give the full derivation tree as follows:

$$\frac{\dfrac{\dfrac{\dfrac{A \vdash A}{A, B \vdash A} WL \qquad \dfrac{\dfrac{\dfrac{B \vdash B}{B, A \vdash B} WL}{A, B \vdash B} EL}{\,}}{A, B \vdash A \land B} \land R}{A \vdash B \to (A \land B)} \to R}{\vdash A \to (B \to (A \land B))} \to R$$

Since every branch is closed, we claim that the proof is complete. $\qquad\qquad\square$

Example 1.13 Consider again the formula $A \to A \land B$ which we could not prove in Example 1.12. Since LK is just as powerful as NK, it is not surprising that we cannot prove this formula in LK, either. Below is a partial derivation tree.

---

[12] Note that, unlike previous lemmas, this lemma does not claim that the formula is valid in classical propositional logic. This is due to the order of writing. In Sect. 1.3, we first give the soundness and completeness theorems for NK, then we know that if the formula can be proved in NK, it must be valid and vice versa. We have not given the soundness and completeness theorems for LK yet, so I am only claiming that the formula is derivable at this stage.

$$\dfrac{\overline{A \vdash A}^{\ id} \qquad A \vdash B}{\dfrac{A \vdash A \land B}{\vdash A \to A \land B}^{\ \to R}}{}^{\land R}$$

Since LK is not concerned with assumptions, we only need to focus on the other two requirements when finding a successful proof: each inference rule is applied correctly, and all branches are closed. In the above case, the branch $A \vdash B$ is open, and there is no logical rule we can apply backwards on this sequent. The identity rule is not applicable as the antecedent does not match the succedent. Structural rules do not help as removing formulae or making copies of existing ones does not make id or any logical rule applicable. The only rule left to consider is the *cut* rule, but in this case, it only closes a branch at the expense of creating another open branch, as shown below.

$$\dfrac{\overline{A \vdash A}^{\ id} \qquad \dfrac{\overline{A \vdash A}^{\ id} \qquad A \vdash B}{A \vdash B}^{\ cut}}{\dfrac{A \vdash A \land B}{\vdash A \to A \land B}^{\ \to R}}{}^{\land R}$$

Alternatively, we can cut on B, but it does not help, either.

$$\dfrac{\overline{A \vdash A}^{\ id} \qquad \dfrac{A \vdash B \qquad \overline{B \vdash B}^{\ id}}{A \vdash B}^{\ cut}}{\dfrac{A \vdash A \land B}{\vdash A \to A \land B}^{\ \to R}}{}^{\land R}$$

The reader can check that there is no way to derive this formula in LK whatsoever.

As with Hilbert's system and the natural deduction system NK, the sequent calculus LK is also sound and complete with respect to propositional logic. This time, we will attempt to prove these theorems. The soundness of a proof theory is usually easy to show—we just need to prove that each rule is correct individually. In the case of sequent calculus, we can show that each rule preserves validity downwards, where sequent validity is defined as follows.

Definition 1.18 (*Sequent Validity*) A sequent $\Gamma \vdash \Delta$ is valid if every formula in Γ is true implies that some formula in Δ is true.

The above definition coincides with the reading of sequent in which each comma in the antecedent is a $\land$, each comma in the succedent is a $\lor$, and $\vdash$ is $\to$. We can then prove the correctness of a rule by showing that if every sequent in the premises is valid, then the sequent in the conclusion is also valid. This reasoning is very similar to the explanation of rules on Page 34.

Recall in the exercises of Sect. 1.3 we have proved the formula $(A \to B) \to (\neg B \to \neg A)$. The opposite direction is also valid: $(\neg B \to \neg A) \to (A \to B)$.

These formulae embed the idea of "proof by contraposition",[13] i.e., if we want to prove that A implies B, we can prove that $\neg B$ implies $\neg A$. Applying this reasoning to the soundness proof, we can alternatively prove that if the sequent in the conclusion is not valid, then at least one of the sequents in the premises is not valid. This style of upward or backward reasoning is similar to the backward proof search shown in the above example. We first formalise the concept of "not valid" as follows.

Definition 1.19 (*Sequent Falsifiability*)   A sequent $\Gamma \vdash \Delta$ is falsifiable if every formula in Γ is true and every formula in Δ is false.

The above definition is obtained by negating the definition of sequent validity. For example, $\neg(A \land B \to C \lor D)$ is equivalent to $\neg(\neg(A \land B) \lor (C \lor D))$, which is equivalent to $((A \land B) \land (\neg C \land \neg D))$. Since logical implication can be confusing at times, not having to deal with it often makes the proof easier to follow.

Backward proof search as proof by contradiction. A backward proof search procedure is effectively a proof by contradiction. A sequent $\Gamma \vdash \Delta$ can be falsified when "everything in Γ is true, and everything in Δ is false". We start from $\vdash A$, which assumes that A is false, and try to find counter-examples to falsify this sequent using backward proof search. If we can complete the proof by closing every branch of the derivation tree, then we know that every possibility where A is false leads to a contradiction, so A must be valid. If a branch in the derivation tree cannot be closed whatsoever, then that branch is indeed a counter-example that falsifies A.

Going back to Example 1.13, in which we obtained a partial derivation tree with an open branch whose top sequent was $A \vdash B$. This sequent provides a counter-example of the formula we tried to prove. More specifically, the sequent $A \vdash B$ is valid when A is true, and B is false. This is exactly a truth assignment that falsifies the formula $A \to A \land B$.

Theorem 1.3 (Soundness of LK) *If a formula can be proved in LK,[14] then it is valid in classical propositional logic.*

Proof   We show that, for each rule in Fig. 1.2, if the conclusion is falsifiable, then at least one of the premises is falsifiable.

The id rule. It is impossible that A is both true and false, so the conclusion of the id rule is not falsifiable. Thus, the above if-then implication vacuously holds.

The cut rule. Assume that every formula in Γ and Γ' is true and every formula in Γ and Γ' is false. We need to show that at least one of the premises is falsifiable. There are two cases:

---

[13] Not to be confused with "proof by contradiction" on Page 21.
[14] The LK in this section refers to the subset of rules for propositional logic.

- If A is true, then the right premise is falsifiable.
- If A is false, then the left premise is falsifiable.

The $\wedge L_1$ rule. Assume that every formula in Γ is true, $A \wedge B$ is true, and every formula in Γ is false. Then A must be true. Thus, the premise is also falsifiable. Similarly, the $\wedge L_2$ rule also preserves falsifiability upwards.

The $\wedge R$ rule. Assume that every formula in Γ is true, $A \wedge B$ is false, and every formula in Γ is false. Note that $\neg(A \wedge B)$ is equivalent to $\neg A \vee \neg B$. Similarly, we deduce that A is false *or* B is false.

- In the former case, the left premise is falsifiable.
- In the latter case, the right premise is falsifiable.

The $\neg L$ rule. Assume that every formula in Γ is true, $\neg A$ is true, and every formula in Γ is false. Then we know that A must be false. Thus the premise is falsifiable.

The $\neg R$ rule. Assume that every formula in Γ is true, $\neg A$ is false, and every formula in Γ is false. Then we know that A must be true. Thus the premise is falsifiable.

The rules for $\vee$ and $\to$ can be proved similarly. We leave them as exercises for the reader.

WL **and** WR. The falsifiability of the conclusion directly implies the falsifiability of the premise.

CL **and** CR. For CL, if we assume that A is true, then we know that both occurrences of A in the premise are true. Thus, the premise is falsifiable. For CR, assuming A is false, we can deduce that both occurrences of A in the premise are false. Thus, the premise is also falsifiable.

EL **and** ER. The commutativity of $\wedge$ and $\vee$ suffices to show that these rules preserve falsifiability upwards.

The above proof shows that every inference rule preserves falsifiability upwards. If we can derive $\vdash A$, but A is not valid, then there must be at least one branch of the derivation tree that preserves falsifiability up to the top, which is an empty sequent and cannot be falsified. Thus, this case cannot happen, and A must be valid. □

Completeness is often a much harder proof—we need to show that we can somehow construct a derivation tree for an arbitrary valid formula. One of the techniques that slightly simplifies the proof is again to prove the contrapositive: every unprovable sequent is invalid. However, even that proof is quite complex and may exceed the assumed background of a reader of the first chapter. Consequently, we present a much simpler proof by taking a shortcut via Hilbert's system. Interested readers can see a proof from scratch in Hunter's book Metalogic [6], which contains a treatment for first-order logic.

Theorem 1.4 (Completeness of LK) *If a formula is valid in classical propositional logic, then it can be proved in LK.*

Proof Since Hilbert's axiomatic system presented on Page 15 is well-known to be sound and complete for classical propositional logic [7], we can stand on the shoulders of giants and develop our result from there. The reasoning of this proof is as follows: we know that the five axioms and the Modus Ponens deduction rule of Hilbert's system are sufficient to prove any valid formula; thus, if we can derive these axioms and rules using LK, then we can show that LK can prove any valid formula. Another purpose of this proof is to demonstrate example derivations in LK.

Proving $A \to (B \to A)$ is straightforward in LK, as shown below.

$$
\cfrac{
\cfrac{
\cfrac{
\cfrac{}{A \vdash A}\ id
}{A, B \vdash A}\ WL
}{A \vdash B \to A}\ {\to}R
}{\vdash A \to (B \to A)}\ {\to}R
$$

The derivation for the second axiom involves several structural rule applications because we need to ensure that the formulae are in the correct order. See the derivation given below.

$$
\cfrac{
\cfrac{
\cfrac{
\cfrac{
\cfrac{
\cfrac{
\cfrac{}{A \vdash A}\ id
\qquad
\cfrac{
\cfrac{
\cfrac{
\cfrac{}{B \vdash B}\ id
\qquad
\cfrac{}{C \vdash C}\ id
}{B, B \to C \vdash C}\ {\to}L
}{B \to C, B \vdash C}\ EL
}{A, B, A \to (B \to C) \vdash C}\ {\to}L
}{B, A, A \to (B \to C) \vdash C}\ EL
}{B, A \to (B \to C), A \vdash C}\ EL
}{A \to (B \to C), B, A \vdash C}\ EL
}{A \to (B \to C), B \vdash A \to C}\ {\to}R
}{A \to (B \to C) \vdash B \to (A \to C)}\ {\to}R
}{\vdash (A \to (B \to C)) \to (B \to (A \to C))}\ {\to}R
$$

Note how we can pattern match the first $\to L$ application (bottom-up) to the corresponding rule: in the conclusion "$A, B, A \to (B \to C) \vdash C$", A is the Γ, B is the Γ', an empty sequence of formulae is the Δ and C is the Δ'.

The derivation for the third axiom is given below. Most of the rule applications are straightforward. We use two EL applications to move the formulae in the appropriate order for later rule applications.

$$\cfrac{\cfrac{}{A \vdash A} \; id \quad \cfrac{\cfrac{}{B \vdash B} \; id \quad \cfrac{}{C \vdash C} \; id}{B, B \to C \vdash C} \to L}{\cfrac{A, B \to C, A \to B \vdash C}{\cfrac{B \to C, A, A \to B \vdash C}{\cfrac{B \to C, A \to B, A \vdash C}{\cfrac{B \to C, A \to B \vdash A \to C}{\cfrac{B \to C \vdash (A \to B) \to (A \to C)}{\vdash (B \to C) \to ((A \to B) \to (A \to C))} \to R} \to R} \to R} EL} EL} \to L}$$

The fourth axiom is again easy to derive.

$$\cfrac{\cfrac{\cfrac{\cfrac{\cfrac{\cfrac{}{A \vdash A} \; id}{A \vdash B, A} \; WR}{A \vdash A, B} \; ER}{A, \neg A \vdash B} \; \neg L}{A \vdash \neg A \to B} \to R}{\vdash A \to (\neg A \to B)} \to R$$

The derivation for the last axiom is shown as follows:

$$\cfrac{\cfrac{\cfrac{\cfrac{\cfrac{}{A \vdash A} \; id \quad \cfrac{}{B \vdash B} \; id}{A, A \to B \vdash B} \to L}{A \to B, A \vdash B} \; EL}{A \to B \vdash \neg A, B} \; \neg R \quad \cfrac{}{B \vdash B} \; id}{\cfrac{A \to B, \neg A \to B \vdash B, B}{A \to B, \neg A \to B \vdash B} \; CR} \to L}{\cfrac{A \to B \vdash (\neg A \to B) \to B}{\vdash (A \to B) \to ((\neg A \to B) \to B)} \to R} \to R$$

The CR rule application in the above derivation is crucial—we may not be able to complete the derivation if we apply the $\to L$ rule first. This shows that we need to be careful when deciding which rule to use in proof search with the original LK. We will improve the rules and remove such inconveniences later.

Finally, we derive the Modus Ponens rule using cut.

$$\cfrac{\vdash A \to B \quad \cfrac{\vdash A \quad \cfrac{}{B \vdash B} \; id}{A \to B \vdash B} \to L}{\vdash B} \; cut$$

The above derivation has two open branches, which require us to prove $A \to B$ and A, respectively. These are exactly the premises of the Modus Ponens rule.

Since we can derive every axiom and deduction rule in Hilbert's system, we can effectively "simulate" every proof in Hilbert's system using LK derivations. Since Hilbert's system is complete, i.e., for every valid classical propositional logic formula, we can always find a proof in Hilbert's system, and we conclude that we can also find a derivation in LK for every valid formula. □

Exercises

1.15 Prove that the rules for $\lor$ and $\rightarrow$ in Fig. 1.2 are sound.

1.16 Prove $(A \rightarrow B) \rightarrow (\neg B \rightarrow \neg A)$ using sequent calculus.

1.17 Prove $A \land (B \lor C) \rightarrow (A \land B) \lor (A \land C)$ using sequent calculus.

1.18 Prove the soundness of sequent calculus w.r.t. classical propositional logic in Isabelle/HOL.

Instruction. Encode each sequent into a logical formula using the translation on Page 33. For an inference rule of the form

$$\frac{premise_0 \quad \cdots \quad premise_n}{conclusion} \; rule$$

We show that if every premise is a valid sequent, then the conclusion is a valid sequent. We can encode this reasoning in several ways.

- The first way is to translation the above into a logical formula, i.e., $premise_0 \land \cdots \land premise_n \rightarrow conclusion$. Then we prove the following:

```
lemma "premise0 /\ ... /\ premisen --> conclusion"
```

- The second way is to use meta-level operators in Isabelle/HOL. To express "assume A and B, prove C", we can write $A \implies B \implies C$, where $\implies$ (typed via "==>" in Isabelle/HOL) is the meta-level implication or entailment. Note that $premise_0 \land \cdots \land premise_n \rightarrow conclusion$ is equivalent to $premise_0 \rightarrow \cdots \rightarrow premise_n \rightarrow conclusion$ (try to prove an instance of this equivalence). Thus, we can alternatively prove the following lemma:

```
lemma "premise0 ==> ... ==> premisen ==> conclusion"
```

- Another way to express the proof goal is to make it very explicit. The Isar style supports the following format:

```
lemma assumes a0: "premise0"
and a1: "premise1"
...
and an: "premisen"
shows "conclusion"
```

Note that when you prove the conclusion in this format, you have to explicitly use the assumptions via "using a0 ..." or "from a0 ...".

We give some examples below, where we write G for Γ and D for Δ. To show the soundness of the *id* rule, we can simply prove the following:

```
lemma "A --> A"
   by simp
```

To prove the soundness of the *cut* rule, we can prove the following:

```
lemma
"G --> D \/ A ==> A /\ G' --> D' ==> G /\ G' --> D \/ D'"
   by auto
```

We use the tactic "auto", which is more powerful than "simp". If we want to write the proofs in a more readable format, we can use the Isar style.

```
lemma
assumes a1: "G --> D \/ A"
and a2: "A /\ G' --> D'"
shows "G /\ G' --> D \/ D'"
proof -
   from a1 a2 show ?thesis by auto
qed
```

In the proof block, we do not use any natural deduction rule. Instead, we write "-" after the keyword "proof" to tell Isabelle/HOL that we are writing proofs in "free-style". This way, we just need to somehow prove the goal "$G \land G' \to D \lor D'$". This is expressed via "show ?thesis", in which "?thesis" is a pre-set variable for the final proof goal in the "proof - qed" block.

Continue and prove the soundness for the other rules in Isabelle/HOL.

References

1. Boole G (1847) The mathematical analysis of logic: being an essay towards a calculus of deductive reasoning. Cambridge University Press, pp 3–14
2. Harrison J (2009) Handbook of practical logic and automated reasoning 1st. Cambridge University Press
3. Gentzen G (1935) Untersuchungen über das logische Schließen I. Mathematische Zeitschrift 39, 176–210. issn: 1432-1823
4. Kleene S, Beeson M (1952) Introduction to metamathematics. Ishi Press International. ISBN: 9780923891572
5. Gentzen G (1964) Investigations into logical deduction. Am Philos Q 1:288–306
6. Hunter G (1971) Metalogic: an introduction to the metatheory of standard first order logic. Macmillan International Higher Education
7. Wasilewska A (2018) Logics for computer science: classical and non-classical. Springer International Publishing, Cham, pp 179–232. ISBN: 978-3-319-92591-2

First-Order Logic

2

Although propositional logic has found many applications, it is sometimes not powerful enough. For example, propositional logic cannot express the very first example in this book because it involves *quantified variables*:

All X are Y.
a is an X.
Therefore, a is Y.

Here is an example from basic mathematics: we can express $x > 1$ and $x < 5$ as propositions, and build a compound formula $(x > 1) \wedge (x < 5)$. However, in propositional logic, we cannot specify that the two instances of x refer to the same variable because x is non-propositional. That is, x may be an integer variable that ranges over more values than 0 and 1.

In this chapter, we will study a much richer logic that allows the above kinds of formulae; this logic is often called *first-order logic* (FOL) or *predicate logic*. It is called "first-order" because it permits quantifiers over variables, ranging from individual items in a set. In comparison, *second-order logic* additionally allows quantifiers over sets of items (e.g., quantifiers over functions and relations). Similarly, *third-order logic* allows quantifiers over sets of sets, and *fourth-order logic* allows quantifiers over sets of sets of sets, and so on. We call the union of second-order logic, third-order logic, and so on *higher-order logic*. We will restrict our attention to first-order logic in this book as it is already a hard topic.

© The Author(s), under exclusive license to Springer Nature Switzerland AG 2021
Z. Hou, *Fundamentals of Logic and Computation*, Texts in Computer Science,
https://doi.org/10.1007/978-3-030-87882-5_2

2.1   Syntax and Semantics of First-Order Logic

We shall use the notations of Fitting [1], Troelstra and Schwichtenberg [2], and
Harrison [3] for the introduction to first-order logic.

For the syntax, we consider the following logical connectives as first-class citizens:
$\neg, \vee, \wedge, \rightarrow, \forall$ and $\exists$. Logical constants are $\bot$ and $\top$. Note that $=$ is not first-class in
this definition; neither are comparison operators $<, \leq, >$, and $\geq$, though they can be
included as extensions. We use the following notation for objects in the language:

- variables are denoted by $x, y, z, \ldots$;
- function symbols are denoted by $f, g, h, \ldots$;
- constants are denoted by $a, b, c, \ldots$;
- terms are denoted by t with subscripts or superscripts;
- atomic formulae are $P, Q, \ldots$;
- relation symbols are denoted by R with subscripts or superscripts;
- arbitrary formulae are written as $F, A, B, C, \ldots$.

The arity of a function or a relation is the number of arguments it takes. Constants
can be seen as functions of arity zero, i.e., functions with no arguments. We explicitly
distinguish between formulae, which can only be true or false, and terms, which are
intended to denote objects in the domain of discussion. The construction of a first-
order logic formula consists of two "stages": the first stage constructs terms and the
second stage the formula.

Definition 2.1 (*Terms*) *Terms* are built up using the following rules:

- any constant is a term;
- any variable is a term;
- any expression $f(t_1, \ldots, t_n)$, where f is a n-ary function symbol and $t_1, \ldots, t_n$
  are terms, is a term.

Constants in the above syntax refer to items in the domain, such as 1, 2, 3 or "red",
"green", "blue", etc. Do not confuse them with the logical constants $\top$ and $\bot$. Variables in first-order logic are non-propositional variables; they can represent naturals,
integers, reals, persons, days, blood types, colours, and whatever. We distinguish
between a *function symbol*, such as f, and $f(x, y)$, which is a *function application* on input parameters x and y. Similarly, in the below definition, we distinguish
between a *relation symbol* R and a *relation application* such as $R(x, y)$.

Definition 2.2 (*Syntax of FOL*) *Formulae* in first-order logic are defined inductively
as follows:

- $\top, \bot$ are *atomic formulae*;
- any expression $R(t_1, \ldots, t_n)$, where R is a n-ary relation symbol and $t_1, \ldots, t_n$
  are terms, is an *atomic formula*;

- if A is a formula, so is $\neg A$;
- if A, B are formulae, so are $A \vee B$, $A \wedge B$, $A \rightarrow B$;
- if A is a formula and x is a variable, then $\forall x.A$ and $\exists x.A$ are formulae.

The symbol $\forall$ is a universal quantifier pronounced "for all", and the symbol $\exists$ is an existential quantifier pronounced "there exists". Quantifiers bind tighter than all the logical connectives. For instance, $\forall x.A \wedge B$ should be read as $(\forall x.A) \wedge B$. We sometimes write $\forall x.\forall y.A$ as $\forall xy.A$ for simplicity.

We can alternatively define the syntax in BNF as below, where t stands for a term and F stands for a formula.

$$t ::= a \mid x \mid f(t, \ldots, t)$$
$$F ::= \top \mid \bot \mid R(t, \ldots, t) \mid$$
$$\neg F \mid F \wedge F \mid F \vee F \mid F \rightarrow F \mid \forall x.F \mid \exists x.F.$$

In mathematical literature, a function is sometimes regarded as a special type of relation where every input is mapped to at most one output. By contrast, the above definition explicitly distinguishes functions and relations in terms of their output: a function application $f(t, \ldots, t)$ is a term, whereas a relation application $R(t, \ldots, t)$ is a formula. Delving deeper into this subtlety, the reader may wonder whether we can define functions that return the logical constants $\top$ or $\bot$. This is not permitted in the syntax, as logical constants are not terms. However, this should in no way restrict the expressiveness of first-order logic—we can use a "user-defined" Boolean type such as $\{1,0\}$ or $\{$"true", "false"$\}$ as a proxy for the formulae $\top$ and $\bot$.

Example 2.1 The following are *not* first-order logic formulae:

$$x, f(y), x \wedge R(x), f(x) \vee R(y) \text{ and } \forall x.f(x).$$

On a related note, the literature sometimes uses the word "predicate" instead of "relation" in the above definitions. Mathematically, a predicate is merely the indicator function for a relation. It can be understood as a Boolean function that maps terms to true or false. For an example of the "$<$" relation over two integers, we can define a predicate $f_<$ such that

$$f_<(x, y) = \begin{cases} \text{true} & \text{if } x < y \\ \text{false} & \text{otherwise.} \end{cases}$$

This predicate is called the indicator function for the relation $<$. Since the only type of atomic formula besides logical constants is relation/predicate, first-order logic is also called predicate logic.

The *type signature* of a function is written in the form $S \rightarrow S'$, which means that the function takes an element from the set S as input and returns an element in the set S' as output. If the function takes two input arguments from the sets S_1 and S_2, respectively, and returns an output in the set S_3, we can write its type signature as $S_1 \times S_2 \rightarrow S_3$. Recall that on Page 19, we wrote it as $S_1 \rightarrow S_2 \rightarrow S_3$. These two representations are equivalent.[1] To simplify the notation, we write D^n as a shorthand for $D \times \cdots \times D$ with n D's.

The semantics of first-order logic is determined by a non-empty *domain* D of objects that we can quantify over, an *interpretation* I that specifies the meaning of functions and relations, and a *valuation* v that specifies the meaning of variables. The pair (D, I) is called a *model*. Formally, the interpretation I

- maps each n-ary function symbol f to a function $f_I : D^n \to D$;
- maps each n-ary relation symbol R to a predicate $R_I : D^n \to \{\text{true}, \text{false}\}$.

The valuation v maps each variable to an item in the domain D. We write $t^{I,v}$ for the value of term t valued by interpretation I and valuation v. The value of terms is defined as follows:

- $a^{I,v} = a$;
- $x^{I,v} = v(x)$;
- $[f(t_1, \ldots, t_n)]^{I,v} = f_I(t_1^{I,v}, \ldots, t_n^{I,v})$.

The value of a constant a is simply a itself. The value of a variable x is $v(x)$, i.e., the mapped item via the valuation function v. To obtain the value of a function application $f(t_1, \ldots, t_n)$, we first find the interpretation of the function symbol, then we apply the function f_I to the valuated arguments $t_1^{I,v}, \ldots, t_n^{I,v}$.

The semantics for each type of formula is given in Table 2.1, where $v[d/x]$ is a valuation that agrees with v except that x is mapped to d. We also use this notation for a substitution that replaces x with d.

We have seen most components of first-order logic in Chapter 1. The semantics for relation is straightforward. The two notable new types of formulae are quantified formulae. To make $\exists x . A$ true, we need to find *some* instance d in the domain D such that when we substitute every occurrence of x with d in A, the resultant formula is true under I and v. To make $\forall x . A$ true, we need to ensure that for *any* d in D, if we substitute every occurrence of x with d in A, the resultant formula is true under I and v.

We say a variable occurrence is *free* if it is not quantified in the formula; otherwise, we say the occurrence is *bound* by a quantifier. For example, in $\forall x . R_1(x, y) \to R_2(x)$, the occurrence of x in R_1 is bound, and the occurrence of x in R_2 is free. The only occurrence of y is free. When we evaluate this formula, the bound occurrence of x is substituted in the semantics of $\forall$; thus, we only need to look at the valuation for the free variable occurrences.

---

[1] Coincidentally, $\times$ in type signatures can be understood as conjunction and $\to$ as implication. And $A \land B \to C$ is equivalent to $A \to B \to C$. We will come back to such correspondences at the end of this book.

Table 2.1 The semantics of first-order logic

$$\perp^{I,v} = \text{false} \qquad \top^{I,v} = \text{true}$$

$$[R(t_1, \cdots, t_n)]^{I,v} = \begin{cases} \text{true} & \text{if } R_I(t_1^{I,v}, \cdots, t_n^{I,v}) \text{ holds} \\ \text{false} & \text{otherwise} \end{cases}$$

$$[\neg A]^{I,v} = \begin{cases} \text{true} & \text{if } A^{I,v} \text{ is false} \\ \text{false} & \text{otherwise} \end{cases}$$

$$[A \wedge B]^{I,v} = \begin{cases} \text{true} & \text{if } A^{I,v} \text{ is true and } B^{I,v} \text{ is true} \\ \text{false} & \text{otherwise} \end{cases}$$

$$[A \vee B]^{I,v} = \begin{cases} \text{true} & \text{if } A^{I,v} \text{ is true or } B^{I,v} \text{ is true} \\ \text{false} & \text{otherwise} \end{cases}$$

$$[A \rightarrow B]^{I,v} = \begin{cases} \text{true} & \text{if } A^{I,v} \text{ is false or } B^{I,v} \text{ is true} \\ \text{false} & \text{otherwise} \end{cases}$$

$$[\exists x.A]^{I,v} = \begin{cases} \text{true} & \text{if for some } d \in D,\ A^{I,v[d/x]} \text{ is true} \\ \text{false} & \text{otherwise} \end{cases}$$

$$[\forall x.A]^{I,v} = \begin{cases} \text{true} & \text{if for all } d \in D,\ A^{I,v[d/x]} \text{ is true} \\ \text{false} & \text{otherwise} \end{cases}$$

Definition 2.3 (*Model of Formula*) A first-order logic formula A is true in the model (D, I) if $A^{I,v}$ is true for *every* valuation v.

Definition 2.4 (*Formula Validity*) A formula is *valid* if it is true in *all* models.

Definition 2.5 (*Formula Satisfiability*) A formula is *satisfiable* if it is true in *some* model.

Example 2.2 Consider the domain $D = \{\text{spring, summer, autumn, winter}\}$. Suppose we have a function symbol *next* and two relation symbols *has3Months* and *before*. We define an interpretation I that

- maps *next* to a function $next : D \rightarrow D$, which returns the next season;
- maps *has3Months* to a predicate $has3Months : D \rightarrow \{\text{true, false}\}$, which maps all elements in D to true, that is, every season has three months;
- maps *before* to a predicate $before : D^2 \rightarrow \{\text{true, false}\}$, where $before(x, y)$ is true iff $next(x) = y$.

The formula $\forall x.has3Months(x)$ is true in the model (D, I) because we can substitute x with *any* element s in D and $has3Months(s)$ is true. The formula $\exists x.has3Months(x)$ is also true in this model because we can use spring as an example and $has3Months(spring)$ holds.

The formula $\exists x.before(x, \text{winter})$ is true in the model (D, I) because there exists an instance autumn such that when we replace x by autumn, the resultant formula $before(\text{autumn, winter})$ holds. However, $\forall x.before(x, \text{winter})$ is not true in this model.

There is only one variable in the above two formulae, namely x, which is bound by a quantifier. Thus, we do not need to check the valuation of variables in the above cases. For an example with free variables, consider the formula $\exists x.before(x, y)$, which is true in the model (D, I). To show this, we need to check that it is true for *every* valuation. Since there is only one free variable y, a valuation can only map y to one of the four possible elements in D. For each valuation v, we can always find some x that is before $v(y)$. Therefore, this formula is true in (D, I).

The formula $\forall x.before(x, next(x))$ is also true in (D, I). We leave the analysis to the reader. However, none of the above-mentioned formulae are valid, because they may not be true if we change the interpretation I. On the other hand, the formula $\forall x.before(x, next(x)) \rightarrow \exists x.before(x, next(x))$ is valid, because if $before(x, next(x))$ is true for every x in the domain, then we must be able to find an instance a in the domain such that $before(a, next(a))$ is true. This analysis is independent of the domain, the interpretation and the valuation.

Exercises

2.1 Let the domain D be the set of integers. The interpretation I maps $<$ to the "less than" relation on integers and maps $+$ to the addition operation on integers. Additionally, I maps pos to an unary relation such that $pos(x)$ is true for all positive integers. You are allowed to write $<$ and $+$ as infix symbols. That is, you can write $x < y$ instead of $< (x, y)$ and $x + y$ instead of $+(x, y)$. Which of the following formulae are true in (D, I)? Which ones are valid? Explain your reasoning using the semantics of first-order logic.

1. $x < (y + 8)$.
2. $\exists x.x < (y + 8)$.
3. $x < (x + 5)$.
4. $\forall x.x < (x + 5)$.
5. $x < y \rightarrow (y < z \rightarrow x < y)$.
6. $\neg\forall x.pos(x) \rightarrow \exists x.\neg pos(x)$.

2.2 Try to prove the above formulae in Isabelle/HOL.

Instruction. You can type $\exists$ and $\forall$ in Isabelle/HOL via "\exists" and "\forall", respectively, and select from the drop-down menu.

When we type the following lemma:

```
1  lemma "\exists x. x < (y + 8)"
```

We do not specify the domain of x and y, nor the interpretation of $<$ and $+$. In this case, Isabelle/HOL finds a counterexample, which shows that this formula is not valid. If we do want to restrict the formula to the domain of integers and the interpretation of $<$ and $+$ over integers, we can simply force Isabelle/HOL to parse x as an integer. To do so, we pick an occurrence of x and change it to $(x::int)$, as follows.

```
1  lemma "\exists (x::int). x < (y + 8)"
```

Once Isabelle/HOL understands that x is an integer, it will automatically understand y and 8 as integers as well because that is the only obvious way to ensure type consistency for this formula. Moreover, Isabelle/HOL will automatically take the common interpretation of $<$ and $+$ over integers. As a result, the above formula is restricted to the domain D and interpretation I in Exercise 2.1. Alternatively, you can restrict y or 8 to an integer; the resultant formulae are equivalent. The above formula requires some arithmetic theories to prove, so instead of using "simp", we can prove by Presburger arithmetic.

```
1  lemma "\exists (x::int). x < (y + 8)"
2    by presburger
```

Thus, this formula is true under the model (D, I) of Exercise 2.1.

Note that Isabelle/HOL has a quite strict parsing method for quantified formulae. The last formula of Exercise 2.1 should be typed as

```
1  lemma "\not (\forall x. pos x) -->
2    (\exists x. \not (pos x))"
```

In Isabelle/HOL, we write $pos(x)$ as $pos\ x$.

Try and prove the other formulae.

2.2 Natural Deduction for First-Order Logic

In this section, we move back to the topic of theorem proving. To show that a first-order logic formula is valid, we need to prove that it is true under *any* valuation and interpretation and in *any* non-empty domain. Therefore, theorem proving for first-order logic is not particularly concerned with these concepts. Indeed, the full natural deduction system NK for first-order logic consists of the inference rules in Sect. 1.3 and four additional rules for the quantifiers, which are detailed below and do not show the components of the semantics explicitly.

The rules for $\forall$. To introduce $\forall x.A$ in the conclusion, we need to show that $A[c/x]$ is true for *every* possible item c in the domain, where the notation $[c/x]$ means that we replace every occurrence of x in A by c. Obviously, we do not want to enumerate all possible cases because the domain may be infinite. Instead, we can simply show that $A[c/x]$ is true *for an arbitrary item* c. To show the arbitrariness of our choice of c, we need to ensure that this choice is independent of all other terms in the current scope of the proof. For simplicity, we require that c is *fresh*, i.e., it does not appear in any undischarged assumption that leads to the formula $A[c/x]$. Such a fresh term is called an *eigenvariable*. The rule $\forall I$ is given below, where we write the side condition explicitly.

$$\frac{A[c/x]}{\forall x.A} \quad \forall I. c \text{ is fresh}$$

The rule for eliminating $\forall$ is quite simple: if we know that $\forall x.A$ is true, then we can replace x by any term t, and $A[t/x]$ must be true. In this rule, the term t does not have to be fresh.

$$\frac{\forall x.A}{A[t/x]} \quad \forall E$$

Lemma 2.1 $\forall x.R_1(x) \rightarrow (\forall x.R_2(x) \rightarrow \forall y.(R_1(y) \wedge R_2(y)))$ *is derivable in* NK.

Proof We give a derivation in NK as follows:

$$\cfrac{\cfrac{\cfrac{[a_1 : \forall x.R_1(x)]}{R_1(y)} \forall E \qquad \cfrac{[a_2 : \forall x.R_2(x)]}{R_2(y)} \forall E}{R_1(y) \wedge R_2(y)} \wedge I}{\cfrac{\cfrac{\forall y.(R_1(y) \wedge R_2(y))}{\forall x.R_2(x) \rightarrow \forall y.(R_1(y) \wedge R_2(y))} \rightarrow I, \text{discharge } a_2}{\forall x.R_1(x) \rightarrow (\forall x.R_2(x) \rightarrow \forall y.(R_1(y) \wedge R_2(y)))}} \rightarrow I, \text{discharge } a_1$$

The reader should be familiar with the applications for $\rightarrow I$ and $\wedge I$ by now. The rules for $\forall$ require more care. The top left $\forall E$ rule application instantiates the relation R_1 with y, and nothing stops us from instantiating R_2 with y as well, since there is no side condition for the $\forall E$ rule. Actually, instantiating both R_1 and R_2 with the same variable is crucial in the remainder of the proof. The $\forall I$ application is correct because y is fresh—it does not appear in any undischarged assumption that leads to $R_1(y) \wedge R_2(y)$. $\qquad\square$

The rules for, $\exists$. Introducing $\exists x.A$ is straightforward: if we can show that $A[t/x]$ holds for some term t, then we can conclude that there exists an x that makes A rule. There is no requirement on the term t.

$$\frac{A[t/x]}{\exists x.A} \quad \exists I$$

On the other hand, the elimination rule for $\exists$ is more complex, and it runs as follows: assume that $A[c/x]$ is true, where c is an *arbitrary* item in the domain. If we can deduce B from $A[c/x]$, then we know that we can also deduce B from any other instance of x in A. At the same time, if $\exists x.A$ is true, then we know that there must be some instance of x that makes A true. Therefore, we deduce that B must be true. This rule is given as follows:

$$
\begin{array}{c}
[a : A[c/x]] \\
\vdots \\
\cfrac{\exists x.A \qquad\qquad B}{B} \;\; \exists E, \text{discharge } a, c \text{ is fresh}
\end{array}
$$

The side condition of this rule is that c must not appear in any premise of the rule ($\exists x.A$ and B) nor any undischarged assumption that leads to the conclusion B. The assumption a does not count since it is discharged by the rule application, and the occurrence of c in a is required fresh. However, if there are other assumptions in the sub-proof for $\exists x.A$ and B, then they must not contain c.

There is an analogy between $\exists$ and $\vee$: $\exists x.A$ can be seen as $A[a/x] \vee A[b/x] \vee \cdots$, for each item $a, b, \ldots$ in the domain. If we consider a special case where there are only two items b and c in the domain, then instead of using a fresh eigenvariable, we can simply enumerate all cases: if we can prove that $A[b/x]$ implies B and $A[c/x]$ implies B, then $\exists x.A$ implies B. This reasoning can be written as follows:

$$
\begin{array}{c}
\qquad\qquad\qquad [a_1 : A[b/x]] \qquad [a_2 : A[c/x]] \\
\qquad\qquad\qquad\qquad \vdots \qquad\qquad\qquad\qquad \vdots \\
\cfrac{[A[b/x] \vee A[c/x]] \qquad\qquad B \qquad\qquad\qquad B}{B} \;\; \text{discharge } a_1 \text{ and } a_2
\end{array}
$$

The above derivation has the same form as the $\vee E$ rule in NK.

Lemma 2.2 $\exists x.R_1(x) \to \exists x.(R_1(x) \vee R_2(x))$ *is derivable in* NK.

Proof Consider the *incorrect* derivation below where we mark the incorrect rule application with question marks.

$$
\cfrac{\cfrac{\cfrac{\cfrac{[a_1 : \exists x.R_1(x)] \qquad [a_2 : R_1(b)]}{R_1(b)} \; \exists E, \text{discharge } a_2 \; ???}{R_1(b) \vee R_2(b)} \; \vee I_l}{\exists x.(R_1(x) \vee R_2(x))} \; \exists I}{\exists x.R_1(x) \to \exists x.(R_1(x) \vee R_2(x))} \to I, \text{discharge } a_1
$$

The problem with the above derivation is that the term b appears in one of the premises of the $\exists E$ rule, which is not allowed. To resolve this issue, we apply the $\vee I_l$ and $\exists I$ rules before the $\exists E$ application. The below derivation is correct.

$$\cfrac{[a_1 : \exists x.R_1(x)] \qquad \cfrac{\cfrac{\cfrac{[a_2 : R_1(b)]}{R_1(b) \vee R_2(b)} \vee I_l}{\exists x.(R_1(x) \vee R_2(x))} \exists I}{\exists x.(R_1(x) \vee R_2(x))} \exists E, \text{ discharge } a_2}{\exists x.R_1(x) \rightarrow \exists x.(R_1(x) \vee R_2(x))} \rightarrow I, \text{ discharge } a_1$$

In the above proof, the term b satisfies the "fresh" condition that it does not appear in either of the premises of the $\exists E$ rule nor in any undischarged assumptions except a_2.   □

We give the full set of inference rules in NK in Fig. 2.1.

As an extension to the theorems in Sect. 1.3, the full set of rules in the natural deduction system NK is sound and complete for first-order logic.

Theorem 2.1 (Soundness of NK) *If a formula can be proved in NK, then it is valid in classical first-order logic.*

Theorem 2.2 (Completeness of NK) *If a formula is valid in classical first-order logic, then it can be proved in NK.*

As another example, we show that the "existential-universal" quantification pair over a formula implies the "universal-existential" quantification pair. Note that this does not apply to quantifiers in sub-formulae.

Lemma 2.3 $\exists x.\forall y.R(x, y) \rightarrow \forall y.\exists x.R(x, y)$ *is valid in first-order logic.*

Proof The reader may be tempted to construct the following *incorrect* derivation where the incorrect rule application is marked with "???":

$$\cfrac{\cfrac{[a_1 : \exists x.\forall y.R(x, y)] \qquad \cfrac{[a_2 : \forall y.R(d, y)]}{R(d, c)} \forall E}{R(d, c)} \exists E, \text{ discharge } a_2 \text{ ???}}{\cfrac{\cfrac{\exists x.R(x, c)}{\forall y.\exists x.R(x, y)} \forall I}{\exists x.\forall y.R(x, y) \rightarrow \forall y.\exists x.R(x, y)}} \rightarrow I, \text{ discharge } a_1$$

As discussed in the proof of Lemma 2.2, the term d does not satisfy the "fresh" condition of the $\exists E$ rule because it appears in the second premise $R(d, c)$. We give a correct derivation as follows:

$$\dfrac{}{\top}\ \top I \qquad \dfrac{\bot}{A}\ \bot E \qquad \begin{array}{c} [a : \neg A] \\ \vdots \\ \dfrac{\bot}{A}\ RAA,\, \text{discharge } a \end{array}$$

$$\begin{array}{c} [a : A] \\ \vdots \\ \dfrac{\bot}{\neg A}\ \neg I,\, \text{discharge } a \end{array} \qquad \dfrac{\neg A}{A \to \bot}\ \neg E \qquad \begin{array}{c} [a : A] \\ \vdots \\ \dfrac{B}{A \to B}\ \to I,\, \text{discharge } a \end{array} \qquad \dfrac{A \qquad A \to B}{B}\ \to E$$

$$\dfrac{A}{A \lor B}\ \lor I_l \qquad \dfrac{B}{A \lor B}\ \lor I_r \qquad \dfrac{A \lor B \qquad \begin{array}{c}[a_1 : A]\\ \vdots \\ C\end{array} \qquad \begin{array}{c}[a_2 : B]\\ \vdots \\ C\end{array}}{C}\ \lor E,\, \text{discharge } a_1 \text{ and } a_2$$

$$\dfrac{A \qquad B}{A \land B}\ \land I \qquad \dfrac{A \land B}{A}\ \land E_l \qquad \dfrac{A \land B}{B}\ \land E_r$$

$$\dfrac{A[c/x]}{\forall x.A}\ \forall I,\, c \text{ is fresh} \qquad \dfrac{\forall x.A}{A[t/x]}\ \forall E$$

$$\dfrac{A[t/x]}{\exists x.A}\ \exists I \qquad \dfrac{\exists x.A \qquad \begin{array}{c}[a : A[c/x]]\\ \vdots \\ B\end{array}}{B}\ \exists E,\, \text{discharge } a,\, c \text{ is fresh}$$

Fig. 2.1 The full natural deduction system NK for classical first-order logic

$$\dfrac{[a_1 : \exists x.\forall y.R(x, y)] \qquad \dfrac{\dfrac{\dfrac{[a_2 : \forall y.R(d, y)]}{R(d, c)}\ \forall E}{\exists x.R(x, c)}\ \exists I}{\forall y.\exists x.R(x, y)}\ \forall I}{\dfrac{\forall y.\exists x.R(x, y)}{\exists x.\forall y.R(x, y) \to \forall y.\exists x.R(x, y)}\ \to I,\, \text{discharge } a_1}\ \exists E,\, \text{discharge } a_2$$

In the above proof, the application of the $\exists E$ rule is correct because d is freshly introduced in a_2 and it does not appear in a_1, nor in any premise of the $\exists E$ rule. The $\forall I$ application is correct because c does not appear in a_2, which is the only undischarged assumption in the sub-proof of the premise $\exists x.R(x, c)$.   □

Example 2.3 Let us consider the other direction of Lemma 2.3, i.e.,

$$\forall y.\exists x.R(x, y) \rightarrow \exists x.\forall y.R(x, y).$$

The reader should now be familiar with the reason why the following derivation is incorrect:

$$
\cfrac{
  \cfrac{
    \cfrac{[a_1 : \forall y.\exists x.R(x, y)]}{\exists x.R(x, c)} \; \forall E
    \qquad
    \cfrac{
      \cfrac{[a_2 : R(b, c)]}{R(b, c)} \; \exists E, \text{discharge } a_2 \; ???
    }{}
  }{
    \cfrac{
      \cfrac{R(b, c)}{\forall y.R(b, y)} \; \forall I
    }{\exists x.\forall y.R(x, y)} \; \exists I
  }
}{\forall y.\exists x.R(x, y) \rightarrow \exists x.\forall y.R(x, y)} \; \rightarrow I, \text{discharge } a_1
$$

The term b above does not satisfy the fresh condition of the $\exists E$ rule. Unfortunately, the technique of moving some rule applications upwards does not always work. Consider the following incorrect derivation:

$$
\cfrac{
  \cfrac{[a_1 : \forall y.\exists x.R(x, y)]}{\exists x.R(x, c)} \; \forall E
  \qquad
  \cfrac{
    \cfrac{\cfrac{[a_2 : R(b, c)]}{\forall y.R(b, y)} \; \forall I \; ???}{\exists x.\forall y.R(x, y)} \; \exists I
  }{\exists x.\forall y.R(x, y)} \; \exists E, \text{discharge } a_2
}{\forall y.\exists x.R(x, y) \rightarrow \exists x.\forall y.R(x, y)} \; \rightarrow I, \text{discharge } a_1
$$

In the above derivation, the $\forall I$ rule application is incorrect because the term c appears in the assumption a_2 which has not been discharged.

In fact, this formula is not derivable at all. We can assign an interpretation to the formula and understand it in a natural language. For instance, let $R(x, y)$ denote "x has read y", where x is a person and y is a book. The formula in Lemma 2.3 says that

If there is a person who has read all books, then every book has been read by a person.

The above is clearly valid. On the other hand, the formula in this example means that

If every book has been read by a (possibly different) person, then there is a person who has read all books.

Suppose there are only two books b_1 and b_2, and two persons p_1 and p_2, and p_1 has only read b_1 and p_2 has only read b_2. In this case, the "if" part is satisfied, but the "then" part is not. Therefore, the above statement is not valid. This reasoning is reflected in the second incorrect derivation that we cannot deduce that a person has read all the books; that is, the $\forall I$ rule application is incorrect.

Hilbert calculus for FOL. We gave the Hilbert calculus for propositional logic on Page 15. Those axioms can be extended with the following three for FOL:

$$\forall x.A \rightarrow A[t/x]$$
$$\forall x.(A \rightarrow B) \rightarrow (\forall x.A \rightarrow \forall x.B)$$
$$A \rightarrow \forall x.A.$$

We can understand the axioms for quantifiers using natural deduction rules. The first axiom is essentially the $\forall E$ rule in NK.

The second axiom shows that we can distribute the $\forall$ quantifier over the logical connective $\rightarrow$. A similar formula is $\forall x.(X \rightarrow Y) \rightarrow (X[a/x] \rightarrow Y[a/x])$, which expresses "all X are Y, a is an X, therefore, a is Y". We prove this axiom using NK as follows.

Lemma 2.4 $\forall x.(A \rightarrow B) \rightarrow (\forall x.A \rightarrow \forall x.B)$ *is valid in classical first-order logic.*

Proof See the derivation in NK given below

$$
\cfrac{
\cfrac{
\cfrac{\cfrac{[a_2 : x.A]}{A[c/x]}\ \forall E \qquad \cfrac{[a_1 : \forall x.(A \rightarrow B)]}{A[c/x] \rightarrow B[c/x]}\ \forall E}{\cfrac{B[c/x]}{\forall x.B}\ \forall I}\ \rightarrow E
}{\forall x.A \rightarrow \forall x.B}\ \rightarrow I, \text{discharge } a_2
}{\forall x.(A \rightarrow B) \rightarrow (\forall x.A \rightarrow \forall x.B)}\ \rightarrow I, \text{discharge } a_1
$$

The term c satisfies the fresh condition of the $\forall I$ rule as it does not appear in any undischarged assumption. $\qquad\square$

The third axiom is an embodiment of the $\forall I$ rule where the side condition is implicit. There is no need for axioms for the existential quantifier because $\exists x.A$ can be encoded as $\neg(\forall x.\neg A)$.

The Hilbert calculus with the above rules is also sound and complete for first-order logic.

Exercises

2.3 Prove the following formulae in natural deduction.

1. $\neg\forall x.R(x) \rightarrow \exists x.\neg R(x)$;
2. $\neg\exists x.R(x) \rightarrow \forall x.\neg R(x)$;
3. $\forall x.\exists y.(R_1(x) \wedge R_2(y)) \rightarrow \forall x.R_1(x) \wedge \exists x.R_2(x)$;
4. $\forall x.(R_1(x) \rightarrow R_2(x)) \rightarrow (\forall x.R_1(x) \rightarrow \forall x.R_2(x))$.

2.4 Prove the above formulae in Isabelle/HOL using Isar style proofs.

Instruction. We give the natural deduction rule templates for quantifiers below. Note again that in Isabelle/HOL, it is custom to write $R\,x$ instead of $R(x)$, though the latter is also permitted. The $\forall I$ rule requires a proof for $R\,t$ in which t is fresh. Then we can deduce $\forall x.\ R\,x$. To ensure that t is fresh in Isabelle/HOL, we use the keyword "fix". In the below template, "fix t" effectively creates an arbitrary/eigenvariable t for the sub-proof. Note that in Isabelle/HOL, there must be a space between the "." and the formula that follows

```
1  have "\forall x. R x"
2  proof
3      fix t
4      show "R t" sorry
5  qed
```

The $\forall E$ rule is much simpler. Whenever we have a proof for $\forall x.\ R\,x$, we can obtain $R\,t$ for any term t.

```
1  have "\forall x. R x" sorry
2  then have "R t" ..
```

The $\exists I$ rule is symmetric to $\forall E$. To deduce $\exists x.\ R\,x$, we only need to prove $R\,t$ for some term t.

```
1  have "\exists x. R x"
2  proof
3      show "R t" sorry
4  qed
```

The built-in $\exists E$ rule in Isabelle/HOL is different from the form shown in this book. In the built-in form, we simply obtain a particular instance t that makes $R\,t$ true. The phrase "obtain xxx where formula" in Isabelle/HOL creates a proof state just as "have" does.

```
1  have "\exists x. R x" sorry
2  then obtain t where "R t" ..
```

The form of $\exists E$ in this book can be presented as follows. Assume that we can prove $\exists x.\ R\,x$, and we can prove that $R\,t\ \rightarrow\ B$ for an arbitrary term t, then we can obtain B. Again, we use "fix t" to create an arbitrary/eigenvariable term for the sub-proof.

```
1  have f1: "\exists x. R x" sorry
2  {
3      fix t
4      have f2: "R t --> B"
5      proof
6      assume a1: "R t"
7      show "B" sorry
8      qed
9  }
10 then have "B" using f1 by auto
```

We use "{" and "}" to create a scope for a sub-proof in which the eigenvariable t is fresh. The "then" after "}" uses the result of the sub-proof in the next proof state.

In addition, we give a template for the RAA rule discussed in Sect. 1.3. The reader may find this rule useful for certain problems.

```
1  have "A"
2  proof -
3      {
4          assume a1: "\not A"
5          have f1: "False" sorry
6      }
7      then show ?thesis by auto
8  qed
```

The proof for Exercise 2.3.1 is a bit tricky. If we simply follow the "backward reasoning then forward reasoning" routine we used in Sect. 1.3, we may end up writing the following partial proof:

```
1  lemma "\not (\forall x. R x) --> (\exists x. \not (R x))"
2  proof
3      assume a1: "\not (\forall x. R x)"
4      show "(\exists x. \not (R x))"
5      proof
6          show "\not (R t)"
7          proof
8          assume a2: "R t"
9          show "False" sorry
10          qed
11      qed
12  qed
```

From there, we seem to hit a dead-end as there is no clear way we can take to prove "False" from the existing assumptions. Instead, we can use the RAA rule and assume that $\neg(\exists x. \neg(R\ x))$ is true and derive a contradiction. In the sub-proof, we will need to prove $\forall x. R\ x$ which contradicts the assumption $a1$. To show this, we can use RAA again and assume $\neg(\forall x. R\ x)$ and derive a contradiction.

Use the above templates and prove the formulae in Exercise 2.3.

2.3 Sequent Calculus for First-Order Logic

As with the natural deduction system NK, the full set of inferences rules in the sequent calculus LK for first-order logic consists of the rules presented in Sect. 1.4 and four additional rules for quantifiers. We give the full LK system in Fig. 2.2.

Let us have a look at the four new rules for quantifiers. In the premise of $\forall L$, we assume that Γ is true and that a term t makes A true, and we can deduce Δ. In the conclusion, we assume that Γ is true and that any term makes A true, and we can also deduce Δ because this assumption implies the assumption in the premise.

Identity and Cut:

$$\frac{}{A \vdash A} \; id \qquad\qquad \frac{\Gamma \vdash \Delta, A \qquad A, \Gamma' \vdash \Delta'}{\Gamma, \Gamma' \vdash \Delta, \Delta'} \; cut$$

Logical Rules:

$$\frac{\Gamma \vdash \Delta}{\Gamma, \top \vdash \Delta} \; \top L \qquad \frac{}{\Gamma \vdash \top, \Delta} \; \top R \qquad \frac{}{\Gamma, \bot \vdash \Delta} \; \bot L \qquad \frac{\Gamma \vdash \Delta}{\Gamma \vdash \bot, \Delta} \; \bot R$$

$$\frac{\Gamma, A \vdash \Delta}{\Gamma, A \wedge B \vdash \Delta} \; \wedge L_1 \qquad \frac{\Gamma, B \vdash \Delta}{\Gamma, A \wedge B \vdash \Delta} \; \wedge L_2 \qquad \frac{\Gamma \vdash A, \Delta}{\Gamma \vdash A \vee B, \Delta} \; \vee R_1 \qquad \frac{\Gamma \vdash B, \Delta}{\Gamma \vdash A \vee B, \Delta} \; \vee R_2$$

$$\frac{\Gamma, A \vdash \Delta \qquad \Gamma, B \vdash \Delta}{\Gamma, A \vee B \vdash \Delta} \; \vee L \qquad\qquad \frac{\Gamma \vdash A, \Delta \qquad \Gamma \vdash B, \Delta}{\Gamma \vdash A \wedge B, \Delta} \; \wedge R$$

$$\frac{\Gamma \vdash A, \Delta \qquad B, \Gamma' \vdash \Delta'}{\Gamma, \Gamma', A \rightarrow B \vdash \Delta, \Delta'} \to L \qquad\qquad \frac{\Gamma, A \vdash B, \Delta}{\Gamma \vdash A \rightarrow B, \Delta} \to R$$

$$\frac{\Gamma \vdash A, \Delta}{\Gamma, \neg A \vdash \Delta} \; \neg L \qquad\qquad \frac{\Gamma, A \vdash \Delta}{\Gamma \vdash \neg A, \Delta} \; \neg R$$

$$\frac{\Gamma, A[t/x] \vdash \Delta}{\Gamma, \forall x.A \vdash \Delta} \; \forall L \qquad \frac{\Gamma \vdash A[a/x], \Delta}{\Gamma \vdash \forall x.A, \Delta} \; \forall R \qquad \frac{\Gamma, A[a/x] \vdash \Delta}{\Gamma, \exists x.A \vdash \Delta} \; \exists L \qquad \frac{\Gamma \vdash A[t/x], \Delta}{\Gamma \vdash \exists x.A, \Delta} \; \exists R$$

Structural Rules:

$$\frac{\Gamma \vdash \Delta}{\Gamma, A \vdash \Delta} \; WL \qquad \frac{\Gamma \vdash \Delta}{\Gamma \vdash A, \Delta} \; WR \qquad \frac{\Gamma, A, A \vdash \Delta}{\Gamma, A \vdash \Delta} \; CL \qquad \frac{\Gamma \vdash A, A, \Delta}{\Gamma \vdash A, \Delta} \; CR$$

$$\frac{\Gamma, A, B, \Gamma' \vdash \Delta}{\Gamma, B, A, \Gamma' \vdash \Delta} \; EL \qquad\qquad \frac{\Gamma \vdash \Delta, A, B, \Delta'}{\Gamma \vdash \Delta, B, A, \Delta'} \; ER$$

Side Condition: in $\forall R$ and $\exists L$, a does not occur in the conclusion.

Fig. 2.2 The full sequent calculus LK for classical first-order logic

In the premise of $\forall R$, from the assumption Γ, we deduce that a makes A true or Δ is true, where a does not appear in the conclusion. This side condition ensures that a is an arbitrary item in the current derivation. Thus, from the same assumption, we can also deduce that $\forall x.A$ is true, or Δ is true, which is the conclusion. This reasoning is similar to the $\forall I$ in NK.

The rules for $\exists$ are symmetric. In the premise of $\exists L$, we assume that an arbitrary item a makes A true, and that Γ is true, then we deduce Δ. Thus, if there is indeed a term that makes A true, and that Γ is true, then we can also deduce Δ. This rule is similar to the $\exists E$ rule in NK.

In the premise of $\exists R$, from the assumption, we can deduce that some term t makes A true or Δ is true. Then from the same assumption, we can derive that there must be some term that makes A true, or Δ is true.

The full LK system is sound and complete for first-order logic.

Theorem 2.3 (Soundness of LK) *If a formula can be proved in LK, then it is valid in classical first-order logic.*

Theorem 2.4 (Completeness of LK) *If a formula is valid in classical first-order logic, then it can be proved in LK.*

Let us see an example derivation for the formula $\neg\forall x.R(x) \to \exists x.\neg R(x)$, which has a non-trivial proof in NK.

Lemma 2.5 $\neg\forall x.R(x) \to \exists x.\neg R(x)$ *is valid in first-order logic.*

Proof We give the derivation tree as follows:

$$
\dfrac{
\dfrac{
\dfrac{
\dfrac{
\dfrac{
\dfrac{
\dfrac{}{R(a) \vdash R(a)}\ id
}{\vdash \neg R(a),\, R(a)}\ \neg R
}{\vdash \exists x.\neg R(x),\, R(a)}\ \exists R
}{\vdash R(a),\, \exists x.\neg R(x)}\ ER
}{\vdash \forall x.R(x),\, \exists x.\neg R(x)}\ \forall R
}{\neg\forall x.R(x) \vdash \exists x.\neg R(x)}\ \neg L
}{\vdash \neg\forall x.R(x) \to \exists x.\neg R(x)}\ \to R
$$

Reading the derivation bottom-up, we see that the $\forall R$ rule requires that the term a in the premise does not occur in the conclusion, which is satisfied by the rule application. The $\exists R$ rule does not have side conditions, so we can simply choose the existing term a to instantiate the bound variable x. $\square$

For another example, we prove Lemma 2.1 in LK as follows.

Lemma 2.6 $\forall x.R_1(x) \to (\forall x.R_2(x) \to \forall y.(R_1(y) \wedge R_2(y)))$ *is derivable in LK.*

Proof We give a derivation in LK as follows:

$$
\cfrac{
  \cfrac{
    \cfrac{
      \cfrac{\overline{R_1(a) \vdash R_1(a)}\ ^{id}}{\forall x.R_1(x) \vdash R_1(a)}\ ^{\forall L}
    }{\forall x.R_1(x), \forall x.R_2(x) \vdash R_1(a)}\ ^{WL}
    \qquad
    \cfrac{
      \cfrac{
        \cfrac{\overline{R_2(a) \vdash R_2(a)}\ ^{id}}{\forall x.R_2(x) \vdash R_2(a)}\ ^{\forall L}
      }{\forall x.R_2(x), \forall x.R_1(x) \vdash R_2(a)}\ ^{WL}
    }{\forall x.R_1(x), \forall x.R_2(x) \vdash R_2(a)}\ ^{EL}
  }{\forall x.R_1(x), \forall x.R_2(x) \vdash R_1(a) \wedge R_2(a)}\ ^{\wedge R}
}{\cfrac{
  \cfrac{
    \cfrac{\forall x.R_1(x), \forall x.R_2(x) \vdash \forall y.(R_1(y) \wedge R_2(y))}{\forall x.R_1(x) \vdash \forall x.R_2(x) \to \forall y.(R_1(y) \wedge R_2(y))}\ ^{\to R}
  }{\vdash \forall x.R_1(x) \to (\forall x.R_2(x) \to \forall y.(R_1(y) \wedge R_2(y)))}\ ^{\to R}
}{}}\ ^{\forall R}
$$

In the above backward proof search, it is essential that we apply $\forall R$ before applying $\forall L$, as the $\forall R$ rule has a side condition that the instantiated variable must be fresh. In contrast, the $\forall L$ rule does not require such a condition.   □

Next, let us prove Lemma 2.3 in LK.

Lemma 2.7 $\exists x.\forall y.R(x, y) \to \forall y.\exists x.R(x, y)$ *is derivable in* LK.

Proof We give the derivation as follows:

$$
\cfrac{
  \cfrac{
    \cfrac{
      \cfrac{
        \cfrac{\overline{R(a, b) \vdash R(a, b)}\ ^{id}}{R(a, b) \vdash \exists x.R(x, b)}\ ^{\exists R}
      }{\forall y.R(a, y) \vdash \exists x.R(x, b)}\ ^{\forall L}
    }{\forall y.R(a, y) \vdash \forall y.\exists x.R(x, y)}\ ^{\forall R}
  }{\exists x.\forall y.R(x, y) \vdash \forall y.\exists x.R(x, y)}\ ^{\exists L}
}{\vdash \exists x.\forall y.R(x, y) \to \forall y.\exists x.R(x, y)}\ ^{\to R}
$$

As a rule of thumb in backward proof search, we always apply $\forall R$ and $\exists L$ as early as we can because they generate fresh terms. When these two rules are not applicable, we apply $\forall L$ and $\exists R$ to instantiate the quantified variable using existing terms.   □

Example 2.4 Consider the following invalid formula again:

$$\forall y.\exists x.R(x, y) \to \exists x.\forall y.R(x, y).$$

We give a partial derivation as follows:

$$
\cfrac{
  \cfrac{
    \cfrac{
      \cfrac{
        \cfrac{
          \cfrac{???}{R(b, a) \vdash R(b, c)}
        }{R(b, a) \vdash \forall y.R(b, y)}\ ^{\forall R}
      }{R(b, a) \vdash \exists x.\forall y.R(x, y)}\ ^{\exists R}
    }{\exists x.R(x, a) \vdash \exists x.\forall y.R(x, y)}\ ^{\exists L}
  }{\forall y.\exists x.R(x, y) \vdash \exists x.\forall y.R(x, y)}\ ^{\forall L}
}{\vdash \forall y.\exists x.R(x, y) \to \exists x.\forall y.R(x, y)}\ ^{\to R}
$$

Reading from the bottom-up, unfortunately, this time we cannot apply $\exists L$ or $\forall R$ before $\exists R$ and $\forall L$. As a result, we choose to apply $\forall L$ first. The case of applying $\exists R$ first is similar. There is no existing free variable to instantiate from, so we create a new term a. Now we can apply $\exists L$ and create another new term b. Then we have to apply $\exists R$, and we instantiate x with b to match the antecedent. The only remaining quantifier is a $\forall$ on the right-hand side. The $\forall R$ rule requires to create a fresh term c; consequently, the formula $R(b, c)$ cannot match the antecedent $R(b, a)$.

If we take the interpretation in Example 2.3, the top $\forall R$ application says that we need to deduce "b has read all books". To prove it, we need to show that "b has read an arbitrary book c", which has not appeared in the proof. There is no way to prove this statement from the fact that "b has read the book a".

By comparing the derivations in LK and NK, the reader may see that many proofs are more straightforward in LK. It is not hard to come up with heuristic methods for selecting inference rules at each step with practice. However, structural rules and *cut* are cumbersome to use in many derivations. For example, the *cut* rule, the contraction rules, and the exchange rules can be applied as often as one wishes; hence, they may lead to an endless reasoning. The weakening rules may accidentally remove some formulae that we later need and result in partial derivations that cannot be closed. On the other hand, Logical rules break the formulae down to smaller sub-formulae and eliminate logical connectives upwards. Therefore, purely logical rule applications from the original LK would eventually terminate. Consequently, there has been ample research on eliminating the need for structural rules and ensuring that proof search is driven by logical connectives.

Definition 2.6 (*Admissibility of Inference Rules*) We say an inference rule

$$\frac{\rho_1 \quad \cdots \quad \rho_n}{\alpha}\ r$$

is *admissible* in a calculus when we can prove that whenever the premises $\rho_1, \ldots, \rho_n$ are all derivable in the calculus, the conclusion α is also derivable in the calculus without using the rule r.

It is easy to make the exchange rules EL and ER admissible—we only need to assume that the antecedent and succedent of a sequent are made of multisets[2] rather than sequences. Since items in a multiset do not have an order, there is no need to exchange them.

The weakening rules WL and WR can be absorbed into zero-premise rules. In fact, the derived rules for $\top R$ and $\bot L$ on Page 36 already have weakening built-in. In those rules, we allow context structures Γ and Δ to appear in the conclusion. Similarly, we can change the rule id to

---

[2] This is just an intermediate step. We will simplify it further soon.

$$\frac{}{\Gamma, A \vdash A, \Delta}\; id$$

With the above id rule, we no longer need to remove formulae in a sequent explicitly. We can simply accumulate all the formulae we obtain in the derivation.

Contraction, handled by the rules CL and CR, needs more care. To eliminate contraction, we have to copy some formulae or structures from the conclusion to the premise(s) when necessary. The following rules for $\wedge L$ and $\vee R$ merge the two cases in the original LK:

$$\frac{\Gamma, A, B \vdash \Delta}{\Gamma, A \wedge B \vdash \Delta}\; \wedge L \qquad\qquad \frac{\Gamma \vdash A, B, \Delta}{\Gamma \vdash A \vee B, \Delta}\; \vee R$$

The new $\wedge L$ rule, for example, builds in a contraction application on $A \wedge B$, and applications of $\wedge L_1$ and $\wedge L_2$ to obtain A and B respectively. The new $\wedge L$ and $\vee R$ rules also align with the interpretation that comma in the antecedent is conjunction and comma in the succedent is disjunction.

In the rule $\rightarrow L$, we now need to copy the entire context to both premises.

$$\frac{\Gamma \vdash A, \Delta \qquad \Gamma, B \vdash \Delta}{\Gamma, A \rightarrow B \vdash \Delta}\; \rightarrow L$$

Finally, reading backwards in a falsifiability-preserving fashion (i.e., "everything in the antecedent is true, and everything in the succedent is false"), the $\forall L$ rule says that $\forall x.A$ is true in order to falsify the conclusion, and replaces x by some t in the premise. Since every item d in the domain makes $A[d/x]$ true, the instance t we choose in the premise may not be the (only) one we need. Therefore, we should keep the formula $\forall x.A$ so that we can instantiate x to other terms in later proofs. Similarly, in the rule $\exists R$, falsifying the conclusion means that $\exists x.A$ is false. Therefore, any instance of x makes A false. In the premise of $\exists R$, we choose an instance t that falsifies A. However, this instance may not be the one we need in the proof. To be able to instantiate x to other terms, we keep the formula $\exists x.A$ in the premise. Accordingly, the rules $\forall L$ and $\exists R$ are modified as follows:

$$\frac{\Gamma, \forall x.A, A[t/x] \vdash \Delta}{\Gamma, \forall x.A \vdash \Delta}\; \forall L \qquad\qquad \frac{\Gamma \vdash \exists x.A, A[t/x], \Delta}{\Gamma \vdash \exists x.A, \Delta}\; \exists R$$

The above modifications yield an alternative version of LK, here called LK', which is given in Fig. 2.3. With the elimination of structural rules, we no longer care about the order of formulae in a sequent, nor the duplication of formulae. Therefore, we can simplify the system further by defining the antecedent and the succedent of a sequent as *sets* instead of sequences or multisets.

A naïve proof search procedure. In LK', the only logical rules that copy the main formula upwards are $\forall L$ and $\exists R$. All other logical rules remove the main connective and break the formula into smaller sub-formulae. As a result, if we do not consider

Identity and logical constants:

$$\overline{\Gamma, A \vdash A, \Delta} \ \ id \qquad \overline{\Gamma \vdash \top, \Delta} \ \ \top R \qquad \overline{\Gamma, \bot \vdash \Delta} \ \ \bot L$$

Logical Rules:

$$\frac{\Gamma, A, B \vdash \Delta}{\Gamma, A \wedge B \vdash \Delta} \wedge L \qquad\qquad \frac{\Gamma \vdash A, \Delta \qquad \Gamma \vdash B, \Delta}{\Gamma \vdash A \wedge B, \Delta} \wedge R$$

$$\frac{\Gamma, A \vdash \Delta \qquad \Gamma, B \vdash \Delta}{\Gamma, A \vee B \vdash \Delta} \vee L \qquad\qquad \frac{\Gamma \vdash A, B, \Delta}{\Gamma \vdash A \vee B, \Delta} \vee R$$

$$\frac{\Gamma \vdash A, \Delta \qquad \Gamma, B \vdash \Delta}{\Gamma, A \rightarrow B \vdash \Delta} \rightarrow L \qquad\qquad \frac{\Gamma, A \vdash B, \Delta}{\Gamma \vdash A \rightarrow B, \Delta} \rightarrow R$$

$$\frac{\Gamma \vdash A, \Delta}{\Gamma, \neg A \vdash \Delta} \neg L \qquad\qquad \frac{\Gamma, A \vdash \Delta}{\Gamma \vdash \neg A, \Delta} \neg R$$

$$\frac{\Gamma, \forall x.A, A[t/x] \vdash \Delta}{\Gamma, \forall x.A \vdash \Delta} \forall L \qquad\qquad \frac{\Gamma \vdash A[a/x]\Delta}{\Gamma \vdash \forall x.A, \Delta} \forall R$$

$$\frac{\Gamma, A[a/x] \vdash \Delta}{\Gamma, \exists x.A \vdash \Delta} \exists L \qquad\qquad \frac{\Gamma \vdash \exists x.A, A[t/x], \Delta}{\Gamma \vdash \exists x.A, \Delta} \exists R$$

Side Condition: in $\forall R$ and $\exists L$, a does not occur in the conclusion.

Fig. 2.3   The alternative sequent calculus LK' for first-order logic

quantifiers, we can develop a systematic and terminating proof search procedure for propositional logic, as shown in Algorithm 1

Algorithm 1 delays creating new branches as much as possible. If the "foreach" loop is completed and all branches are closed, then we obtain a derivation of the formula A. If we enter the "else" part and stop, then we obtain a partial derivation, and the formula is not provable. In this case, we can extract a counterexample from the open branch of the partial derivation.

Example 2.5 Let us see an example derivation generated by Algorithm 1 for the formula $(A \rightarrow B) \rightarrow ((\neg A \rightarrow B) \rightarrow B)$, which we have proved in Sect. 1.4.

Algorithm 1: A naïve backward proof search strategy for classical propositional logic using LK'.

Data: A classical propositional logic formula A.
Result: A derivation tree in LK'.
build the bottom sequent $\vdash A$;
foreach *top sequent on an open branch* **do**
    if *any of the rules* id, $\top R$ *and* $\bot L$ *is applicable* **then**
      | apply the rule backwards and close the branch;
    else if *any of the rules* $\wedge L$, $\vee R$, $\to R$, $\neg L$ *and* $\neg R$ *is applicable* **then**
      | apply the rule backwards;
    else if *any of the rules* $\wedge R$, $\vee L$ *and* $\to L$ *is applicable* **then**
      | apply the rule backwards and create a new branch;
    else
      | stop;
    end
end

$$\dfrac{\dfrac{\overline{A \vdash A, B}^{\;id} \quad \overline{A, B \vdash B}^{\;id}}{\dfrac{A \to B, A \vdash B}{A \to B \vdash \neg A, B}^{\;\neg R}} {}^{\to L} \quad \dfrac{\overline{A \to B, B \vdash B}^{\;id}}{}^{\to L}}{\dfrac{A \to B, \neg A \to B \vdash B}{\dfrac{A \to B \vdash (\neg A \to B) \to B}{\vdash (A \to B) \to ((\neg A \to B) \to B)}^{\;\to R}}^{\;\to R}}$$

Compared to the derivation in Sect. 1.4, the above derivation is simpler. More importantly, we no longer need to pay attention to the contraction rule application, without which we may obtain a partial derivation that cannot be closed in the original LK.[3] With the above proof search strategy for LK', if a propositional formula is valid, then any choice of rule application is guaranteed to lead to a full derivation, and we will never have dead-ends nor the need for backtracking.

Example 2.6 Let us try to prove the formula $A \vee B \to A \wedge B$, which is not valid. We obtain the partial derivation below using Algorithm 1.

$$\dfrac{\dfrac{\overline{A \vdash A}^{\;id} \quad A \vdash B}{A \vdash A \wedge B}^{\wedge R} \quad \dfrac{B \vdash A \quad \overline{B \vdash B}^{\;id}}{B \vdash A \wedge B}^{\wedge R}}{\dfrac{A \vee B \vdash A \wedge B}{\vdash A \vee B \to A \wedge B}^{\;\to R}}^{\vee L}$$

There are two open branches in the derivation, and no rule in LK' is applicable to the top sequent on those branches. Such top sequents correspond to counterexamples

---

[3] This does not contradict with the completeness proof, which only guarantees that *there is* a derivation.

in the following sense: backward proof search is essentially a refutation procedure that tries the falsify the bottom sequent. Recall in Definition 1.19 that a sequent is falsifiable if everything in the antecedent is true and everything in the succedent is false. By assuming that the bottom sequent is falsifiable, we are trying to show that the formula $A \vee B \rightarrow A \wedge B$ is false. If every branch is closed, then there is no way to falsify the bottom sequent; therefore, the formula is true in all cases, so it is valid. A branch that cannot be closed corresponds to an example that falsifies the bottom sequent.

In the above example, the top sequent on the left open branch is $A \vdash B$. In the falsifiability reading, we assume that A is true and B is false. This assignment falsifies the formula $A \vee B \rightarrow A \wedge B$ as the left-hand side of the implication is true, and the right-hand side is false. The other open branch gives another counterexample: B is true, and A is false.

I called the above proof search algorithm *naïve* because there are many other more sophisticated algorithms, heuristic methods, and optimisations in modern theorem provers that make proof search for propositional logic much more efficient than Algorithm 1. These are not in the scope of this book.

Proof search for first-order logic may not terminate. We can extend the naïve proof search for propositional logic with quantifiers as in Algorithm 2.

Algorithm 2: A naïve backward proof search strategy for first-order logic using LK'.

Data: A first-order logic formula A.
Result: A derivation tree in LK'.
build the bottom sequent $\vdash A$;
foreach *top sequent on an open branch* **do**
    if *any of the rules id, $\top R$ and $\bot L$ is applicable* **then**
       | apply the rule backwards and close the branch;
    else if *any of the rules $\wedge L$, $\vee R$, $\rightarrow R$, $\neg L$, $\neg R$, $\forall R$ and $\exists L$* **then**
       | apply the rule backwards;
    else if *any of the rules $\wedge R$, $\vee L$ and $\rightarrow L$ is applicable* **then**
       | apply the rule backwards and create a new branch;
    else if *$\forall L$ or $\exists R$ is applicable and there is a term t which has not been used to instantiate the quantified variable x in said formula* **then**
       | apply the rule backwards by substituting x with t;
    else if *$\forall L$ or $\exists R$ is applicable* **then**
       | apply the rule backwards and create a fresh term;
    else
       | stop;
    end
end

The main trouble in first-order reasoning is in the rules $\forall L$ and $\exists R$, which do not eliminate the corresponding quantifier in the premise, and they may be applied infinitely many times. One can certainly find a more efficient proof search than the above, but unfortunately, this problem is generally inevitable in first-order logic reasoning. In the worst case, we can still apply the rules *fairly*, e.g., iteratively apply each rule in every possible way so that each possible rule application could eventually be considered. In this way, if a first-order logic formula is valid, we will eventually find a derivation; but our algorithm may never stop if the formula is invalid. Indeed, we will discuss in later chapters that theorem proving for first-order logic is generally a much harder problem than that for propositional logic.

Example 2.7 Consider the sequent

$$\Gamma, \forall x.A \vdash \Delta.$$

The rule $\forall L$ is always applicable because the formula $\forall x.A$ remains in the antecedent in all cases of backward rule applications. Consequently, Algorithm 2 cannot be used to provide counterexamples for this sequent.

We will formally prove the admissibility of structural rules and show the completeness of LK' in the next section, so right now, the reader just needs to trust me that if a formula is valid, then it is provable in LK'.

Note that the completeness of a proof theory is a separate issue from the same property for a proof search algorithm. We do not formally prove that Algorithm 1 and 2 are complete in this book. However, the completeness of these algorithms is implied by the results of the next section. That is, invertibility of inference rules (cf. Lemma 2.13) entails that each rule application preserves the provability of sequents. As a result, when we exhaust all possible rule applications, we must be able to find a derivation for a valid formula. It is straightforward to check that Algorithm 1 and 2 exhaust all possible rule applications for their respective proof theory.

Exercises

2.5 Prove the formulae in Exercise 1.16 and 1.17 of Sect. 1.4 using LK'.

Hint: use Algorithm 1.

2.6 Prove the formulae in Exercise 2.3 of Sect. 2.2 using LK'.

Hint: use Algorithm 2.

2.7 Prove the above formulae in Isabelle/HOL using "apply"-style proofs.

2.4   The Cut-Elimination Theorem

This section goes back to Gentzen's attempt on showing that a proof with a "detour"[4] can always be normalised into a proof without one. He finally succeeded in proving it with sequent calculus. In the sequent calculus LK, the *cut* rule

$$\frac{\Gamma \vdash \Delta, A \qquad A, \Gamma' \vdash \Delta'}{\Gamma, \Gamma' \vdash \Delta, \Delta'} \; cut$$

has two premises: one has a formula A in the succedent and the other has A in the antecedent. The rule application removes A (called the *cut* formula) and joins the other structures into one sequent. The top-down reading of the rule is somewhat analogous to the "detour": we introduce the formula A in the premises and then eliminate it. Reading the rule backwards as in proof search, we have to guess the formula A in the premise. The cut formula can be any (sub)formula in the conclusion, or *even a new formula*. Consequently, the *cut* rule is a means of introducing uncertainty and infinite steps in proof search, and its removal is critical in automated reasoning.

Cut-elimination is the central result of sequent calculus. It was first proved in Gentzen's paper "Investigations into Logical Deduction" [4]. This theorem is also called Gentzen's *Hauptsatz*, which translates to the "main theorem".

Before we present a proof for Gentzen's main theorem, we need to prove quite a few lemmas that are used as components of the proof. To reduce the number of cases in proofs, we give a smaller set of rules that are equivalent to LK'. We have discussed the "minimal" set of logical connectives required for propositional logic in Sect. 1.2. In practice, having only the "nand" connective is often inconvenient. Therefore, we take a step back and simplify the presentation to only the rules for $\neg$, $\wedge$, $\forall$, and id. We call this subset of rules LK'' and show it in Fig. 2.4. Clearly, since the other logical constants, connectives, and quantifier can be derived from this subset, we have the following result:

Lemma 2.8 LK'' *is equivalent to* LK'.

Proof We define the other elements of the first-order logic language using $\neg$, $\wedge$, and $\forall$ as follows:

$$\top ::= \neg(A \wedge \neg A)$$
$$\bot ::= (A \wedge \neg A)$$
$$A \vee B ::= \neg(\neg A \wedge \neg B)$$
$$A \rightarrow B ::= \neg(A \wedge \neg B)$$
$$\exists x.A ::= \neg(\forall x.\neg A)$$

---

[4] The word "detour" on Page 32 refers to some proof steps in natural deduction that introduces a formula via an introduction rule and then eliminates the formula via an elimination rule. Such "detours" do not necessarily contribute to longer proofs. In fact, in sequent calculus, a detour in the form of the *cut* rule often shortens proofs.

Fig. 2.4 A smaller set of rules LK'' for first-order logic

Identity:

$$\frac{}{\Gamma, A \vdash A, \Delta}\ id$$

Logical Rules:

$$\frac{\Gamma, A, B \vdash \Delta}{\Gamma, A \wedge B \vdash \Delta}\ \wedge L \qquad \frac{\Gamma \vdash A, \Delta \qquad \Gamma \vdash B, \Delta}{\Gamma \vdash A \wedge B, \Delta}\ \wedge R$$

$$\frac{\Gamma \vdash A, \Delta}{\Gamma, \neg A \vdash \Delta}\ \neg L \qquad \frac{\Gamma, A \vdash \Delta}{\Gamma \vdash \neg A, \Delta}\ \neg R$$

$$\frac{\Gamma, \forall x.A, A[t/x] \vdash \Delta}{\Gamma, \forall x.A \vdash \Delta}\ \forall L \qquad \frac{\Gamma \vdash A[a/x]\Delta}{\Gamma \vdash \forall x.A, \Delta}\ \forall R$$

Side Condition: in $\forall R$, a does not occur in the conclusion.

It is straightforward to prove that these definitions are sound using LK derivations. We leave it for the readers to check. □

Previously we have discussed how we transform some inference rules to get rid of the structural rules. Now we formally prove that the structural rules in LK are indeed admissible in LK''.

Lemma 2.9 (Admissibility of Exchange) *If the sequent* $\Gamma, A, B, \Gamma' \vdash \Delta$ *is derivable in* LK'', *so is* $\Gamma, B, A, \Gamma' \vdash \Delta$. *Also, if the sequent* $\Gamma \vdash \Delta, A, B, \Delta'$ *is derivable in* LK'', *so is* $\Gamma \vdash \Delta, B, A, \Delta'$.

Proof The antecedent and the succedent in a sequent of LK'' are sets, which do not impose order over the elements. By definition, $\Gamma, A, B, \Gamma' \vdash \Delta$ is equivalent to $\Gamma, B, A, \Gamma' \vdash \Delta$ and $\Gamma \vdash \Delta, A, B, \Delta'$ is equivalent to $\Gamma \vdash \Delta, B, A, \Delta'$. □

Next, we prove that substituting a fresh item in the domain for an item that already occurs in the sequent preserves provability. This lemma will be useful in subsequent proofs.

Lemma 2.10 (Substitution of Items) *Assume that* $\Gamma \vdash \Delta$ *has a derivation* Π *in* LK'' *and that an item m in the domain occurs in this sequent. Then we can replace every occurrence of m by a fresh item n that does not occur in the above sequent,*

and the new sequent $\Gamma[n/m] \vdash \Delta[n/m]$ *has a derivation* Π' *in* LK'', *and* Π *and* Π'
have the same number of rule applications on each branch.

Proof Let Π be a derivation tree for $\Gamma \vdash \Delta$, which is visualised as follows:

$$\frac{\Pi}{\Gamma \vdash \Delta}$$

Let n be an item that does not appear anywhere in the above derivation. If the above
derivation uses all the items in the domain, we can extend the language by adding a
new item to the domain. Thus, after replacing every occurrence of m by n, we obtain
the following derivation:

$$\frac{\Pi[n/m]}{\Gamma[n/m] \vdash \Delta[n/m]}$$

Since n is fresh, it appears in the new derivation exactly where m appears in the
old one, and the above substitution is simply a renaming of items. Thus, $\Pi[n/m]$
is a correct derivation for $\Gamma[n/m] \vdash \Delta[n/m]$ and it has the same number of rule
applications as Π on every branch.   □

Proof by induction. Admissibility for the other structural rules requires more
detailed analysis. We will need a technique called *proof by induction*. Such proof
works on inductively defined mathematical structures. An *inductive definition* often
contains some *base cases* and some *inductive cases*. Recall the BNF format definition
of the syntax of proposition logic as follows.

$$F ::= \top \mid p \mid \neg F \mid F \wedge F.$$

The base cases are $\top$ and p because we cannot break them down any further, and
we build up other cases from these base cases. The inductive cases are $\neg F$ and
$F \wedge F$. That is, assuming that we have built a formula F, then $\neg F$ is also a formula.
Similarly, if F_1 and F_2 are formulae, so is $F_1 \wedge F_2$.

For another example, we can define the set of natural numbers as below, where
suc is a function that takes a natural number n as input and returns its successor
$n + 1$.

Base case: 0 is a natural number.
Inductive case: if n is a natural number, so is $suc(n)$.

Analogously, the proof by induction technique has two steps: the first step is to
prove the base cases, and the second step is the inductive cases. For example, if we
want to prove a property P on natural numbers, we first prove the base case that P
is true for 0. For the inductive case, we assume that P is true for an arbitrary number
n (this assumption is called the *induction hypothesis*), and we prove that P is also

true for $suc(n)$. Once we have done these two steps, we can conclude that P holds for any natural number.

We can also view a derivation tree as an inductively generated structure. The induction is on the length of the derivation, which is defined as follows.

Definition 2.7 (*Length of Derivation*) The length of a derivation Π, denoted by $|\Pi|$, is the number of rule applications on the longest branch of Π.

Example 2.8 The length of the derivation in Example 2.5 is 6, which is the number of rule applications on the leftmost branch. Alternatively, one can use the number of rule applications on the second branch from the left, as it also has 6 rule applications.

Let us prove another lemma that is related to substitution. In this lemma, we assume that the substitution $[t/a]$ does not clash with any bound variable. That is, when we perform the substitution $[t/a]$ on a formula such as $\forall x.A$, we assume that t does not contain the bound variable x; otherwise, the substitution may change the semantics of the formula. If the clash were to happen, we could always rename all the bound variables so that they do not clash with t.

Lemma 2.11 (Substitution of Terms) *If there is a derivation Π for the sequent $\Gamma \vdash \Delta$, then there is also a derivation Π' for the sequent $\Gamma[t/a] \vdash \Delta[t/a]$, where t is a term, and the substitution $[t/a]$ does not clash with any bound variable, and $|\Pi'| \leq |\Pi|$.*

Proof By induction on the length of the derivation.

(Base case) The derivation only has a single rule application, which must be the id rule of LK''. In this case, the sequent after substitution must also be derivable by applying id.

(Inductive case) The induction hypothesis is that for any sequent $\Gamma_0 \vdash \Delta_0$, if it has a derivation of length n, then $\Gamma_0[t/a] \vdash \Delta_0[t/a]$ also has a derivation of length at most n. The inductive case is that $\Gamma \vdash \Delta$ has a derivation of length $n+1$. We need to prove that $\Gamma[t/a] \vdash \Delta[t/a]$ also has a derivation of length at most $n+1$. We prove by a case analysis on the lowest rule application.

- The cases for $\wedge L, \wedge R, \neg L$ and $\neg R$ are straightforward. We give the case for $\forall L$ as an example. If the lowest rule application is this rule, then Γ contains some $\forall x.A$. We can rewrite Γ as $\Gamma'' \cup \{\forall x.A\}$. The derivation for $\Gamma \vdash \Delta$ has the following form:

$$
\frac{\begin{array}{c} \Pi \\ \Gamma'', \forall x.A, A[t'/x] \vdash \Delta \end{array}}{\Gamma'', \forall x.A \vdash \Delta} \; \forall L
$$

The premise Γ'', $\forall x.A$, $A[t'/x] \vdash \Delta$ has a derivation Π of length n. By the induction hypothesis, there is a derivation Π' of length at most n for the sequent $\Gamma''[t/a]$, $\forall x.A[t/a]$, $A[t'/x][t/a] \vdash \Delta[t/a]$.

- If a does not appear in t', then the order of the two substitutions in $A[t'/x][t/a]$ can be exchanged. So $A[t'/x][t/a] = A[t/a][t'/x]$. Then we obtain the following derivation:

$$\Pi'$$
$$\frac{\Gamma''[t/a], \forall x.A[t/a], A[t/a][t'/x] \vdash \Delta[t/a]}{\Gamma''[t/a], \forall x.A[t/a] \vdash \Delta[t/a]} \; {\scriptstyle \forall L}$$

- If a appears in t', then $A[t'/x][t/a]$ does not directly equal $A[t/a][t'/x]$. However, we can choose the term that instantiates x in the new derivation. For example, instead of instantiating x by t', we can instantiate x by $t'[t/a]$. The reader can check that the following is still a correct derivation:

$$\Pi'$$
$$\frac{\Gamma''[t/a], \forall x.A[t/a], A[t'/x][t/a] \vdash \Delta[t/a]}{\Gamma''[t/a], \forall x.A[t/a] \vdash \Delta[t/a]} \; {\scriptstyle \forall L}$$

In this case, the term t plays the role of a just fine.

- The case for $\forall R$ is more tricky. In this case, Δ contains some $\forall x.A$, and we can rewrite Δ as $\Delta'' \cup \{\forall x.A\}$. The derivation of $\Gamma \vdash \Delta$ takes the following form:

$$\Pi$$
$$\frac{\Gamma \vdash A[b/x], \Delta''}{\Gamma \vdash \forall x.A, \Delta''} \; {\scriptstyle \forall R}$$

The premise $\Gamma \vdash A[b/x], \Delta''$ has a derivation Π of length n. However, a problem arises: the term t in the lemma may contain the item b. If we directly apply the induction hypothesis and obtain a derivation for $\Gamma[t/a] \vdash A[b/x][t/a], \Delta''[t/a]$, the following derivation may be incorrect:

$$\vdots$$
$$\frac{\Gamma[t/a] \vdash A[b/x][t/a], \Delta''[t/a]}{\Gamma[t/a] \vdash \forall x.A[t/a], \Delta''[t/a]} \; {\scriptstyle \forall R}$$

The issue here is that b may appear in the conclusion, thus violating the side condition of the rule $\forall R$. To proceed with the proof, we apply Lemma 2.10 and globally replace b by a new item c which does not appear anywhere in the discussion.

Lemma 2.10 ensures that there is a derivation Π' for $\Gamma \vdash A[c/x], \Delta''$, and Π' is also of length n. Now we can apply the induction hypothesis and obtain another derivation Π'' of length at most n for $\Gamma[t/a] \vdash A[c/x][t/a], \Delta''[t/a]$. Since c is an item in the domain, it naturally does not contain a. Also, the assumption of the lemma ensures that t does not clash with x. Then we obtain the following derivation:

$$\cfrac{\begin{array}{c} \Pi'' \\ \Gamma[t/a] \vdash A[c/x][t/a], \Delta''[t/a] \end{array}}{\Gamma[t/a] \vdash \forall x.A[t/a], \Delta''[t/a]} \; {\scriptstyle \forall R}$$

Note that the side condition of $\forall R$ is satisfied because c does not appear in the conclusion.

$\square$

Now we are ready to prove that weakening is admissible in LK''.

Lemma 2.12 (Admissibility of Weakening) *If there is a derivation Π for $\Gamma \vdash \Delta$ in LK'', then there is also a derivation Π' for $\Gamma, \Gamma' \vdash \Delta, \Delta'$ in LK'', where Γ' and Δ' are additional sets of formulae, and $|\Pi'| \leq |\Pi|$.*

Proof By induction on the length of the derivation.

(Base case) The derivation only has a single rule application, which must be the id rule of LK''. If

$$\cfrac{}{\Gamma \vdash \Delta} \; {\scriptstyle id}$$

is a correct derivation, then there is a formula A that appears on both sides of $\vdash$. Thus,

$$\cfrac{}{\Gamma, \Gamma' \vdash \Delta, \Delta'} \; {\scriptstyle id}$$

must also be a correct derivation.

(Inductive case) The induction hypothesis is that for any sequent $\Gamma_0 \vdash \Delta_0$ that has a derivation of length n, we can also find a derivation of length at most n for $\Gamma_0, \Gamma_1 \vdash \Delta_0, \Delta_1$, for any sets Γ_1 and Δ_1 of formulae. In the inductive case, $\Gamma \vdash \Delta$ has a derivation of length $n + 1$, and we need to show that $\Gamma, \Gamma' \vdash \Delta, \Delta'$ also has a derivation of length at most $n + 1$, for any sets Γ' and Δ' of formulae. We prove this by case analysis of the lowest rule application in the derivation of $\Gamma \vdash \Delta$.

- If the lowest rule application is $\wedge L$, then Γ must contain some $A \wedge B$. So we can rewrite Γ as $\Gamma'' \cup \{A \wedge B\}$. The derivation for $\Gamma \vdash \Delta$ looks like the following:

$$\frac{\begin{array}{c}\Pi\\ \Gamma'', A, B \vdash \Delta\end{array}}{\Gamma'', A \wedge B \vdash \Delta} \wedge L$$

And the premise $\Gamma'', A, B \vdash \Delta$ has a derivation Π of length n. By the induction hypothesis, there is a derivation Π' of length at most n for $\Gamma'', A, B, \Gamma' \vdash \Delta, \Delta'$. We then obtain a derivation of length at most $n + 1$ for $\Gamma'', A \wedge B, \Gamma' \vdash \Delta, \Delta'$ by applying the $\wedge L$ rule downwards.

$$\frac{\begin{array}{c}\Pi'\\ \Gamma'', A, B, \Gamma' \vdash \Delta, \Delta'\end{array}}{\Gamma'', A \wedge B, \Gamma' \vdash \Delta, \Delta'} \wedge L$$

- The cases where the lowest rule application is $\wedge R$, $\neg L$, $\neg R$ and $\forall L$ are similar. We leave them as an exercise for the reader.
- If the lowest rule application is $\forall R$, then Δ must contain some $\forall x.A$. We rewrite Δ as $\Delta'' \cup \{\forall x.A\}$. The derivation for $\Gamma \vdash \Delta$ looks like the following, where the fresh item a does not appear in the conclusion:

$$\frac{\begin{array}{c}\Pi\\ \Gamma \vdash A[a/x], \Delta''\end{array}}{\Gamma \vdash \forall x.A, \Delta''} \forall R$$

The derivation Π is of length n, so we can apply the induction hypothesis on it. However, since the additional sets Γ' and Δ' of formulae are arbitrary, they may contain occurrences of a. In this case, we use Lemma 2.10 to perform the substitution $\Gamma[b/a] \vdash A[a/x][b/a], \Delta''[b/a]$, where b is a new item that does not appear in $\Gamma, \Gamma' \vdash \forall x.A, \Delta'', \Delta'$, and we know that there is a derivation Π' for the substituted sequent, and Π' is also of length n. Since a does not appear in the conclusion of the above rule application, it also does not appear in Γ, A and Δ''. Thus, we have

$$\Gamma[b/a] \vdash A[a/x][b/a], \Delta''[b/a] = \Gamma \vdash A[b/x], \Delta''$$

Now that the above sequent can be derived by Π', we apply the induction hypothesis and obtain a derivation Π'' of length at most n for $\Gamma, \Gamma' \vdash A[b/x], \Delta'', \Delta'$. We then obtain the following derivation:

$$\frac{\Pi''}{\Gamma, \Gamma' \vdash A[b/x], \Delta'', \Delta'} \forall R$$
$$\overline{\Gamma, \Gamma' \vdash \forall x.A, \Delta'', \Delta'}$$

The lowest rule application is correct because the new item b does not appear in the conclusion.

$\square$

The admissibility of the weakening rules in LK is a special case of the above lemma. We state the special cases in the corollary as follows.

Corollary 2.1 *If* $\Gamma \vdash \Delta$ *is derivable in* LK'', *then both* $\Gamma, A \vdash \Delta$ *and* $\Gamma \vdash A, \Delta$ *are derivable in* LK''.

Using the same technique, we can also prove the following two lemmas:

Lemma 2.13 (Invertibility of Rules) *For each inference rule in* LK'', *if there is a derivation* Π *for the conclusion in* LK'', *then there is also a derivation* Π' *for each premise in* LK'', *and* $|\Pi'| \leq |\Pi|$.

The above lemma implies that we do not need to worry about the case where a wrong choice of rule application leads to a dead-end in the proof. Since each rule is invertible, any backward rule application preserves provability. However, there may still be cases where a rule application leads to a much shorter proof than others.

Lemma 2.14 (Admissibility of Contraction) *If there is a derivation* Π *for* $\Gamma, \Gamma \vdash \Delta, \Delta$ *in* LK'', *then there is also a derivation* Π' *for* $\Gamma \vdash \Delta$ *in* LK'', *and* $|\Pi'| \leq |\Pi|$.

Admissibility of contraction rules CL and CR are special cases of the above lemma, which we state as follows.

Corollary 2.2 *If* $\Gamma, A \vdash \Delta$ *is derivable in* LK'', *so is* $\Gamma, A, A \vdash \Delta$. *If* $\Gamma \vdash A, \Delta$ *is derivable in* LK'', *so is* $\Gamma \vdash A, A, \Delta$.

The above lemmas conclude the admissibility of all structural rules in LK''. A careful reader should have noticed that we do not present the *cut* rule in LK' and LK''. Since we have shown that LK' is equivalent to LK'', the admissibility of the *cut* rule in LK'' is the only missing link towards the equivalence of LK, LK', and LK''.

Next, we give some definitions that are essential to proving the cut-elimination theorem.

Definition 2.8 (*Size of Formula*) The size of a first-order logic formula A, denoted by $|A|$, is defined as the number of logical connectives and quantifiers in A.

Definition 2.9 (*Cut Rank and Cut Length*) The *cut rank* of a *cut* rule application is the pair $(|A|, |\Pi_1| + |\Pi_2|)$, where A is the cut formula, and $|\Pi_1|$ and $|\Pi_2|$ are the lengths of the derivations above the *cut* rule, respectively. The sum of $|\Pi_1|$ and $|\Pi_2|$ is called the *cut length*.

Cut ranks are ordered *lexicographically*, where each component of a rank is ordered according to the ordering $<$ on natural numbers. That is, when comparing two cut ranks (x_1, y_1) and (x_2, y_2), we first compare the left component. If $x_1 < x_2$, then the first cut rank is smaller. If the left components are equal, then we compare the right component. For example, $(4, 18) < (5, 15)$ and $(5, 15) < (5, 20)$.

We denote the union of LK'' rules and *cut* as $LK'' + cut$. We now proceed and prove the cut-elimination theorem.

Note that the statement of the theorem below simply says that *cut* is admissible. On the other hand, Gentzen's proof is more than that—he gives a proof transformation algorithm that systematically removes each *cut* rule application from a proof. A cut-admissibility theorem proved by such a procedure is called *cut-elimination*. The proof presented below follows the general ideas of Gentzen's proof but is adapted to the presentation of this book, which is inherited from my PhD thesis [5].

Theorem 2.5 (Cut-admissibility) *If $\Gamma \vdash \Delta$ is derivable in $LK'' + cut$, then it is also derivable in LK''.*

Proof By induction on the cut rank of the proof in $LK'' + cut$. We show that each application of *cut* can either be

- eliminated, or
- replaced by one or more *cut* rule applications of smaller cut ranks.

We start by eliminating the topmost *cut* and repeat this procedure until there is no *cut* in the derivation. The base cases show that a *cut* application can be eliminated when the *cut length* is the shortest, i.e., at least one premise can be proved in one step. We can think of a derivation tree as a glass of water and a cut application as a bubble. In this metaphor, cut length is the distance between the bubble and the surface of the water, and the size of the cut formula is the size of the bubble. The base cases show that a bubble can be removed when it is at the surface.

Then we show that the *cut length* is reduced in all cases in which the cut formula is not the main formula in both premises of cut. That is, in these cases, the bubble moves up. The proof transformation looks like

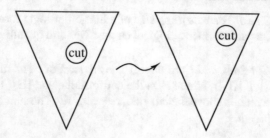

If the cut formula is the main formula in both premises, then the *cut* application is reduced to one or more *cut*s on smaller formulae or shorter derivations. In these cases, the bubble breaks up into smaller bubbles, and the smaller bubbles may move up in position but never move down. This proof transformation is illustrated below

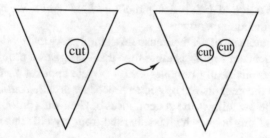

In the worst case, we apply the second method of proof transformation repeatedly until the cut formula is reduced to an atomic formula. Since atomic formulae cannot be the main formula in logical rules, we must be able to apply the first proof transformation in such cases and move the bubble up, and eventually remove it.

(Base case) If at least one premise of the *cut* rule is an *id* application, we consider the following cases:

1. The left premise of *cut* is an application of *id*, and the cut formula is *not* the main formula, then the derivation is transformed as follows:

$$\cfrac{\cfrac{}{\Gamma, B \vdash B, A, \Delta}\ id \qquad \cfrac{\Pi}{\Gamma', A \vdash \Delta'}}{\Gamma, \Gamma', B \vdash B, \Delta, \Delta'}\ cut \quad \Rightarrow \quad \cfrac{}{\Gamma, \Gamma', B \vdash B, \Delta, \Delta'}\ id$$

2. The left premise of *cut* is an application of *id*, and the cut formula is the main formula, then the derivation is transformed as follows:

$$\cfrac{\cfrac{}{\Gamma, A \vdash A, \Delta}\ id \qquad \cfrac{\Pi}{\Gamma', A \vdash \Delta'}}{\Gamma, \Gamma', A \vdash \Delta, \Delta'}\ cut \quad \Rightarrow \quad \cfrac{\cfrac{\Pi}{\Gamma', A \vdash \Delta'}}{\Gamma, \Gamma', A \vdash \Delta, \Delta'}\ \text{Lemma 2.12}$$

3. The right premise of *cut* is an application of *id*, and the cut formula is not the main formula. This case is similar to Case 1.
4. The right premise of *cut* is an application of *id*, and the cut formula is the main formula. This case is similar to Case 2.

(Inductive case) If both premises are not in one of the base cases, we distinguish three cases here: 1) the cut formula is not the main formula in the left premise; 2) the cut formula is only the main formula in the left premise; 3) the cut formula is the main formula in both premises.

1. In this case, the cut formula is not the main formula in the left premise. We permute the *cut* application upwards in the derivation tree to reduce the cut length.

   a. If the rule application r on the left premise is one of $\wedge L$, $\neg L$, $\neg R$ and $\forall L$, then the original derivation takes the following form:

   $$\cfrac{\cfrac{\Pi_1}{\cfrac{\Gamma_1 \vdash A, \Lambda_1}{\Gamma \vdash A, \Delta}\, r} \qquad \cfrac{\Pi_2}{\Gamma', A \vdash \Delta'}}{\Gamma, \Gamma' \vdash \Delta, \Delta'} \; cut$$

   Then we can permute the application of *cut* upwards as follows:

   $$\cfrac{\cfrac{\Pi_1}{\Gamma_1 \vdash A, \Lambda_1} \qquad \cfrac{\Pi_2}{\Gamma', A \vdash \Delta'}}{\cfrac{\Gamma_1, \Gamma' \vdash \Lambda_1, \Delta'}{\Gamma, \Gamma' \vdash \Delta, \Delta'}\, r} \; cut$$

   The reader can check that the above scheme works for all the covered rule applications.

   b. If the rule application on the left premise is $\forall R$, then the original derivation looks like the following, where a is an item that does not occur in Γ, B, A, and Δ:

   $$\cfrac{\cfrac{\Pi_1}{\cfrac{\Gamma \vdash B[a/x], A, \Delta}{\Gamma \vdash x.B, A, \Delta}\, \forall R} \qquad \cfrac{\Pi_2}{\Gamma', A \vdash \Delta'}}{\Gamma, \Gamma' \vdash \forall x.B, \Delta, \Delta'} \; cut$$

   Since a may occur in Γ' and Δ', the transformation in Case (a) does not work. Instead, we first apply Lemma 2.10 with a substitution $[b/a]$ on Π_1 to obtain a new derivation Π_3 of length $|\Pi_1|$ where b is a fresh item that does not occur in Γ, Γ', B, A, Δ, and Δ':

$$\Pi_3$$
$$\Gamma \vdash B[b/x], A, \Delta$$

We can then construct the following derivation in which *cut* is moved upwards:

$$\frac{\dfrac{\Pi_3}{\Gamma \vdash B[b/x], A, \Delta} \qquad \dfrac{\Pi_2}{\Gamma', A \vdash \Delta'}}{\dfrac{\Gamma, \Gamma' \vdash B[b/x], \Delta, \Delta'}{\Gamma, \Gamma' \vdash \forall x.B, \Delta, \Delta'} \scriptstyle{\forall R}} \scriptstyle{cut}$$

In the above cases, the cut rank of the original *cut* is $(|A|, |\Pi_1| + 1 + |\Pi_2|)$, whereas the cut rank of the new *cut* is $(|A|, |\Pi_1| + |\Pi_2|)$, so the cut *length* is reduced.

c. If the rule application on the left premise is $\wedge R$, we transform the derivation as follows:

$$\frac{\dfrac{\dfrac{\Pi_1}{\Gamma \vdash B, A, \Delta} \qquad \dfrac{\Pi_2}{\Gamma \vdash C, A, \Delta}}{\Gamma \vdash B \wedge C, A, \Delta} \scriptstyle{\wedge R} \qquad \dfrac{\Pi_3}{\Gamma', A \vdash \Delta'}}{\Gamma; \Gamma' \vdash B \wedge C, \Delta, \Delta'} \scriptstyle{cut}$$

$$\Downarrow$$

$$\frac{\dfrac{\dfrac{\Pi_1}{\Gamma \vdash B, A, \Delta} \qquad \dfrac{\Pi_3}{\Gamma', A \vdash \Delta'}}{\Gamma, \Gamma' \vdash B, \Delta, \Delta'} \scriptstyle{cut} \qquad \dfrac{\dfrac{\Pi_2}{\Gamma \vdash C, A, \Delta} \qquad \dfrac{\Pi_3}{\Gamma', A \vdash \Delta'}}{\Gamma, \Gamma' \vdash C, \Delta, \Delta'} \scriptstyle{cut}}{\Gamma, \Gamma' \vdash B \wedge C, \Delta, \Delta'} \scriptstyle{\wedge R}$$

The cut rank of the original *cut* is $(|A|, max(|\Pi_1|, |\Pi_2|) + 1 + |\Pi_3|)$, and that of the two new *cut*s are $(|A|, |\Pi_1| + |\Pi_3|)$ and $(|A|, |\Pi_2| + |\Pi_3|)$, respectively. Both of the new cut lengths are reduced.

2. In this case, the cut formula is only the main formula in the left premise, which means that it is not the main formula in the right premise. Thus, we only need to consider the lowest rule application in the right branch. The proof of this case is symmetric to that of Case 1. The cut length is reduced in all sub-cases.
3. In this case, the cut formula is the main formula in both premises. We do a case analysis based on the main connective/quantifier of the cut formula.

a. If the main connective is $\wedge$, we transform the derivation as follows:

$$\frac{\dfrac{\dfrac{\Pi_1}{\Gamma \vdash A, \Delta} \qquad \dfrac{\Pi_2}{\Gamma \vdash B, \Delta}}{\Gamma \vdash A \wedge B, \Delta} \scriptstyle{\wedge R} \qquad \dfrac{\dfrac{\Pi_3}{\Gamma', A, B \vdash \Delta'}}{\Gamma', A \wedge B \vdash \Delta'} \scriptstyle{\wedge L}}{\Gamma, \Gamma' \vdash \Delta, \Delta'} \scriptstyle{cut}$$

$$\Downarrow$$

$$
\cfrac{
\Pi_1 \quad\quad
\cfrac{
\Pi_2 \qquad\qquad \Pi_3
}{
\cfrac{\Gamma \vdash B, \Delta \qquad \Gamma', A, B \vdash \Delta'}{\Gamma, \Gamma', A \vdash \Delta, \Delta'}\ cut
}
}{
\cfrac{\Gamma \vdash A, \Delta \qquad\qquad \Gamma, \Gamma', A \vdash \Delta, \Delta'}{\Gamma, \Gamma, \Gamma' \vdash \Delta, \Delta, \Delta'}\ cut
}
$$

$$\Gamma, \Gamma, \Gamma' \vdash \Delta, \Delta, \Delta' \cdots\cdots\cdots\cdots \text{Lemma 2.14}$$
$$\Gamma, \Gamma' \vdash \Delta, \Delta'$$

The original cut rank is $(|A \wedge B|, max(|\Pi_1|, |\Pi_2|) + |\Pi_3| + 2)$. In the new derivation, the upper cut rank is $(|B|, |\Pi_2| + |\Pi_3|)$, the lower cut rank is $(|A|, |\Pi_1| + max(|\Pi_2|, |\Pi_3|) + 1)$, both are reduced from the original cut rank because both cut formulae are smaller.

b. If the main connective is $\neg$, we transform the derivation as follows:

$$
\cfrac{
\cfrac{
\cfrac{\Pi_1}{\Gamma, A \vdash \Delta}}{\Gamma \vdash \neg A, \Delta}\ \neg R
\qquad
\cfrac{
\cfrac{\Pi_2}{\Gamma' \vdash A, \Delta'}}{\Gamma', \neg A \vdash \Delta'}\ \neg L
}{
\Gamma, \Gamma' \vdash \Delta, \Delta'
}\ cut
$$

$$\Downarrow$$

$$
\cfrac{
\cfrac{\Pi_2}{\Gamma' \vdash A, \Delta'} \qquad \cfrac{\Pi_1}{\Gamma, A \vdash \Delta}
}{
\Gamma, \Gamma' \vdash \Delta, \Delta'
}\ cut
$$

The original cut rank is $(|\neg A|, |\Pi_1| + |\Pi_2| + 2)$, whereas the new cut rank is $(|A|, |\Pi_1| + |\Pi_2|)$, which is clearly smaller.

c. If the main quantifier is $\forall$, the original derivation has the following form, where a does not occur in Γ, A and Δ:

$$
\cfrac{
\cfrac{
\cfrac{\Pi_1}{\Gamma \vdash A[a/x], \Delta}}{\Gamma \vdash \forall x.A, \Delta}\ \forall R
\qquad
\cfrac{
\cfrac{\Pi_2}{\Gamma', \forall x.A, A[t/x] \vdash \Delta'}}{\Gamma', \forall x.A \vdash \Delta'}\ \forall L
}{
\Gamma, \Gamma' \vdash \Delta, \Delta'
}\ cut
$$

Using Lemma 2.11, we can take the derivation Π_1 and substitute the term t for the item a, and obtain a derivation Π_3 of length at most $|\Pi_1|$, as shown below

$$\cfrac{\Pi_3}{\Gamma \vdash A[t/x], \Delta}$$

Note that the term t does not clash with any bound variables in the bottom sequent, as it appears in the same way in the derivation Π_2. Therefore, the assumptions of Lemma 2.11 are satisfied. Finally, We transform the original derivation into the following:

$$
\cfrac{
  \Pi_3 \atop \Gamma \vdash A[t/x], \Delta
}{}
$$

$$
\cfrac{
  \cfrac{
    \cfrac{\Pi_1 \atop \Gamma \vdash A[a/x], \Delta}{\Gamma \vdash \forall x.A, \Delta}\ {\scriptstyle \forall R}
    \qquad
    \Pi_2 \atop \Gamma', \forall x.A, A[t/x] \vdash \Delta'
  }{\Gamma, \Gamma', A[t/x] \vdash \Delta, \Delta'}\ {\scriptstyle cut}
}{
  \cfrac{\Gamma, \Gamma, \Gamma' \vdash \Delta, \Delta, \Delta'}{\Gamma, \Gamma' \vdash \Delta, \Delta'}\ {\scriptstyle Lemma\ 2.14}
}\ {\scriptstyle cut}
$$

The original cut rank is $(|\forall x.A|, |\Pi_1| + |\Pi_2| + 2)$. In the new derivation, the upper cut rank is $(|\forall x.A|, |\Pi_1| + |\Pi_2| + 1)$, which has a reduced cut length, and the lower cut rank is $(|A|, |\Pi_3| + max(|\Pi_1| + 1, |\Pi_2|) + 1)$, which cuts on a smaller formula.

The above includes all the cases.   □

Implications of the cut-elimination theorem. With the above proof, we can finally state the following results:

Corollary 2.3 *The sequent calculi* LK, LK', *and* LK'' *are equivalent to each other.*

Therefore, we also have

Corollary 2.4 *The sequent calculi* LK' *and* LK'' *are both sound and complete for first-order logic.*

We say a derivation is *analytic* if it does not use the *cut* rule. An analytic proof is often longer than a proof with *cut*. On the other hand, a direct consequence of the cut-elimination theorem is that when we try to prove a formula, we only need to reason about its sub-formulae. This is stated in the corollary as follows.

Corollary 2.5 (Sub-formula Property) *If* $\Gamma \vdash \Delta$ *is derivable in* LK'', *then we can derive it using only the sub-formulae that appear in the sequent.*

Despite having potentially longer proofs, the sub-formula property significantly reduces the search space of rule applications.

There are many other significant consequences of cut-elimination, such as Craig's interpolation theorem [6], resolution-based proof search [7], the Prolog programming language [8], and proof transformation as program reduction via the Curry-Howard Isomorphism [9]. Interested readers are referred to the cited books and papers to learn more.

Exercises

2.8 Prove Lemma 2.13 by induction.

2.9 Prove Lemma 2.14 by induction.

2.10 Prove the following by induction using Isar style proofs in Isabelle/HOL.

1. For any natural number n, if n can be divided by 2, then n^2 can also be divided by 2.

Instruction. Recall the proof by induction technique for natural numbers on Page 71. In Isabelle/HOL, the proof structure has the following form:

```
1  fix n::nat
2  have "P n"
3  proof (induction n)
4      case 0
5      then show ?case sorry
6  next
7      case (Suc n)
8      then show ?case sorry
9  qed
```

where the "sorry" parts are placeholders for sub-proofs. To formalise this question in Isabelle/HOL, we write $n \ mod \ 2 = 0$ to mean n can be divided by 2. After typing the line "proof (induction n)", Isabelle/HOL will automatically generate a code template (shown in the Output window) for induction proofs based on the type of n. The reader is recommended to utilise this feature for efficient coding. This question can be stated in Isabelle/HOL as follows.

```
1  lemma
2      fixes n::nat
3      shows "n mod 2 = 0 ==> n^2 mod 2 = 0"
```

Use the above proof template and prove this question.

2. $1 + \cdots + n = \frac{n \times (n+1)}{2}$, for any natural number n.[5]

Instruction. We can define the summation from 1 to n using the following recursive function in Isabelle/HOL:

---

[5] Fun fact: the German mathematician Gauss (1777–1855) found this equation for $n = 100$ when he was seven years old.

```
1 primrec sum :: "nat => nat" where
2 "sum 0 = 0" |
3 "sum (Suc n) = (sum n) + Suc n"
```

This question can be written as follows in Isabelle/HOL

```
1 lemma
2    fixes n::nat
3    shows "sum n = n * (n + 1) div 2"
```

3. Let us consider some other inductively defined structures. For example, lists in Isabelle/HOL are defined as follows.

```
1 datatype (set: 'a) list =
2 Nil   ("[]")
3 | Cons (hd: 'a) (tl: "'a list")   (infixr "#" 65)
```

There is a type variable $'a$ in the definition, which can be instantiated by any data type, such as *bool* (Booleans), *nat* (naturals), *int* (integers), etc. The base case is an empty list, denoted by *Nil* or []. The inductive case takes the form "*Cons hd tl*", where *hd* (the "head" of the list) is a single item of type $'a$, and *tl* (the "tail" of the list) is a list of such items. This case represents the concatenation of *hd* and *tl*, which can also be written as *hd#tl*. Concatenation of two lists *xs* and *ys* is written as $xs@ys$.

We define the following function that adds the elements of the first list to the second list in reverse order.

```
1 primrec itrev :: "'a list => 'a list => 'a list" where
2 "itrev [] ys = ys" |
3 "itrev (x#xs) ys = itrev xs (x#ys)"
```

As the first example of "program verification", prove the following, where *rev* is a built-in function that reverses a list.

```
1 lemma "itrev xs ys = (rev xs) @ ys"
```

Instruction. Note that a simple induction on the list *xs* may fail because the proof also depends on the structure of the list *ys*. In this case, we need to strengthen the induction hypothesis by assuming that *ys* is an *arbitrary* list instead of a fixed list. To do so in Isabelle/HOL, we can use the following line:

```
1 proof (induction xs arbitrary: ys)
```

4. Prove the following where the built-in function *length* gives the length of a list:

```
1 lemma "length (itrev xs ys) = length xs + length ys"
```

References

1. Fitting M (1996) First-order logic and automated theorem proving, 2nd ed. Springer, New York, Inc., Secaucus, NJ, USA. ISBN: 0-387-94593-8
2. Troelstra AS, Schwichtenberg H (1996) Basic proof theory. CUP
3. Harrison J (2009) Handbook of practical logic and automated reasoning, 1st ed. Cambridge University Press
4. Gentzen G (1964) Investigations into logical deduction. Am Philos Q 1:288–306
5. Hóu Z (2016) Labelled sequent calculi and automated reasoning for assertions in separation logic PhD thesis. The Australian National University
6. Lyndon RC et al (1959) An interpolation theorem in the predicate calculus. Pac J Math 9:129–142
7. Davis M, Putnam H (1960) A computing procedure for quantification theory. J ACM (JACM) 7:201–215
8. Clocksin WF, Mellish CS (2012) Programming in prolog: using the ISO standard. Springer Science & Business Media
9. Howard WA (1980) The formulae-as-types notion of construction. To HB Curry: essays on combinatory logic, lambda calculus and formalism vol 44, pp 479–490

Non-classical Logics

Propositional logic and first-order logic are both *classical* logics. There are many other logics, some called *non-classical* logics, that have different syntax or semantics than classical logics and cater to different reasoning tasks. Nobody stops us from inventing a logic of our own, and new logics arise all the time.

For example, a joke from a stand-up comedy show gives the "logic of marriage" in the "truth table" below. This "logic" is certainly non-classical—but the take away is that I would rather be happy than being right!

Zhé	Sarah	Result
Wrong	Right	Sarah's right
Right	Right	Sarah's right
Right	Wrong	Sarah's right
Wrong	Wrong	Zhé's wrong

3.1 Intuitionistic Logic

The need for *intuitionism*, dating back to the early 20th century in Brouwer's constructivist movement, comes from the notion of *constructive proof*, which shows each step of reasoning by giving evidence of a mathematical object [1]. By contrast,

© The Author(s), under exclusive license to Springer Nature Switzerland AG 2021
Z. Hou, *Fundamentals of Logic and Computation*, Texts in Computer Science,
https://doi.org/10.1007/978-3-030-87882-5_3

a *non-constructive proof*[1] shows the existence of an object without providing an example. Classical logic permits non-constructive proofs. Let us see two well-known examples [2] given below.

Lemma 3.1 *At least one of $e + \pi$ and $e - \pi$ is irrational.*[2]

Proof Proof by contradiction. Assume that both $e + \pi$ and $e - \pi$ are rational, then their sum $2e$ must also be rational, which is false, therefore at least one of them is irrational.   □

The proof by contradiction technique, embodied in the RAA rule of natural deduction (cf. Page 21), can be expressed as the formula below, which is called *double negation elimination*.

$$\neg\neg A \rightarrow A$$

Lemma 3.2 *There are two irrational numbers x and y such that x^y is rational.*

Proof Consider the number $\sqrt{2}^{\sqrt{2}}$. If it is rational, then $x = y = \sqrt{2}$ is a solution; otherwise, let $x = \sqrt{2}^{\sqrt{2}}$ and $y = \sqrt{2}$, then $x^y = \sqrt{2}^2 = 2$ is rational.   □

The proof technique used above is a case analysis of whether $\sqrt{2}^{\sqrt{2}}$ is rational. Let us write "$\sqrt{2}^{\sqrt{2}}$ is rational" as A and the lemma as C. The above inference is essentially a $\vee E$ rule application in natural deduction:

$$\cfrac{A \vee \neg A \qquad \cfrac{[a_1 : A]}{\vdots} \atop C \qquad \cfrac{[a_2 : \neg A]}{\vdots} \atop C}{C} \; {\vee E, \text{ discharge } a_1 \text{ and } a_2}$$

There is an implicit step: either A is true, or its negation is true; there is nothing in between. This can be expressed in the formula below, which is called the *law of excluded middle*.

$$A \vee \neg A$$

The above two proofs are legitimate but non-constructive—we still do not know which one of $e + \pi$ and $e - \pi$ is irrational, nor which x and y make x^y rational. Intuitionism forbids such proofs. Research has shown that double negation elimination and the law of excluded middle have the same effect on classical logic—if we

---

[1] Also called (pure) existence proof.
[2] e is a constant called *Euler's number,* which is an irrational number that is approximately equal to 2.71828. π is also an irrational number, which is approximately equal to 3.14159.

reject one of them as a valid formula, we reject both. *Intuitionistic logic*, also called constructive logic, is defined as a variant of classical logic where these two formulae are *not* valid.[3]

Definition 3.1 (*Syntax of Intuitionistic Logic*) The syntax of intuitionistic logic is the same as the syntax of classical logic.

Algebraically, intuitionistic logic corresponds to Heyting[4]'s algebra [3], which removes double negation elimination and the law of excluded middle from Boolean Algebra.

The removal of such important laws is not without controversy. The German mathematician David Hilbert argued that:

> Taking the principle of excluded middle from the mathematician would be the same, say, as proscribing the telescope to the astronomer or to the boxer the use of his fists. To prohibit existence statements and the principle of excluded middle is tantamount to relinquishing the science of mathematics altogether.

Naturally, intuitionistic logic is a weakening of classical logic: every valid formula in intuitionistic logic is valid in classical logic, but not conversely.

Nonetheless, intuitionism has found many significant applications. For example, through the Curry-Howard Isomorphism, a constructive proof that an object exists can be transformed into an algorithm that generates the object.

Informal semantics of intuitionistic logic. We give an informal reading of the semantics of intuitionistic logic. Instead of understanding A as "A is true", we understand it as "I have a (constructive) proof of A". This reading can be extended to logical connectives as follows:

- A proof of $\top$ is trivial.
- A proof of $\bot$ does not exist.
- A proof of $A \wedge B$ is a pair (a, b) where a is a proof of A and b a proof of B.
- A proof of $A \vee B$ is a pair (i, p) where $i \in \{1, 2\}$, and p is a proof of A if $i = 1$, else p is a proof of B.
- A proof of $A \rightarrow B$ is a (proof-transformation) function that maps each proof of A to a proof of B.
- A proof of $\neg A$ is a function that maps a proof of A to a proof of absurdity. That is, a proof of A should not exist.

---

[3] In fact, the law of contraposition $(\neg B \rightarrow \neg A) \rightarrow (A \rightarrow B)$ and Peirce's law $((A \rightarrow B) \rightarrow A) \rightarrow A$ do not hold in intuitionism, either. Accepting any of the four formulae as a valid formula makes the logic classical.

[4] Unsurprisingly, he was a student of Brouwer.

Identity and Cut:

$$\frac{}{A \vdash A} \ id \qquad\qquad \frac{\Gamma \vdash A \qquad A, \Gamma' \vdash C}{\Gamma, \Gamma' \vdash C} \ cut$$

Logical Rules:

$$\frac{\Gamma, A \vdash C}{\Gamma, A \wedge B \vdash C} \ {}^{\wedge L_1} \qquad\qquad \frac{\Gamma, B \vdash C}{\Gamma, A \wedge B \vdash C} \ {}^{\wedge L_2}$$

$$\frac{\Gamma \vdash A}{\Gamma \vdash A \vee B} \ {}^{\vee R_1} \qquad\qquad \frac{\Gamma \vdash B}{\Gamma \vdash A \vee B} \ {}^{\vee R_2}$$

$$\frac{\Gamma, A \vdash C \qquad \Gamma, B \vdash C}{\Gamma, A \vee B \vdash C} \ {}^{\vee L} \qquad\qquad \frac{\Gamma \vdash A \qquad \Gamma \vdash B}{\Gamma \vdash A \wedge B} \ {}^{\wedge R}$$

$$\frac{\Gamma \vdash A \qquad B, \Gamma' \vdash C}{\Gamma, \Gamma', A \rightarrow B \vdash C} \ {}^{\rightarrow L} \qquad\qquad \frac{\Gamma, A \vdash B}{\Gamma \vdash A \rightarrow B} \ {}^{\rightarrow R}$$

$$\frac{\Gamma \vdash A}{\Gamma, \neg A \vdash} \ {}^{\neg L} \qquad\qquad \frac{\Gamma, A \vdash}{\Gamma \vdash \neg A} \ {}^{\neg R}$$

Structural Rules:

$$\frac{\Gamma \vdash C}{\Gamma, A \vdash C} \ {}^{WL} \qquad \frac{\Gamma \vdash}{\Gamma \vdash A} \ {}^{WR} \qquad \frac{\Gamma, A, A \vdash C}{\Gamma, A \vdash C} \ {}^{CL} \qquad \frac{\Gamma, A, B, \Gamma' \vdash C}{\Gamma, B, A, \Gamma' \vdash C} \ {}^{EL}$$

Fig. 3.1 The subset of sequent calculus LJ for propositional intuitionistic logic

Clearly, it is not always the case that we have a proof of A, or its proof does not exist; thus, the law of excluded middle does not hold. Also, just because we do not have a proof that A cannot be proved does not imply A can be proved. That is, double negation cannot be eliminated.

The sequent calculus LJ. Proof theoretically, Gentzen proposed the sequent calculus LJ for intuitionistic logic. Interestingly, Gentzen showed that a minor modification of LK suits exactly the semantics of intuitionistic logic: only allowing at most one formula in the succedent. The propositional fragment of the system LJ is presented in Fig. 3.1. Naturally, contraction and exchange on the right-hand side are not allowed in LJ.

The LJ calculus is sound and complete for intuitionistic logic and admits a similar cut-elimination proof.

Theorem 3.1 *The sequent calculus LJ shown in Fig. 3.1 is sound and complete for propositional intuitionistic logic.*

Theorem 3.2 *The cut rule is admissible in LJ.*

Double negation elimination and the law of excluded middle are provable in LK but are not provable in LJ. Let us see some proof attempts below.

Example 3.1 The formula $\neg\neg A \rightarrow A$ is not provable in LJ. Starting from the sequent $\vdash \neg\neg A \rightarrow A$, we build the following derivation tree:

$$\frac{\neg\neg A \vdash A}{\vdash \neg\neg A \rightarrow A} {\scriptstyle \rightarrow R}$$

Since the $\neg L$ rule requires that the succedent of the conclusion is empty, we cannot apply it backwards. Indeed, none of the logical rules is applicable at this point, so we can only choose from the structural rules WL, WR and CL. Making a copy of $\neg\neg A$ via CR will not help as both copies can only appear on the same side of the sequent. Removing either of the existing formulae using weakening will eliminate the chance of using id to close the branch. The reader can check that there is no way to derive this sequent whatsoever.

Example 3.2 The formula $A \vee \neg A$ is not provable in LJ. Similarly, we start from the sequent $\vdash A \vee \neg A$. Since there is no contraction rule on the right-hand side, the only obvious rules to use at this point are $\vee R_1$ and $\vee R_2$. However, these rules will remove one of the disjuncts, resulting in an unprovable sequent.

It is later proved that an even simpler modification works for the propositional fragment of intuitionistic logic: we just need to take Figure 1.2 and only change the $\rightarrow R$ rule to the below form.

$$\frac{\Gamma, A \vdash B}{\Gamma \vdash A \rightarrow B, \Delta} {\scriptstyle \rightarrow R}$$

More specifically, when applying the $\rightarrow R$ rule backwards, we need to remove the context Δ in the succedent. The resultant calculus is equivalent to the subset of LJ in Fig. 3.1. This modification shows that implication plays an important role in distinguishing intuitionistic logic from classical logic.

Let us see an example of a provable formula.

Lemma 3.3 $(A \rightarrow B) \rightarrow ((A \rightarrow \neg B) \rightarrow \neg A)$ *is valid in intuitionistic logic.*

Proof We give the bottom part of a derivation in LJ as follows:

$$\dfrac{\dfrac{\dfrac{\dfrac{\dfrac{\dfrac{\dfrac{\dfrac{A, A \to \neg B, A, A \to B \vdash}{A \to \neg B, A, A, A \to B \vdash} \, {}^{EL}}{A \to \neg B, A, A \to B, A \vdash} \, {}^{EL}}{A \to \neg B, A \to B, A, A \vdash} \, {}^{EL}}{A \to B, A \to \neg B, A, A \vdash} \, {}^{EL}}{A \to B, A \to \neg B, A \vdash} \, {}^{CL}}{A \to B, A \to \neg B \vdash \neg A} \, {}^{\neg R}}{A \to B \vdash (A \to \neg B) \to \neg A} \, {}^{\to R}}{\vdash (A \to B) \to ((A \to \neg B) \to \neg A)} \, {}^{\to R}$$

Following the above derivation upwards, we give the remainder of the proof as follows:

$$\dfrac{A \vdash A \,{}^{id} \quad \dfrac{\dfrac{A \vdash A \,{}^{id} \quad \dfrac{\dfrac{\dfrac{B \vdash B \,{}^{id}}{B, \neg B \vdash} \, {}^{\neg L}}{\neg B, B \vdash} \, {}^{EL}}{A, B, A \to \neg B \vdash} \, {}^{\to L}}{\dfrac{B, A, A \to \neg B \vdash}{B, A \to \neg B, A \vdash} \, {}^{EL}} \, {}^{EL}}{A, A \to \neg B, A, A \to B \vdash} \, {}^{\to L}$$

Notice that there is at most one formula in the succedent of each sequent.   □

Except for the restriction that the succedent cannot have more than one formula, derivations in LJ are similar to derivations in LK. See another example below.

Lemma 3.4 $(A \to (B \to C)) \to ((A \to B) \to (A \to C))$ *is valid in intuitionistic logic.*

Proof

$$\dfrac{\dfrac{\dfrac{\dfrac{\dfrac{\dfrac{\dfrac{\dfrac{A \vdash A \,{}^{id} \quad \dfrac{\dfrac{A \vdash A \,{}^{id} \quad \dfrac{\dfrac{\dfrac{B \vdash B \,{}^{id} \quad C \vdash C \,{}^{id}}{B, B \to C \vdash C} \, {}^{\to L}}{B \to C, B \vdash C} \, {}^{EL}}{A, B, A \to (B \to C) \vdash C} \, {}^{\to L}}{\dfrac{B, A, A \to (B \to C) \vdash C}{B, A \to (B \to C), A \vdash C} \, {}^{EL}} \, {}^{EL}}{A, A \to (B \to C), A, A \to B \vdash C} \, {}^{\to L}}{A \to (B \to C), A, A, A \to B \vdash C} \, {}^{EL}}{A \to (B \to C), A, A \to B, A \vdash C} \, {}^{EL}}{A \to (B \to C), A \to B, A, A \vdash C} \, {}^{EL}}{A \to (B \to C), A \to B, A \vdash C} \, {}^{CL}}{A \to (B \to C), A \to B \vdash A \to C} \, {}^{\to R}}{A \to (B \to C) \vdash (A \to B) \to (A \to C)} \, {}^{\to R}}{(A \to (B \to C)) \to ((A \to B) \to (A \to C))} \, {}^{\to R}$$

The above derivation is a proof.   □

The natural deduction system NJ. The natural deduction system NJ for intuition-istic logic is simply NK (cf. Fig. 1.1) without the RAA rule. We shall define NJ as below, where $\setminus$ denotes set minus/difference.

$$NJ = NK \setminus \{RAA\}.$$

Conversely and alternatively, if we add RAA or any of the following rules, for double negation elimination and the law of excluded middle respectively, to NJ, we get back to NK:

$$\frac{\neg\neg A}{A}\ \neg\neg E \qquad \frac{}{A \vee \neg A}\ EM$$

Example 3.3 To see the role of RAA when proving $\neg\neg A \to A$ in natural deduction, see the derivation in NK as follows:

$$\frac{\frac{[a_2 : \neg A] \quad \dfrac{[a_1 : \neg\neg A]}{\neg A \to \bot}\ \neg E}{\dfrac{\bot}{A}\ RAA,\ \text{discharge } a_2} \to E}{\neg\neg A \to A}\ \to I,\ \text{discharge } a_1$$

With NJ, we get stuck after deriving $\bot$, and we cannot discharge the assumption a_2.

Since proof theories for intuitionistic logic are essentially restricted versions of those for classical logic, it is not surprising that if a formula is provable in NJ (or LJ), it is also provable in NK (or LK). By the soundness and completeness of NJ and LJ, we have the following result:

Lemma 3.5 *If a formula is valid in intuitionistic logic, then it is also valid in classical logic.*

Proofs in NJ are the same as proofs in NK except that the rule RAA cannot be used, so we will not give more examples of NJ proofs.

Exercises

3.1 Prove the following formulae using LJ.

1. $A \to \neg\neg A$
2. $(A \to B) \to (\neg B \to \neg A)$
3. $A \to (\neg A \to B)$

4. $(A \rightarrow B) \rightarrow ((A \rightarrow \neg B) \rightarrow \neg A)$
5. $(A \rightarrow B) \rightarrow ((C \rightarrow B) \rightarrow (A \vee C \rightarrow B))$

3.2 Prove the above formulae using the alternative sequent calculus discussed at the end of this section.

3.3 Prove the above formulae using NJ.

3.2 Linear Logic

> Linear logic is a logic behind logic, more precisely, it provides a continuation of the constructivisation that began with intuitionistic logic.
>
> —Jean-Yves Girard

Reasoning about resources is another scenario where classical logic is inappropriate. For example, we can express "if I have a coin, then I can buy a bar of chocolate" as $coin \rightarrow choc$. But the idempotence[5] of $\wedge$ in classical logic (i.e., $A \leftrightarrow A \wedge A$) makes the above formula equivalent to $coin \rightarrow choc \wedge choc$, which, depending on the interpretation of $\wedge$, might be understood as "if I have a coin, then I can buy two bars of chocolate", which is obviously not the same as the original sentence. So logical connectives such as conjunction need to be interpreted carefully when reasoning about resources. If we understand $A \wedge A$ as two copies of a resource A, then we should not make $\wedge$ idempotent.

Girard's linear logic [4] solves this problem by allowing two different flavours of logical connectives: *additive* connectives as in classical logic, and *multiplicative* connectives, which are not idempotent.

Even at the propositional level, the syntax of linear logic is more involved than propositional (classical) logic. We shall adopt a hybrid notation of classical logic and that of Girard to be more consistent with the presentation of other logics in this book.

Definition 3.2 (*Syntax of Linear Logic*) We give the syntax of linear logic below and a comparison of notations in Table 3.1.

$$F ::= \top \mid \bot \mid p \mid F \wedge F \mid F \vee F \mid$$
$$1 \mid 0 \mid F^{\perp} \mid F \otimes F \mid F \,\&\, F \mid F \multimap F \mid$$
$$!F \mid ?F$$

---

[5] An operation $\circ$ is said to be *idempotent* over a set S of items if $\forall x \in S.\ x \circ x = x$.

Table 3.1 A comparison of notations used in this book and those used by Girard

Type	In this book	Girard	Pronunciation
Additive	$\top$	$\top$	Truth
	$\bot$	0	Falsity
	$A \wedge B$	$A \mathbin{\&} B$	And/with
	$A \vee B$	$A \oplus B$	Or/plus
Multiplicative	1	1	Unit
	0	$\bot$	Zero
	$A^{\neg}$	$A^{\bot}$	Nil
	$A \otimes B$	$A \otimes B$	Tensor/times
	$A \mathbin{⅋} B$	$A \mathbin{⅋} B$	Par
	$A \multimap B$	$A \multimap B$	Lollipop
Exponential	$!A$	$!A$	Of course/bang
	$?A$	$?A$	Why not

Intuitively, additive constants and connectives behave the same way as in classical logic. Multiplicative constants and connectives operate with a "resource" reading, which does not permit adding (contraction) or removing (weakening) copies of a formula arbitrarily. Note that there is only a multiplicative negation. To preserve the expressiveness compared to classical logic, Girard allows "controlled" contraction and weakening via *exponentials* ? and !.

We assume that exponentials bind tighter than other connectives. For instance, $!A \wedge B$ should be read as $(!A) \wedge B$ rather than $!(A \wedge B)$.

Informal semantics of linear logic. We can understand (most of) linear logic in a classic example of "consumer and vending machine".

- $A \multimap B$ is generally an *action* that transforms a resource A into another resource B. For example, $\$1 \multimap choc$ transforms a dollar into a chocolate bar, which represents a transaction in the vending machine example.
- $A^{\neg}$ is the dual of A. If we understand A as having a resource, then $A^{\neg}$ consumes that resource. Generally, if we understand A as a type of action, then $A^{\neg}$ is the corresponding type of reaction.
- $A \otimes B$ represents two resources A and B that occur *simultaneously*, to be used as the consumer wishes. For example, if a chocolate bar is \$1 and so is a can of coke, then we have $\$2 \multimap (choc \otimes coke)$. That is, we can buy a chocolate bar and a can of coke with \$2.
- 1 represents the absence of a resource, and it is the unit of $\otimes$. That is, $1 \otimes A$ is equivalent to just A.
- $A \wedge B$ represents two resources A and B that occur *alternatively* by the *consumer's* choice. For example, we have $\$1 \multimap (choc \wedge coke)$, which says that the consumer

can buy a chocolate bar with $1, *and* he can buy a can of coke with $1. He can choose one of them but not both.

- $\top$ is a bin for unneeded items. $\top$ is the unit of $\wedge$, that is, selling $A \wedge \top$ is the same as just selling A because we do not need $\top$ anyway. By contrast, $A \otimes \top$ means "A and some other stuff", which cannot be reduced to A.
- $A \vee B$ represents two resources A and B that occur *alternatively* by the *vending machine's* choice. For example, if the machine has a loot box button which gives you an item that is worth $1 by some algorithm, then we have $1 \multimap (choc \vee coke)$.
- $\bot$ (additive falsity) is a product that is not on sale. $\bot$ is the unit of $\vee$, and selling $A \vee \bot$ is the same as selling A.
- $A \,\mathscr{B}\, B$ is somewhat difficult to explain, so the literature often translates it to $A^\neg \multimap B$ or $B^\neg \multimap A$. An explanation could be "if I consume A, then I have exactly the resource to get B". For example, if I have $2, then $1 \,\mathscr{B}\, choc$ says that I can give away $1 and then have the exact money to buy a chocolate bar. Or, I can buy a chocolate bar and eat it, then I will have $1 left.
- $!A$ means that we are rich enough that we can spend as many copies of A as we wish (of course we have $A!$).
- $?A$ means that we have a big enough pocket to receive as many copies of A as we wish (why not get another A?).

Example 3.4 The chemical equation

$$2H_2 + O_2 \rightarrow 2H_2O$$

can be written as

$$H_2 \otimes H_2 \otimes O_2 \multimap H_2O \otimes H_2O$$

Definition 3.3 (*Duality of Linear Logic Formulae*) Every formula A in linear logic has a dual $A^\neg$ defined as follows:

$$
\begin{array}{ll}
\top^\neg ::= \bot & \bot^\neg ::= \top \\
1^\neg ::= 0 & 0^\neg ::= 1 \\
(p)^\neg ::= p^\neg & (p^\neg)^\neg ::= p \\
(A \otimes B)^\neg ::= A^\neg \,\mathscr{B}\, B^\neg & (A \,\mathscr{B}\, B)^\neg ::= A^\neg \otimes B^\neg \\
(A \wedge B)^\neg ::= A^\neg \vee B^\neg & (A \vee B)^\neg ::= A^\neg \wedge B^\neg \\
(!A)^\neg ::= \; ?A^\neg & (?A)^\neg ::= \; !A^\neg
\end{array}
$$

The connective $\multimap$ does not appear in the above table because it can be encoded using nil and par as follows:

$$A \multimap B ::= A^\neg \,\mathscr{B}\, B$$

Relation with classical logic and intuitionistic logic. Linear logic is a refinement of classical logic and intuitionistic logic. Although linear logic does not have a classical negation, we can obtain the full expressiveness of both classical logic and intuitionistic logic via implication. Intuitionistic implication can be recovered in linear logic via the following encoding:

$$!A \multimap B$$

Classical implication can be encoded as

$$!?A \multimap ?B \quad \text{or} \quad !A \multimap ?!B$$

It follows that both intuitionistic logic and classical logic can be translated into linear logic.

Proof theoretically, linear logic is a typical *substructural logic*, as it lacks some of the structural rules in LK; in this case, the rules for weakening and contraction. Girard's sequent calculus for linear logic is presented using one-sided sequents. That is, a sequent

$$\Gamma \vdash \Delta$$

is written as

$$\vdash \Gamma^{\neg}, \Delta$$

This presentation removes the need for left-hand side rules and the rules for negation. To be consistent with our previous presentations, we give a two-sided sequent calculus for linear logic in Fig. 3.2 as a modification and extension of the system LK in Fig. 1.2.

In the sequent calculus for linear logic, commas in the antecedent behave like a $\otimes$ and in the succedent like a $\invamp$. This can be observed from the $1L$ and $0R$ rules, which reflect that 1 is the unit of $\otimes$ and 0 is the unit of $\invamp$. Also, there are no rules for $\top$ on the left and $\bot$ on the right because we cannot remove the constants in these cases. The turnstile $\vdash$ acts like a $\multimap$.

The main difference between the rules for additives and those for multiplicatives is that the context (Γ, Δ, $\cdots$) in a sequent is treated differently. For example, the $\top R$ and $\bot L$ rules allow contexts in the sequent, while $1R$ and $0L$ do not. The $\wedge R$ rule copies the context to both premises, whereas the $\otimes R$ rule *splits* the context into two parts and sends them to the premises, respectively. The $\wedge L$ rule obtains only one of A and B, by the logician's choice, which is analogous to the vending machine example. By contrast, the $\otimes L$ rule obtains both A and B in the premise. The rules for $\vee$ and $\invamp$ are duals to the rules for $\wedge$ and $\otimes$, respectively.

By the encoding of $\multimap$, we can derive inference rules for it as follows:

$$\frac{\Gamma \vdash A, \Delta \qquad B, \Gamma' \vdash \Delta'}{\Gamma, \Gamma', A \multimap B \vdash \Delta, \Delta'} \, {\scriptstyle \multimap L} \qquad\qquad \frac{\Gamma, A \vdash B, \Delta}{\Gamma \vdash A \multimap B, \Delta} \, {\scriptstyle \multimap R}$$

The exponential ! indicates that A can be used as one wishes. Thus, we can perform weakening and contraction on ! formulae in the antecedent. The rule $!L$ and $!R$ obtain a single copy of A. The duality for exponentials is lost in Girard's one-sided sequents but is recovered in our two-sided sequents presentation.

The *cut* rule can be eliminated in this system while maintaining completeness. We give the results in the following theorems:

Identity and Cut:

$$\overline{A \vdash A}\ id \qquad\qquad \frac{\Gamma \vdash \Delta, A \qquad A, \Gamma' \vdash \Delta'}{\Gamma, \Gamma' \vdash \Delta, \Delta'}\ cut$$

Logical Rules:

$$\overline{\Gamma \vdash \top, \Delta}\ \top R \qquad\qquad \overline{\Gamma, \bot \vdash \Delta}\ \bot L$$

$$\frac{\Gamma \vdash \Delta}{\Gamma, 1 \vdash \Delta}\ 1L \qquad \overline{\vdash 1}\ 1R \qquad \overline{0 \vdash}\ 0L \qquad \frac{\Gamma \vdash \Delta}{\Gamma \vdash 0, \Delta}\ 0R$$

$$\frac{\Gamma, A \vdash \Delta}{\Gamma, A \wedge B \vdash \Delta}\ \wedge L_1 \qquad\qquad \frac{\Gamma, B \vdash \Delta}{\Gamma, A \wedge B \vdash \Delta}\ \wedge L_2$$

$$\frac{\Gamma \vdash A, \Delta}{\Gamma \vdash A \vee B, \Delta}\ \vee R_1 \qquad\qquad \frac{\Gamma \vdash B, \Delta}{\Gamma \vdash A \vee B, \Delta}\ \vee R_2$$

$$\frac{\Gamma, A \vdash \Delta \qquad \Gamma, B \vdash \Delta}{\Gamma, A \vee B \vdash \Delta}\ \vee L \qquad\qquad \frac{\Gamma \vdash A, \Delta \qquad \Gamma \vdash B, \Delta}{\Gamma \vdash A \wedge B, \Delta}\ \wedge R$$

$$\frac{\Gamma \vdash A, \Delta}{\Gamma, A^{\neg} \vdash \Delta}\ \neg L \qquad\qquad \frac{\Gamma, A \vdash \Delta}{\Gamma \vdash A^{\neg}, \Delta}\ \neg R$$

$$\frac{\Gamma, A, B \vdash \Delta}{\Gamma, A \otimes B \vdash \Delta}\ \otimes L \qquad\qquad \frac{\Gamma \vdash A, \Delta \qquad \Gamma' \vdash B, \Delta'}{\Gamma, \Gamma' \vdash A \otimes B, \Delta, \Delta'}\ \otimes R$$

$$\frac{\Gamma, A \vdash \Delta \qquad \Gamma', B \vdash \Delta'}{\Gamma, \Gamma', A \,\&\, B \vdash \Delta, \Delta'}\ \&L \qquad\qquad \frac{\Gamma \vdash A, B, \Delta}{\Gamma \vdash A \,\&\, B, \Delta}\ \&R$$

$$\frac{\Gamma, A \vdash \Delta}{\Gamma, !A \vdash \Delta}\ !L \qquad \frac{!\Gamma, \vdash A, ?\Delta}{!\Gamma \vdash !A, ?\Delta}\ !R \qquad \frac{\Gamma \vdash \Delta}{\Gamma, !A \vdash \Delta}\ !W \qquad \frac{\Gamma, !A, !A \vdash \Delta}{\Gamma, !A \vdash \Delta}\ !C$$

$$\frac{!\Gamma, A \vdash ?\Delta}{!\Gamma, ?A \vdash ?\Delta}\ ?L \qquad \frac{\Gamma \vdash A, \Delta}{\Gamma \vdash ?A, \Delta}\ ?R \qquad \frac{\Gamma \vdash \Delta}{\Gamma \vdash ?A, \Delta}\ ?W \qquad \frac{\Gamma \vdash ?A, ?A, \Delta}{\Gamma \vdash ?A, \Delta}\ ?C$$

Structural Rules:

$$\frac{\Gamma, A, B, \Gamma' \vdash \Delta}{\Gamma, B, A, \Gamma' \vdash \Delta}\ EL \qquad\qquad \frac{\Gamma \vdash \Delta, A, B, \Delta'}{\Gamma \vdash \Delta, B, A, \Delta'}\ ER$$

Fig. 3.2 The sequent calculus LL for propositional linear logic

Theorem 3.3 *The sequent calculus LL is sound and complete for propositional linear logic.*

Theorem 3.4 *The cut rule is admissible in the sequent calculus LL.*

For a simple example, let us prove $1 -\!\circ choc \wedge coke$ with all three resources replaced by A.

Lemma 3.6 $A -\!\circ A \wedge A$ *is valid in linear logic.*

Proof

$$
\cfrac{\cfrac{\overline{A \vdash A}^{\;id} \quad \overline{A \vdash A}^{\;id}}{A \vdash A \wedge A}{}^{\wedge R}}{\vdash A -\!\circ A \wedge A}{}^{-\!\circ}
$$

Since the $\wedge R$ rule copies the context in the conclusion to both premises, we can close both branches with id applications.   □

On the other hand, if each of *choc* and *coke* is worth $1, then we cannot derive $1 -\!\circ choc \otimes coke$.

Example 3.5 The formula $A -\!\circ A \otimes A$ is not derivable in LL. To illustrate this, we show a partial derivation as follows:

$$
\cfrac{\cfrac{\overline{A \vdash A}^{\;id} \quad \cfrac{???}{\vdash A}}{A \vdash A \otimes A}{}^{\otimes R}}{\vdash A -\!\circ A \otimes A}{}^{-\!\circ}
$$

Since there is no contraction rule without !, we cannot make a copy of the A in the antecedent. The $\otimes R$ rule splits the antecedent of the conclusion into $[A]$ and $[]$,[6] and send them to the premises, respectively. Consequently, there must be a premise that has an empty antecedent, which results in an open branch.

But if we have as many copies of $1 bill as we wish, then, *of course*, we can afford a bar of chocolate and a can of coke!

---

[6] We use [] to denote an empty list.

Lemma 3.7 $!A \multimap A \otimes A$ *is valid in linear logic.*

Proof

$$
\cfrac{
\cfrac{
\cfrac{
\cfrac{
\cfrac{
\cfrac{\overline{A \vdash A}^{\ id} \quad \overline{A \vdash A}^{\ id}}{A, A \vdash A \otimes A}^{\ \otimes R}
}{A, !A \vdash A \otimes A}^{\ !L}
}{!A, A \vdash A \otimes A}^{\ EL}
}{!A, !A \vdash A \otimes A}^{\ !L}
}{!A \vdash A \otimes A}^{\ !C}
}{\vdash !A \multimap A \otimes A}^{\ \multimap}
$$

The above derivation is the proof.   □

Let us see another example derivation below. We prove that if we have as many copies of $A \wedge B$ as we like, then we can obtain as many copies of A and as many copies of B as we like at the same time.

Lemma 3.8 $!(A \wedge B) \multimap (!A \otimes !B)$ *is valid in linear logic.*

Proof We give the derivation as follows:

$$
\cfrac{
\cfrac{
\cfrac{
\cfrac{\overline{A \vdash A}^{\ id}}{A \wedge B \vdash A}^{\ \wedge L_1}}{!(A \wedge B) \vdash A}^{\ !L}}{!(A \wedge B) \vdash !A}^{\ !R}
\quad
\cfrac{
\cfrac{\overline{B \vdash B}^{\ id}}{A \wedge B \vdash B}^{\ \wedge L_2}}{!(A \wedge B) \vdash B}^{\ !L}}{!(A \wedge B) \vdash !B}^{\ !R}
}{
\cfrac{
\cfrac{!(A \wedge B), !(A \wedge B) \vdash (!A \otimes !B)}{!(A \wedge B) \vdash (!A \otimes !B)}^{\ !C}
}{\vdash !(A \wedge B) \multimap (!A \otimes !B)}^{\ \multimap R}
}^{\ \otimes R}
$$

Note that when applying the rules backwards, we need first to use the $!R$ rule to instantiate the $!$ formula in the succedent because this rule requires that the context must be in exponentials. If we apply $!L$ backwards first, then we can no longer apply $!R$.   □

Exercises

3.4 Prove the following formulae using the sequent calculus LL.

1. $A \otimes (B \vee C) \multimap (A \otimes B) \vee (A \otimes C)$
2. $(A \otimes B) \vee (A \otimes C) \multimap A \otimes (B \vee C)$
3. $A \otimes (B \otimes C) \multimap (A \otimes B) \otimes C$

3.5 Prove the formulae in Exercise 3.1 of Sect. 3.1 using the translation of intuitionistic logic into linear logic.

Instruction. We have discussed the translation of the intuitionistic implication. You can translate $\top$ and $\bot$ to the corresponding constants in linear logic. You can translate $\neg A$ to $A \rightarrow \bot$ and then to linear logic. You can encode the other connectives in intuitionistic logic using $\rightarrow$, $\neg$ and the constants.

3.6 Prove the formulae in Exercises 1.10–1.13 of Sect. 1.3 using the translation of classical logic into linear logic.

Instruction. Similarly, you can translate $\top$ and $\bot$ to the corresponding constants in linear logic. You can translate $\neg A$ to $A \rightarrow \bot$ and then to linear logic. You can encode the other connectives in classical logic using $\rightarrow$, $\neg$ and the constants.

3.3 Linear Temporal Logic

We have primarily been dealing with *truth-functional* logical connectives in the previous logics. For example, the truth value of $\neg A$ entirely depends on the truth value of A; therefore, $\neg$ can be seen as a function that takes a truth value as input and returns a truth value as output. Similarly, $\wedge$ takes two truth values as input and returns a truth value as output. There are two exceptions, however, in linear logic. The exponentials ? and ! are non-truth-functional: we cannot decide whether we can spend as many copies of A as we wish simply from the fact that we have a copy of A; there are other factors in play here. Such non-truth-functional connectives[7] are called *modalities* or modal operators. A modal operator expresses a modal attitude such as necessity, possibility, belief, knowledge, and so on. In the case of linear logic, $!A$ indicates the possibility of using A at one's discretion.

Linear temporal logic (LTL), developed by Pnueli [5] in 1977, has modalities that express beliefs in a linear time-space.

Definition 3.4 (*Syntax of LTL*) The syntax of (propositional) LTL extends propositional logic as follows:

$$F ::= \top \mid p \mid \neg F \mid F \wedge F \mid \mathbf{X} F \mid F \mathbf{U} F$$

The modality $\mathbf{X}$ is called "next", and $\mathbf{U}$ is called "until".

The semantics of LTL can be defined in terms of Kripke structures [6,7].

Definition 3.5 (*Kripke Structure*) A Kripke structure, defined over a set AP of atomic propositions, is a tuple $M = (S, I, R, L)$ where

- S is a finite set of states,

---

[7] Quantifiers are not considered modalities as they quantify over variables and are not logical connectives.

Table 3.2 Kripke-style semantics of LTL

$M, w \models \top$	Iff	Always
$M, w \models p$	Iff	$p \in L(w[0])$
$M, w \models \neg A$	Iff	$M, w \not\models A$
$M, w \models A \wedge B$	Iff	$M, w \models A$ and $M, w \models B$
$M, w \models \mathbf{X} A$	Iff	$M, w^1 \models A$
$M, w \models A \mathbf{U} B$	Iff	There exists $i \geq 0$ such that $M, w^i \models B$ and For all $0 \leq k < i, M, w^k \models A$

- $I \subseteq S$ is a set of initial states,
- $R \subseteq S \times S$ is a transition relation between states,
- $L : S \to 2^{AP}$ is a labelling function that maps a state to a subset of atomic propositions.

Let w be a *path*,[8] which is a (possibly infinite) sequence of states. That is, $w = s_0 s_1 s_2 \cdots$. Let $w[i] = s_i$, i.e., the ith state in the path, and $w^i = s_i s_{i+1} s_{s+2} \cdots$, i.e., the sub-path starting from the ith state. We give the Kripke-style semantics of LTL as follows.

Definition 3.6 (*Semantics of LTL*) The Kripke-style semantics for LTL is defined via a *forcing* relation $\models$ as in Table 3.2.

We say the pair M, w *force* an atomic proposition p iff p is in the subset of propositions at the *first* state in w. The semantics for classical connectives are straightforward, so we will only discuss temporal modalities in what follows. M, w force $\mathbf{X} A$ iff the path starting from the next state in w forces A. That is, if $\mathbf{X} A$ is true in the current state, then A is true in the *next* state. We visualise it as follows:

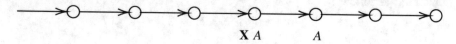

$$\mathbf{X} A \qquad\qquad A$$

M, w force $A \mathbf{U} B$ iff B is true sometime in the future, and before that, A must be true. That is, A is true *until* B is true. This is visualised as follows:

$$A \mathbf{U} B, A \qquad A \qquad\qquad A \qquad \cdots \qquad A \qquad\qquad B$$

---

[8] Sometimes called a word or an ω-word, hence the notation w.

We can define other temporal modalities as follows:

$$\mathbf{F}\,A :: = \top \mathbf{U}\,A$$
$$\mathbf{G}\,A :: = \neg(\mathbf{F}\,\neg A)$$
$$A\,\mathbf{R}\,B :: = \neg(\neg A\,\mathbf{U}\,\neg B)$$

The modality **F** is called "eventually"; it means that the formula is true sometime in the *future*. We draw it in the figure given below.

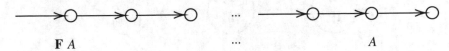

F A   ···   A

The modality **G** is pronounced "globally"; it means that the formula is always true starting from the current state. We draw it in the figure given below.

G A, A   A   A   ···   A   A   A

The modality **R** is pronounced "release". The formula $A\,\mathbf{R}\,B$ says that B must remain true until and including the point when A is true. That is, A *releases* B. If A never becomes true, then B must be true forever. These two cases are visualised below, respectively.

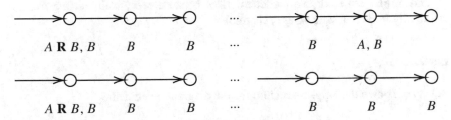

$A\,\mathbf{R}\,B, B$ B   B   ···   B   A, B

$A\,\mathbf{R}\,B, B$ B   B   ···   B   B   B

An LTL formula F is *satisfiable* if there is *some* Kripke structure M such that for *every* path w it produces, $M, w \models F$. In this case, M is called a *model* of F. Note that w must start with one of the initial states of M. A formula is *unsatisfiable* if it has no model. A formula is *valid* if *every* Kripke structure is its model.

Example 3.6 Let us consider the following example of a Kripke structure $M = (S, I, R, L)$:

- $S = \{s_1, s_2, s_3, s_4\}$
- $I = \{s_1\}$
- $R = \{(s_1, s_2), (s_2, s_3), (s_2, s_4), (s_3, s_3), (s_3, s_4), (s_4, s_2)\}$
- $L = \{(s_1 \mapsto \{\}), (s_2 \mapsto \{p\}), (s_3 \mapsto \{p, r\}), (s_4 \mapsto \{p, q\})\}$

This example is illustrated in the diagram below, where circles are states and arrows are transitions given by R. There is only one initial state, which is s_1. This is indicated by an arrow going to s_1 from nowhere. All other arrows have a source and a destination. The mappings of the labelling function L are written at the bottom of each state.

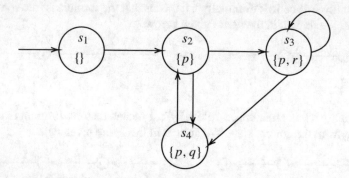

This Kripke structure may produce many paths. For example, $w_1 = s_1 s_2 s_3 s_4 \cdots$ is a valid path, and $w_2 = s_1 s_2 s_4 s_2 s_3 s_3 s_4 \cdots$ is another valid path.

For the second path, we have $M, w_2 \models \mathbf{X} p$. If we consider the sub-path w_2^1, which starts from the second state s_2, then $M, w_2^1 \models \mathbf{G} p$. We also have $M, w_2^1 \models \mathbf{F} r$ and $M, w_2^1 \models \mathbf{F} q$ as these propositions eventually become true in the future.

If we consider the sub-path $w_2^4 = s_3 s_3 s_4 \cdots$, then we have $M, w_2^4 \models r \mathbf{U} q$.

This Kripke structure is a model for $\mathbf{F} p$ because every path starting from s_1 eventually leads to a state where p is true.

Exercises

3.7 Write down the Kripke structure for the diagram given below.

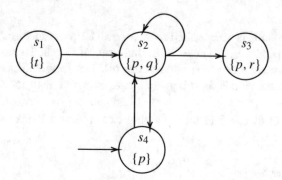

3.8 Write down a path that can be generated from the above Kripke structure.

3.9 Consider the sub-path $w = s_2 s_2 s_2 s_4 s_2 s_3$. Write down three formulae that are forced by the above Kripke structure and w.

3.10 Write down three formulae of which the above Kripke structure is a model.

3.11 Can the state s_1 be reached on any path?

3.12 Can the above Kripke structure produce an infinite path that involves s_3?

3.13 A Kripke-style semantics for intuitionistic logic is given below. A *rooted* Kripke model is a quadruple $M = (W, r, R, L)$ where W is a non-empty set of "worlds" containing a root world r which is minimal w.r.t. R, $R \subseteq W \times W$ is a reflexive and transitive (cf. Page 7) binary relation over W, and $L : W \to 2^{AP}$ is a labelling function that maps a world to a subset of atomic propositions. The relation R is often written infix as $\leq$ in the literature. When $x \leq y$ holds, we say the world y can be reached from the world x. The function L obeys the *persistence* condition. The conditions of a rooted Kripke model are summarised below for any $x, y, z \in W$.

- Minimality of r: $r \leq x$.
- Reflexivity: $x \leq x$.
- Transitivity: if $x \leq y$ and $y \leq z$ then $x \leq z$.
- Persistence: if $x \leq y$ and $p \in L(x)$ then $p \in L(y)$.

The forcing relation with intuitionistic implication is given below for a world $w \in W$.

$$w \models A \to B \text{ iff } \forall x. w \leq x \text{ and } x \models A \text{ implies } x \models B$$

Give the forcing relation for an atomic proposition p, logical constants $\top$ and $\bot$, and logical connectives $\neg, \wedge, \vee$ in intuitionistic logic.

More on modal operators. First-order logic and most other branches of mathematics are *extensional*: they deal with reference or designation of objects. For example, we write $1 + 3 = 2 + 2$ because both sides of the equation designate the same number (cf. Sect. 1.6). However, some statements carry more meaning than extensions, and we call such meanings *intensions*.[9] The Standford Encyclopedia has a nice example of morning star vs evening star[10]: If the reader is not familiar with astronomy, then the statement "the morning star is the evening star" provides new knowledge. However, knowing that both stars refer to Venus, we can substitute the terms and obtain a "mathematically equivalent" statement "the morning star is the morning star", which is quite different from the original one. This subtle difference is an example of

---

[9] Do not confuse intension, which is the opposite to extension, with intention, which is about the will to act in a certain way.

[10] https://plato.stanford.edu/entries/logic-intensional/.

intension. Intensions often invalidate trivial substitutions of equality. Other examples of intensional contexts are "it is possible that...", "it is necessary that...", etc. "The reader has not studied logic" may be wrong for many people, but few would question me if I said "It is possible that the reader has not studied logic". Such intensions are captured in modal logic by modalities: $\square$ for necessity and $\lozenge$ for possibility. Informally, $\square A$ is true iff it must be the case that A is true, and $\lozenge A$ is true iff it is possible that A is true. Modal logic is another non-classical logic.

3.4   Model Checking

Mathematically, *model checking* is the problem of verifying whether a model M makes a formula F true. That is, $M \models F$. On the other hand, *satisfiability checking* (often called SAT[11]) is the problem of verifying whether a formula F has a model; this is denoted by $SAT(F)$. In comparison, theorem proving (assuming soundness of the proof theory) is the problem of proving the validity of a formula, i.e., $\vdash F$. The three problems are related. For example, if we only have a SAT solver, we can perform theorem proving of F by checking $SAT(\neg F)$; that is, if $\neg F$ is unsatisfiable, then F must be valid. Similarly, if we can encode the model M into a formula, then we can perform model checking $M \models F$ by verifying if $SAT(M \wedge (\neg F))$ is unsat(isfiable)—if it is unsat, then M is a model of F.

Example 3.7 The model of a propositional logic formula is a set of truth assignments for the propositions that make the formula true.

The model of a first-order logic (FOL) formula F (cf. Page 48) is a pair $M = (D, I)$ of a domain and an interpretation of functions and relations. $M \models F$ when F is true for *every* valuation under the model.

The model of an LTL formula F is a Kripke structure $M = (S, I, R, L)$. In Sect. 3.3, we have defined the forcing relation $M, w \models F$, where w is a path. We can extend this definition to a model and a state as follows:

$$M, s \models F \quad \text{iff} \quad M, w \models F \text{ for } every \text{ path } w \text{ starting with the state } s$$

The above definition gives rise to the problem of LTL model checking.

Definition 3.7 (*LTL Model Checking*) $M \models F$ iff $M, s_0 \models F$ for *every* initial state $s_0 \in I$ of the Kripke structure M.

---

[11] Without the context of which logic it refers to, SAT usually means satisfiability checking for classical propositional logic. In this paragraph, we just assume that we are talking about the three problems for the same logic.

Note the asymmetry of quantifiers in the above definitions for FOL and LTL. A formula F is satisfiable if it is true in *some* model M. But for FOL, $M \models F$ requires that F is true under *all* valuations. For LTL, $M, s_0 \models F$ requires checking *every* initial state s_0 and *all* paths starting with s_0.

From the verification technique point of view, theorem proving is related to deductive or inductive proofs. In contrast, model checking, especially for temporal logics, is usually an exhaustive search of the states and paths of a model.

Model checking as a verification technique is pioneered by Clarke, Emerson, Queille and Sifakis in the 1980s [8–10]. Their founding of this field of research later won the 2007 Turing Award, which is the most prestigious award for computer scientists.

There are numerous impactful examples of formal verification in the industry [11]. A prominent one is a bug in the floating-point unit of Intel's Pentium II processor, which was released in the early 1990s. For example, the following operation is the correct behaviour:

$$\frac{4,195,835}{3,145,727} = 1.333820449136241002$$

However, on an affected Intel processor, the result is:

$$\frac{4,195,835}{3,145,727} = 1.333739068902037589$$

The error is caused by missing entries in the lookup table of the floating-point division circuitry. This issue cost Intel about 475 million US dollars[12] to replace flawed products and even more to fix their damaged reputation. Another disastrous example was the Ariane-5 launch in 1996; the rocket self-destructed 37 s after launch due to a conversion of a 64-bit floating-point into a 16-bit integer. In such mission-critical tasks, *testing* does not provide sufficient confidence to the user.

> Program testing can be used to show the presence of bugs, but never to show their absence!
>
> – Edsger Dijkstra [12]

Model checking, on the other hand, can show the absence of bugs by exhaustive search.[13] Companies such as Airbus and Intel have been heavily investing in verification techniques in the past decades to provide a high level of guarantee for their products.[14]

Figure 3.3 illustrates Clarke's description of model checking in a nutshell [13]. The system under investigation is modelled into a Kripke structure (or a state-transition

---

[12] US$475 million in 1994 is roughly US$838 million in 2020.

[13] Assuming that the model is correct, the model checking algorithm is correct, and their implementation is correct, etc. There will always be assumptions such as these, and we will not descend into this rabbit hole in this book.

[14] See John Harrison's account of formal verification at Intel here: https://shemesh.larc.nasa.gov/NFM2010/talks/harrison.pdf.

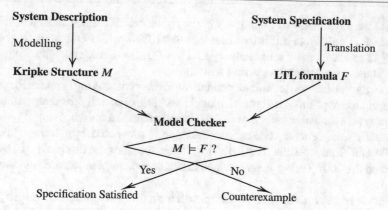

Fig. 3.3 A summary of the model checking technique

graph) M. The specification is translated into an LTL formula F. We then ask the model checker whether $M \models F$. The model checker usually implements an algorithm that systematically checks whether F is true on *every possible* path produced by M. If we get a positive output, we can conclude that the model satisfies the specification. Otherwise, we can obtain a witness path that falsifies the specification; this path is used as a counterexample to inform the system designer how the issue occurs.

There are several common properties expressible in LTL. For example, an *unconditional fairness* property ensures that some action A happens infinitely often along a path. This property can be written as

$$\mathbf{G}\ \mathbf{F}\ A$$

That is, from every state, there is always a future state that makes A true.

A *strong fairness* property says that if A is enabled infinitely often, then B happens infinitely often.

$$\mathbf{G}\ \mathbf{F}\ A \to \mathbf{G}\ \mathbf{F}\ B$$

A *weak fairness* property says that if A is enabled continuously in the future, then B happens infinitely often.

$$\mathbf{F}\ \mathbf{G}\ A \to \mathbf{G}\ \mathbf{F}\ B$$

In general, unconditional fairness implies strong fairness, which in turn implies weak fairness. The converse is not true.

A *safety* property ensures that a bad thing (e.g., a bug A) does not happen. This property can be expressed as follows:

$$\mathbf{G}\ \neg A$$

A *liveness* property states that a good thing will eventually happen. The simplest liveness property can be expressed as follows:

$$\mathbf{F}\ A$$

Example 3.8   The operations of a vending machine can be modelled in the following Kripke structure:

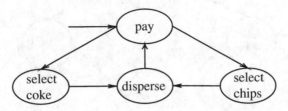

We can check the vending machine's liveness from a consumer's point of view, i.e., eventually, it will disperse goods. Clearly, **F** *disperse* is true in this model.

Example 3.9   Let us consider a semaphore-based mutual exclusion algorithm [11]. In this example, two processes are competing to enter a critical region to use a resource.

The semaphore algorithm uses a variable s to indicate the number of units of available resources. In this example, we only consider one unit of resource, so s is at most 1.

Each competing process is equipped with two atomic operations: wait and signal.[15] These operations are atomic in the sense that all the steps in the operation are done as if they were one step.

The wait (P) operation decrements s. If the new value of s is negative, then the process which executes the operation is blocked and waits for the resource to become available. Otherwise, the process uses the resource, which in this example means that it goes to the critical region.

```
P(semaphore s) = {
    while (1) {
        if (s >= 1) {
            --s;
            break;
        }
        // wait
    }
}
```

The signal (V) operation increments s. If the previous value of s was negative, then the previously blocked process is unblocked and enters the critical region.

```
V(semaphore s) = {
    ++s;
```

[15] The original algorithm is invented by the Dutch computer scientist Edsger Dijsktra, and he used letters P and V for these two operations; they stand for Dutch words "passering" (passing), and "vrijgave" (release).

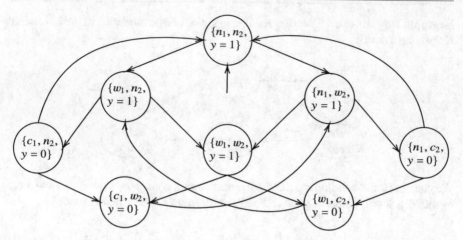

Fig. 3.4 The model of a semaphore-based mutual exclusion algorithm

```
3  }
```

The pseudocode of both processes is given below.

```
1  ...
2  P(s)
3  ... // Do things in critical region
4  V(s)
5  ...
```

We model the above mutual exclusion algorithm in Fig. 3.4. We denote the availability of the resource by $y = 1$ and unavailability by $y = 0$. When the processes are executing non-critical code, their statuses are n_1 and n_2, respectively. Before entering the critical region, a process must first *wait* until the resource is available. The waiting statuses are denoted by w_1 and w_2 respectively for the two processes. Finally, when the two processes are in the critical region, their statuses are c_1 and c_2, respectively. The state-transition graph is drawn below, where we give the labelling function by writing the set of true propositions inside each state.

For the safety of the program, we need to check that the two processes will never enter the critical region at the same time. This property can be expressed as follows:

$$\mathbf{G} \neg (c_1 \wedge c_2)$$

And this property holds in the above model, as none of the states has c_1 and c_2 at the same time.

Another interesting property is that the program should be fair to both processes. Unconditionally, both processes should be able to enter the critical region infinitely often. We can express this unconditional fairness property for Process 1 as follows:

$$\mathbf{G} \ \mathbf{F} c_1$$

However, the semaphore algorithm is not fair in this sense, as we can obtain a counterexample cyclic path as follows:

$$\{n_1, n_2, y = 1\} \rightarrow \{n_1, w_2, y = 1\} \rightarrow \{n_1, c_2, y = 0\} \rightarrow \{n_1, n_2, y = 1\} \rightarrow \cdots$$

On this path, Process 1 will never get access to the critical region. We call this phenomenon a *starvation* of Process 1. Similarly, there is another path on which Process 2 will never get access to the critical region.

Moreover, the semaphore algorithm does not satisfy the strong fairness property for both processes. This property can be expressed as follows: if a process waits infinitely often, then it can enter the critical region infinitely often. Formally, the property below does not hold in this model:

$$\mathbf{G}\ \mathbf{F}\ w_1 \rightarrow \mathbf{G}\ \mathbf{F}\ c_1$$

The following cyclic path is a witness that Process 1 waits infinitely often but can never enter the critical region:

$$\{n_1, n_2, y = 1\} \rightarrow \{w_1, n_2, y = 1\} \rightarrow \{w_1, w_2, y = 1\} \rightarrow \{w_1, c_2, y = 0\} \rightarrow$$
$$\{w_1, n_2, y = 1\} \rightarrow \cdots$$

The above path is also a counterexample of the weak fairness property given below.

$$\mathbf{F}\ \mathbf{G}\ w_1 \rightarrow \mathbf{G}\ \mathbf{F}\ c_1$$

A liveness property for this model can be stated as "it is always the case that if a process waits, then it can eventually enter the critical region". This property is translated to the following formula:

$$\mathbf{G}\ (w_1 \rightarrow \mathbf{F}\ c_1)$$

Clearly, this property does not hold in the above model either.

The above example gives some intuitions on model checking LTL properties. Modern model checkers often adopt automata-based algorithms by translating Kripke structures into Büchi automata [14] to perform verification systematically. This advanced topic is not in the scope of this book, but we will study the basics of automata theory and formal languages from the next chapter.

Exercises

3.14 Peterson's algorithm [15] for mutual exclusion allows two or more processes to share resources without conflict. The algorithm runs as below for an instance of two processes P0 and P1, which run in parallel.

```
1  bool flag[2] = {false, false};
2  int turn;
3  // Code for P0.
4  flag[0] = true; // P0 wants to enter critical region.
5  turn = 1; // P0 gives priority to P1.
6  while (flag[1] == true && turn == 1) {
```

```
 7     // P0 waits
 8 }
 9 // P0 enters critical region
10 ...
11 // P0 exitx critical region
12 flag[0] = false; // P0 resets flag.
```

The code for P1 is symmetric:

```
 1 // Code for P1.
 2 flag[1] = true; // P1 wants to enter critical region.
 3 turn = 0; // P1 gives priority to P0.
 4 while (flag[0] == true && turn == 0) {
 5     // P1 waits
 6 }
 7 // P1 enters critical region
 8 ...
 9 // P1 exits critical region
10 flag[1] = false; // P1 resets flag.
```

There are two important variables: flag and turn. The former indicates which process wants to enter the critical region, the latter indicates who has the priority. P0 must wait if flag[1] == true *and* turn == 1. We can negate this condition as follows:

$$\neg(\texttt{flag[1]} \; == \; \texttt{true} \, and \, \texttt{turn} \; == \; 1)$$
$$\updownarrow$$
$$\texttt{flag[1]} \; == \; \texttt{false} \, or \, \texttt{turn} \; == \; 0.$$

In other words, P0 can only enter the critical region if P1 does not want to enter the critical region *or* P1 has given priority to P0.

Verify the following properties for Peterson's algorithm:

1. Safety: P0 and P1 will never be in the critical region at the same time.
2. Unconditional fairness: P0 visits the critical region infinitely often.
3. Strong fairness: if P0 waits infinitely often, then it visits the critical region infinitely often.
4. Weak fairness: if P0 waits continuously in the future, then it visits the critical region infinitely often.
5. Liveness 1: P0 will eventually visit the critical region.
6. Liveness 2: it is always the case that if P0 waits, then it will eventually visit the critical region.

Instruction. Download the Process Analysis Toolkit (PAT) [16–18], which is a modern model checker, from the link below.

https://pat.comp.nus.edu.sg/?page_id=2587

Linux users can run PAT via Mono and (Intel-based) Mac users can run PAT via Wine. See the instructions in the link below.

https://formal-analysis.com/research/monopat/

Both Intel-based and ARM-based (Apple Silicon) Mac users can run PAT on a Ubuntu guest OS in a virtual machine. ARM-based Macs may require a virtual machine such as

https://mac.getutm.app/,

and that the guest OS may need to be ARM-based as well, for example:

https://ubuntu.com/download/server/arm.

Open PAT and create a new CSP model. The most common modelling language in PAT is CSP#, which is a fusion of Hoare's Communicating Sequential Processes (CSP) [19] and C#. Under the hood, PAT translates CSP# models into labelled transition systems (Kripke structures) and invokes various automata-based or binary decision diagram (BDD)-based model checking algorithms to verify different forms of properties. We give a brief tutorial of CSP# below. The reader can refer to the "Help" menu (press F1) in PAT for detailed documentation (The CSP module is described in Sect. 3.1 of the PAT user manual).

Constants and variables in CSP#. Constants in CSP# can be written in the same syntax as macros in C++. For example, the following code defines N as the constant 2.

```
#define N 2;
```

We then define three variables in the model.

```
var turn;
var flag[N];
var counter = 0;
```

For simplicity, we will encode other data types into integers. For example, flag[N] is an integer array of size 2, and 1 represents "true" and 0 represents "false". We use an extra variable named counter to record how many processes are in the critical region at a time.

Syntax of processes in CSP#. A model in CSP# is encoded as a *process*, which can be thought of as a function. One of the most common forms of processes is a process P with a prefix event, written in the following form:

```
event ->P();
```

The event can be simply used as a label or attached to a piece of C# code that manipulates data. The latter is written in the following form:

```
event{C# code}->P();
```

An event can be guarded by a condition. In this case, the event is only executed when the condition holds; otherwise, the event waits until the condition is met. A guarded event with a condition can be written as follows:

```
[condition]event{C# code}->P();
```

Processes can be composed sequentially using semicolon (think statements in C++):

```
P() ; Q()
```

Parallel composition without synchronisation (also called interleaving) is written as

```
P() ||| Q()
```

Processes can be composed via a deterministic choice using [ ]. For example,

```
event1->P() [] event2->Q()
```

allows lazy evaluation of events. In the above code, if `event1` occurs first, then `P()` is executed; otherwise, `Q()` is executed. We can also compose processes via a non-deterministic choice using <>.

```
P() <> Q()
```

The above code will execute one of the two processes non-deterministically. Finally, the process `Skip` terminates the execution.

The model of Peterson's algorithm. The process P0 can be modelled as follows:

```
Process0() = w0{flag[0] = 1; turn = 1;} -> Wait0(); c0{counter =
    counter+1;} -> reset{flag[0] = 0; counter = counter-1;} ->
    Process0();
```

P0 first initialises the variables `flag[0]` and `turn` and waits by calling the process `Wait0()`. When the wait is over, P0 enters the critical region and increases the counter. To be consistent with the example of this section, we use the events w0 and c0 to denote that P0 waits and enters the critical region, respectively. Finally, when P0 exits the critical region, it resets `flag[0]` and decreases the counter, and then repeats by calling `Process0()`. The wait process is modelled as follows:

```
Wait0() = [turn == 0 || flag[1] == 0]enter0 -> Skip;
```

The event `enter0` is guarded by the condition that P1 does not want to enter the critical region or P1 has given priority to P0. If this condition is not met, the event `enter0` will wait indefinitely. The model for P1 is symmetric. The two processes are composed by a parallel operator: `P0() ||| P1()`. Putting everything together, we give the full model in the code given below.

```
#define N 2;
var turn;
var flag[N];
var counter = 0;

Process0() = w0{flag[0] = 1; turn = 1;} -> Wait0(); c0{counter =
    counter+1;} -> reset{flag[0] = 0; counter = counter-1;} ->
    Process0();
```

```
7  Wait0() = [turn == 0 || flag[1] == 0]enter0 -> Skip;
8
9  Process1() = w1{flag[1] = 1; turn = 0;} -> Wait1(); c1{counter =
        counter+1;} -> reset{flag[1] = 0; counter = counter-1;} ->
        Process1();
10 Wait1() = [turn == 1 || flag[0] == 0]enter1 -> Skip;
11
12 Peterson() = Process0() ||| Process1();
```

Specifying properties. CSP# follows a different set of notations for LTL where **G** is [ ] and **F** is <>. The other temporal modalities are typed the same way as the syntax used in this book. For example, **X** A is simply X A. Conjunction is && and disjunction is | |, similar to C++. Note that parallel events are eventually executed sequentially in all possible orders; thus, c1 && c2 will never be true, but this is not what we should verify! To express that the two processes will never enter the critical region at the same time, we can simply check that the counter is never greater than 1. We define the safety property as below (write the below properties after the above code for the model in the *same* file).

```
1  #define unsafe counter > 1;
2  #assert Peterson() reaches unsafe;
```

That is, we translate the safety property into a reachability property of unsafe states. The syntax for defining a condition (e.g., unsafe) is similar to the syntax for defining constants. The keyword assert defines a property to be checked. The other properties can be expressed using LTL. For example, unconditional fairness can be coded as follows:

```
1  #assert Peterson() |= []<> c0;
```

Refer to Example 3.9 for other properties.

Click the verification button and see which properties are true and which ones are false. Give your analyses on why for each case.

References

1. Troelstra A, Dalen D (1988) Constructivism in mathematics: an introduction. North-Holland. ISBN: 9780444703583
2. Harrison J (2009) Handbook of practical logic and automated reasoning, 1st ed. Cambridge University Press
3. Heyting A (1930) Die formalenRegeln der intuitionistischen Logik. I, II, III German Sitzungsber Preuß Akad Wiss, Phys-Math Kl 1930, 42–56, 57–71, 158–169
4. Girard J-Y (1995) Linear logic: its syntax and semantics in proceedings of the workshop on advances in linear logic. Cambridge University Press, New York, NY, USA, pp 1–42. ISBN: 0-521-55961-8
5. Pnueli A (1977) The temporal logic of programs in proceedings of the 18th annual symposium on foundations of computer science. IEEE Computer Society, USA, pp 46–57

6. Kripke SA (1963) Semantical considerations on modal logic. Acta Philosophica Fennica 16:83–94

7. Clarke E, Peled E, Grumberg O, Peled D (1999) EBSCO. Model checking. MIT Press. ISBN: 9780262032704

8. Emerson EA, Clarke EM (1980) Characterizing correctness properties of parallel programs using fixpoints in automata, languages and programming. In: de Bakker J, van Leeuwen J (eds). Springer Berlin Heidelberg, Berlin, Heidelberg, pp 169–181. ISBN: 978-3-540-39346-7

9. Queille JP, Sifakis J (1982) Specification and verification of concurrent systems in CESAR in international symposium on programming. In: Dezani-Ciancaglini M, Montanari U (eds). Springer Berlin Heidelberg, Berlin, Heidelberg, pp 337–351. ISBN: 978-3-540-39184-5

10. Clarke EM, Emerson EA, Sistla AP (1986) Automatic verification of finite state concurrent systems using temporal logic specifications. ACM Trans Program Lang Syst 8:244–263

11. Baier C, Katoen J-P (2008) Principles of model checking. Representation and mind series. The MIT Press. ISBN: 026202649X

12. Dijkstra EW (1970) Notes on structured programming

13. Handbook of Model Checking. In: Clarke EM, Henzinger TA, Veith H, Bloem R (eds). Springer, Berlin. ISBN: 978-3-319-10574-1

14. Büchi JR (1990) The collected works of J. Richard Büchi. In: Mac Lane S, Siefkes D (eds). Springer New York, New York, NY, pp 425–435

15. Peterson G (1981) Myths about the mutual exclusion problem. Inf Process Lett 12:115–116

16. Sun J, Liu Y, Dong JS, Pang J (2009) PAT: towards flexible verification under fairness in computer aided verification. In: 21st international conference, CAV 2009, Grenoble, France, June 26–July 2, 2009. proceedings, pp 709–714

17. Liu Y, Sun J, Dong JS (2011) PAT 3: an extensible architecture for building multi-domain model checkers. In: IEEE 22nd international symposium on software reliability engineering, ISSRE 2011, Hiroshima, Japan, November 29–December 2, 2011, pp 190–199

18. Bride H, et al (2020) N-PAT: a nested model-checker—(System description). In: Automated reasoning—10th international joint conference, .CAR 2020, Paris, France, July 1–4, 2020, Proceedings, Part II, pp 369–377

19. Hoare CAR (1978) Communicating sequential processes. Commun ACM 21, 666–677. ISBN: 0001–0782

Part II
Computation

Automata Theory and Formal Languages

In this and the next chapter, we will be dealing with automata, formal languages, and problems, and we adopt the definitions from Hopcroft, Motwani, and Ullman's book "Introduction to Automata Theory, Languages, and Computation" [1].

We start with the concept of an *alphabet*, which is a finite and non-empty set of symbols and is often denoted by the Greek letter Σ. For example, $\{0, 1\}$ is an alphabet of two symbols, $\{A, B, \ldots, Z\}$ is the alphabet of English uppercase letters, and $\{a, b, \ldots, z\}$ is the alphabet of English lowercase letters.

A *string*, or a word, is a finite sequence of symbols chosen from an alphabet. For example, 010101 and 10101 are both strings from the alphabet $\{0, 1\}$. We denote an empty string by ϵ and the size of a string w by $|w|$. Naturally, $|\epsilon| = 0$. We denote the set of all possible strings of length k over an alphabet Σ by Σ^k. For example, $\Sigma^0 = \{\epsilon\}$ and $\{0, 1\}^2 = \{00, 01, 10, 11\}$. The set of all possible strings (of any length) over an alphabet Σ is written as Σ^*.

An *automaton* is a state-transition abstract machine that takes a string as input and outputs either success or failure. If the output is a success, then we say the automaton *accepts* the string; otherwise, the automaton *rejects* the string.

A *language* is a set of strings over an alphabet. For example, $\{010101, 10101\}$ is a language over the alphabet $\{0, 1\}$. An automaton *accepts a language* when it accepts every string in the language and nothing else. Any language over an alphabet Σ is a subset of Σ^*.

Given a language L, the corresponding *problem* P_L asks whether a string is in L. Language and problem are two sides of the same coin, and every computational problem can be expressed in the above form. We say that an automaton solves a problem if it accepts the corresponding language.

The study of automata and languages are also interconnected in the following two tasks:

- Given an automaton, find the language that is accepted by this automaton.
- Given a language, find the automaton that accepts this language.

© The Author(s), under exclusive license to Springer Nature Switzerland AG 2021
Z. Hou, *Fundamentals of Logic and Computation*, Texts in Computer Science,
https://doi.org/10.1007/978-3-030-87882-5_4

Automata can be classified by the type of languages they accept, languages can be classified by the way they are generated, and problems can be classified by their corresponding languages. These classifications are central problems in the study of the theory of computation, a field of research initiated by mathematicians and logicians in the early twentieth century. Notably, David Hilbert (1862–1943) put together a proposal in the 1920s, later referred to as *Hilbert's program*, that called for a finite formalisation of *all* of mathematics in an axiomatic form, a proof that the formalisation is consistent, and a systematic method that decides the truth or falsity of any mathematical statement. This line of research has now developed into different sub-fields, such as

> Automata theory: how to formalise computational models? What class of problems can a type of machine solve?
> Complexity theory: how hard is a problem?
> Computability theory: can a problem be solved at all?

We will focus on the first problem in this chapter and look at the other two problems in the next chapter.

4.1 Finite Automata

We have seen state-transition graphs in Kripke structures. However, Kripke structures do not specify what triggers a transition and when does the computation terminate. Let us consider the former by writing an "action" that triggers a transition over the corresponding arrow. The vending machine example can be redrawn as below with different operational semantics: here, we first select then pay, whereas in Example 3.8 we first pay then select.

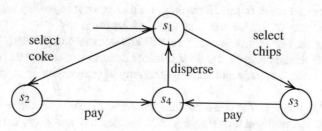

In this example, the state s_1 is the initial state. Each state transition is labelled with an action, and the actions we can perform at each state are distinct, so we can always determine where to go based on the actions that are allowed. However, it is unclear what to do if we are at state s_1 and the action is "pay". It is also unclear what *finite* sequences of actions are permitted by this machine since it does not specify when to stop.

Fig. 4.1 An example of a coin processing machine

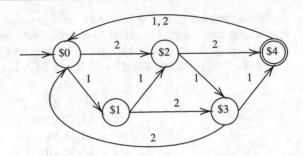

If we restrict the scope to the part of a vending machine that accepts coins, we can draw a state-transition graph for accepting $4 in Fig. 4.1. In this example, the state "$0" is the initial state, and we draw the final state "$4" with two circles. Each transition in this diagram is labelled with either 1 or 2, so this automaton processes a language over the alphabet {1, 2}. We can think of 1 as an action that inserts a $1 coin and 2 likewise. From each state, there are Exactly two transitions for 1 and 2, respectively. Therefore, this automaton is *deterministic*, that is, given any symbol in the alphabet and any state, we always know where to go next.

The above example contains all the ingredients for a *deterministic finite automaton* (DFA), which is formally defined as follows.

Definition 4.1 (*DFA*) A DFA as a five-tuple (Σ, S, s_0, F, N).

- Σ is the input alphabet.
- S is a finite set of states.
- $s_0 \in S$ is an initial state.
- $F \subseteq S$ is a set of final states.
- $N : S \times \Sigma \to S$ is a transition function that maps the current state and a symbol in the alphabet to the next state.

We write $N(s, x) = s'$ if the machine in state s "consumes" a symbol x and transits to the next state s'.

Example 4.1 The DFA in Fig. 4.1 can be defined as follows:

- $\Sigma = \{1, 2\}$.
- $S = \{\$0, \$1, \$2, \$3, \$4\}$.
- $s_0 = \$0$.
- $F = \{\$4\}$.
- $N = \{(\$0, 1) \mapsto \$1, (\$0, 2) \mapsto \$2, (\$1, 1) \mapsto \$2, (\$1, 2) \mapsto \$3, (\$2, 1) \mapsto \$3, (\$2, 2) \mapsto \$4, (\$3, 1) \mapsto \$4, (\$3, 2) \mapsto \$0, (\$4, 1) \mapsto \$0, (\$4, 2) \mapsto \$0\}$.

Although this example only has one final state, there can be multiple in general. However, unlike Kripke structures, there can only be one initial state. Also, the transition function of a DFA must be a *total function*, that is, any pair of state and symbol must be mapped to exactly one state. For a counterexample, the first state-transition graph in this section is not a DFA because there are undefined transitions.

We often write the transition function of a DFA in a table format as follows:

	1	2
\$0	\$1	\$2
\$1	\$2	\$3
\$2	\$3	\$4
\$3	\$4	\$0
\$4	\$0	\$0

We can extend the transition function to an *eventual transition function* N^* : $S \times \Sigma^* \to S$ that takes a state and a string as input and outputs a state. This function can be defined inductively as follows:

Base case: $N^*(s, \epsilon) = s$.
Inductive case: $N^*(s, \alpha x) = N(N^*(s, \alpha), x)$.

If we are in the state s and given an empty string ϵ, then we stay in s. If we are given a string αx, we first transit to the state $N^*(s, \alpha)$ and then process the last symbol x.

The function N^* is transitive. That is, starting from a state s, if N^* takes us to s' by processing a string α, and then from s' we arrive at s'' by processing a string β, then we can go from s to s'' by processing the concatenated string $\alpha\beta$. This property is proved by induction given below.

Lemma 4.1 (Append Lemma) *For all states $s \in S$ and all strings $\alpha, \beta \in \Sigma^*$, $N^*(s, \alpha\beta) = N^*(N^*(s, \alpha), \beta)$.*

Proof By induction on the length of β,

Base case: $\beta = \epsilon$. Then we have
$$N^*(s, \alpha\beta) = N^*(s, \alpha\epsilon) = N^*(s, \alpha)$$
$$N^*(N^*(s, \alpha), \beta) = N^*(N^*(s, \alpha), \epsilon) = N^*(s, \alpha).$$

Inductive case: the inductive hypothesis is that $N^*(s, \alpha\beta) = N^*(N^*(s, \alpha), \beta)$ for any β. We now need to prove that $N^*(s, \alpha\beta x) = N^*(N^*(s, \alpha), \beta x)$ for an extra symbol x. We prove it as follows:
$$N^*(s, \alpha\beta x) = N(N^*(s, \alpha\beta), x) = N(N^*(N^*(s, \alpha), \beta), x)$$
$$N^*(N^*(s, \alpha), \beta x) = N(N^*(N^*(s, \alpha), \beta), x).$$

Thus the left-hand side equals the right-hand side.   □

We can process a string by starting from the initial state and consume a bit of the string (left to right) each time we go through a corresponding transition. If we end up in a final state when the string is depleted, then we say the automaton accepts the string. For example, the DFA of Fig. 4.1 accepts 22, 112, and 2222 but does not accept 2 or 221.

More precisely, let $A = (\Sigma, S, s_0, F, N)$ be a DFA; A *accepts* a string $w \in \Sigma^*$ if $N^*(s_0, w) \in F$. The *language* accepted by A, denoted by $L(A)$, is the set of all strings accepted by A. This definition can be expressed in a "set-former" in the format

$$\{element \mid conditions\}$$

as follows:

$$L(A) = \{w \in \Sigma^* \mid N^*(s_0, w) \in F\}.$$

For example, the language accepted by the DFA in Fig. 4.1 is the set of strings over $\{1, 2\}$ such that when we sum up all the digits in a string, the result is a multiple of 4.

Example 4.2 The language accepted by the following DFA is the set of strings over $\{0, 1\}$ that end with 01:

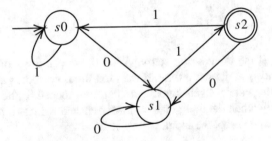

A *nondeterministic finite automaton* (NFA) is a variant of DFA that has a transition *relation* instead of a total function. In an NFA, there can be multiple transitions labelled with the same symbol that go from the same state to different states, and there can also be states that do not have a transition for each symbol in the alphabet. For example, if we take the vending machine diagram and add a final state, then it would become an NFA.

Definition 4.2 (*NFA*) An NFA is a five-tuple (Σ, S, s_0, F, R) where the first four items are the same as the definition of DFA, but $R \subseteq S \times \Sigma \times S$ is a ternary relation that relates a state and a symbol in the alphabet to a state.

Similarly, we can extend the definition of the transition relation of an NFA to an *eventual transition relation* $R^* \subseteq S \times \Sigma^* \times S$ as follows:

Base case: $R^*(s, \epsilon, s')$ holds iff $s = s'$.
Inductive case: $R^*(s, \alpha x, s') = \exists s''. R^*(s, \alpha, s'') \wedge R(s'', x, s')$.

The base case states that we can stay in a state by processing the empty string ϵ. The inductive case says that we can reach s' from s by processing the string αx if there is an intermediate state s'' such that we can reach s'' by processing α, and then reach s' from s'' by processing the last symbol x.

The nondeterminism of NFA can be understood as having the ability to start from the initial state and explore all possible state transitions in parallel. If *one of* the paths ends in a final state, then the input string is accepted. In this sense, an NFA can be in multiple states at the same time.

Formally, a string w is *accepted* by an NFA $A = (\Sigma, S, s_0, F, R)$ if $\exists s \in F$ such that $R^*(s_0, w, s)$. The *language* $L(A)$ accepted by A is defined as follows:

$$L(A) = \{w \in \Sigma^* \mid \exists s \in F. \; R^*(s_0, w, s)\}.$$

Example 4.3 It is often easier to find an NFA for a language than to find a DFA. For example, an NFA for the language in Example 4.2 is given as follows:

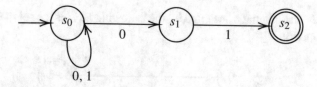

In this example, if the input string starts with a 0, we can think of the NFA going to the state s_0 and s_1 at the same time. If the next input symbol is also a 0, then the "path" through the state s_1 "gets stuck" and cannot proceed further; thus, we need to discard it. Only when the input ends with 01 will we witness a path that ends in the final state s_2 and accept the input.

Perhaps surprisingly, although having the ability of nondeterminism, NFAs are not generally more powerful than DFAs in terms of the class of languages they accept. In fact, for each NFA, one can always construct a DFA that accepts the same language via an algorithm called the *subset construction*,[1] which we describe in Algorithm 3, where we write an assignment of y to x as $x \leftarrow y$.

Algorithm 3: The subset construction Algorithm.

Data: An NFA $A_N = (\Sigma, S_N, s_0, F_N, R)$
Result: A DFA $A_D = (\Sigma, S_D, \{s_0\}, F_D, N)$
$S_D \leftarrow$ the set of subsets of S_N;
$F_D \leftarrow$ the set of subsets of S_N such that $F_D \cap F_N \neq \emptyset$;
$N \leftarrow \emptyset$;
foreach $S \subseteq S_N$ **do**
    foreach $a \in \Sigma$ **do**
       $N(S, a) \leftarrow \{q \in S_N \mid p \in S \wedge R(p, a, q)\}$
    end
end

---

[1] Sometimes called powerset construction.

Example 4.4 We explain how Algorithm 3 works using the NFA of Example 4.3.

The alphabet of the constructed DFA is the same as that of the NFA. The states of the DFA are the subsets of the states of the NFA. That is, the NFA has three states: s_0, s_1, and s_2; thus, the states of the DFA are the following: $S_D = \{\emptyset, \{s_0\}, \{s_1\}, \{s_2\}, \{s_0, s_1\}, \{s_0, s_2\}, \{s_1, s_2\}, \{s_0, s_1, s_2\}\}$.

The initial state of the DFA is precisely the set $\{s_0\}$ of the initial states of the NFA.

The final states of the DFA are those that contain the final states of the NFA. There is only one final state s_2 in the NFA. Thus, the final states of the DFA are $F_D = \{\{s_2\}, \{s_0, s_2\}, \{s_1, s_2\}, \{s_0, s_1, s_2\}\}$.

For each $S \subseteq S_N$, which must be a state of the DFA, and for each symbol $a \in \Sigma$, the transition $N(S, a)$ results in the set of states that are related with p, a by R for all $p \in S$. In other words, we check each state p in S, and see which state q is related with $R(p, a, q)$. Then we take the union of all such qs. We can write the transition function N of this example in Table 4.1. Remember to write the transitions for the emptyset!

A naïve construction generates a DFA with 2^n states from an NFA with n states. In practice, many of the generated states can be removed, and an equivalent DFA often has about as many states as the NFA (cf. Example 4.2). For example, in Table 4.1, the state $\{s_1\}$, $\{s_1, s_2\}$, and $\{s_0, s_1, s_2\}$ cannot be accessed by other states, which means that we can never reach them from the initial state $\{s_0\}$, so they can be safely removed. On the other hand, an equivalent DFA usually has more transitions than the corresponding NFA.

In the lemma below, we prove that the subset construction algorithm yields a DFA that mimics the transitions of the original NFA. For instance, starting from the initial state s_0, if the NFA is able to go to either s_1 or s_2 by processing a string w, then the resulting DFA goes from the initial state $\{s_0\}$ to the state $\{s_1, s_2\}$ by processing w.

Lemma 4.2 *Let $A_D = (\Sigma, S_D, \{s_0\}, F_D, N)$ be the DFA constructed by the subset construction algorithm (Algorithm 3) from the NFA $A_N = (\Sigma, S_N, s_0, F_N, R)$, then $N^*(\{s_0\}, w) = \{s \in S_N \mid R^*(s_0, w, s)\}$ for any string w.*

Table 4.1 The transition function for the DFA of Example 4.4

	0	1
$\emptyset$	$\emptyset$	$\emptyset$
$\{s_0\}$	$\{s_0, s_1\}$	$\{s_0\}$
$\{s_1\}$	$\emptyset$	$\{s_2\}$
$\{s_2\}$	$\emptyset$	$\emptyset$
$\{s_0, s_1\}$	$\{s_0, s_1\}$	$\{s_0, s_2\}$
$\{s_0, s_2\}$	$\{s_0, s_1\}$	$\{s_0\}$
$\{s_1, s_2\}$	$\emptyset$	$\{s_2\}$
$\{s_0, s_1, s_2\}$	$\{s_0, s_1\}$	$\{s_0, s_2\}$

Proof By induction on the length of w,

Base case: $|w| = 0$, that is, $w = \epsilon$ is an empty string. By definition, $N^*(\{s_0\}, \epsilon) = \{s_0\}$, and $R^*(s_0, \epsilon, s)$ holds only when $s_0 = s$, therefore $N^*(\{s_0\}, \epsilon) = \{s \in S_N \mid R^*(s_0, \epsilon, s)\} = \{s_0\}$.

Inductive case: assume that $N^*(\{s_0\}, w) = \{s \mid R^*(s_0, w, s)\}$ for any string w of length up to n. We prove that $N^*(\{s_0\}, w') = \{s \in S_N \mid R^*(s_0, w', s)\}$ for any string w' of length $n + 1$. Without loss of generality, assume that $w' = \alpha x$, that is, w' is a concatenation of a sub-string α of length n and a final symbol x. By the induction hypothesis, we have $N^*(\{s_0\}, \alpha) = \{s \in S_N \mid R^*(s_0, \alpha, s)\}$. Let us call this intermediate set of states I.

By the definition of R^*, we have $R^*(s_0, \alpha x, s) = \exists s'. R^*(s_0, \alpha, s') \wedge R(s', x, s)$. In other words, $\{s \in S_N \mid R^*(s_0, \alpha x, s)\} = \{s \in S_N \mid s' \in I \wedge R(s', x, s)\}$. On the other hand, by the subset construction algorithm, we have $N(I, x) = \{s \in S_N \mid s' \in I \wedge R(s', x, s)\}$. Combining the above, we have the following:

$$N^*(\{s_0\}, \alpha x) = N(N^*(\{s_0\}, \alpha), x) = N(I, x)$$
$$= \{s \in S_N \mid s' \in I \wedge R(s', x, s)\}.$$
$$= \{s \in S_N \mid R^*(s_0, \alpha x, s)\}.$$

The above concludes the inductive case.   □

It is then straightforward to show that the subset construction algorithm is correct in the sense that the resulting DFA accepts the same language as the original NFA.

Lemma 4.3 *Let $A_D = (\Sigma, S_D, \{s_0\}, F_D, N)$ be the DFA constructed by the subset construction algorithm (Algorithm 3) from the NFA $A_N = (\Sigma, S_N, s_0, F_N, R)$, then $L(A_D) = L(A_N)$.*

Proof We show that a string w is accepted by A_N if and only if it is accepted by A_D, that is,

$$\exists s \in F_N. R^*(s_0, w, s) \text{ iff } N^*(\{s_0\}, w) \in F_A.$$

Lemma 4.2 shows that $N^*(\{s_0\}, w) = \{s \in S_N \mid R^*(s_0, w, s)\}$. Let us call this set of states S. If $S \cap F_N \neq \emptyset$, then w is accepted by A_N. By the subset construction algorithm, S in this case is also a final state of A_D, thus w is also accepted by A_D. If $S \cap F_N = \emptyset$, then w is not accepted by A_N. In this case, S by definition is not a final state of A_D. We conclude that the two automata accept the same language. □

Finally, we show that the computational power of the NFAs is equivalent to that of the DFAs.

Theorem 4.1 *A language L is accepted by some DFA iff L is accepted by some NFA.*

Proof Recall from propositional logic that to prove A iff B ($A \leftrightarrow B$), we need to prove A if B ($B \to A$) and A only if B ($A \to B$).

(If:) This part shows that if L is accepted by some NFA, then it can be accepted by some DFA. The proof of Lemma 4.3 for the subset construction algorithm shows exactly this.

(Only if:) This part shows that if L is accepted by some DFA, then it can be accepted by some NFA. To prove this part, we only need to demonstrate that any DFA can be converted to an NFA that accepts the same language. Let $A_D = (\Sigma, S, s_0, F_D, N)$ be a DFA, we construct an NFA $A_N = (\Sigma, S, s_0, F_D, R)$ as follows:

$$R(s, x, s') \text{ iff } N(s, x) = s'.$$

The other components of the two automata are the same. It is straightforward to show that these two automata accept the same language. $\square$

NFAs with ϵ transitions. We can extend the definition of the NFA to the ϵ-NFA, which allows ϵ-transitions. In an ϵ-NFA, the transition relation R is defined as

$$R \subseteq S \times \Sigma \cup \{\epsilon\} \times S.$$

Example 4.5 When an ϵ-NFA makes an ϵ-transition, it does not consume an input symbol. We give an example below.

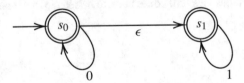

The above ϵ-NFA accepts strings such as ϵ, 0, 0001, 00111, and 1111.

The ability to make ϵ-transitions does *not* increase the power of the automata, and ϵ-NFAs accept the same class of languages as NFAs and DFAs.

Limitations of finite automata. The below language is a well-known example that is not accepted by *any* DFA or NFA. In the definition, we denote the set of natural numbers by $\mathbb{N}$.

$$L = \{0^n 1^n \mid n \in \mathbb{N}\}.$$

This language consists of the strings with a number of 0s followed by the same number of 1s. The main limitation of finite automata is that they do not have a "memory" that can record how many 0s they have processed, so there is no way to ensure that the accepted string must end with the same number of 1s. This problem can be solved by having an infinite number of states, but that is impractical.

To prove that no finite automata can accept the above language, we use the *pigeon-hole principle*: if there are more pigeons than holes, then at least two pigeons must be in the same hole.

Lemma 4.4 *There does not exist a DFA that accepts the language*

$$L = \{0^n 1^n \mid n \in \mathbb{N}\}.$$

Proof Prove by contradiction. Assume that there is a DFA $A = (\Sigma, S, s_0, F, N)$ that accepts L. That is, $L = L(A)$. Consider the following states:

$$N^*(s_0, 0), N^*(s_0, 00), N^*(s_0, 000), N^*(s_0, 0^4), \ldots$$

Since the set $\mathbb{N}$ of natural numbers is infinite, the above list of states is also infinite. However, by definition of the DFA, the set S of states must be finite. Therefore, some items in the above list must be the same state. That is, we can find some natural numbers i and j such that $i \neq j$ and $N^*(s_0, 0^i) = N^*(s_0, 0^j)$.

Since $0^i 1^i$ is in L, $N^*(s_0, 0^i 1^i) \in F$ must be a final state. By Lemma 4.1, $N^*(s_0, 0^i 1^i) = N^*(N^*(s_0, 0^i), 1^i)$. Replacing $N^*(s_0, 0^i)$ with $N^*(s_0, 0^j)$, we have that $N^*(s_0, 0^i 1^i) = N^*(N^*(s_0, 0^j), 1^i) = N^*(s_0, 0^j 1^i) \in F$, thus the string $0^j 1^i$, where $i \neq j$, is accepted by A, contradicting the assumption. Therefore, such a DFA does not exist. $\square$

The above lemma shows that finite automata are not powerful enough to recognise some simple languages. It is thus necessary to explore more powerful machines and more expressive languages. We will come back to this issue in the second half of this chapter.

Exercises

4.1 What language does the following NFA accept?

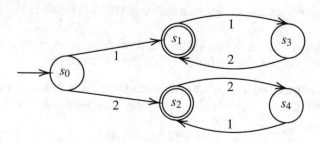

4.2 Find an NFA that accepts the following language:

$$L = \{(12)^n \mid n \in \mathbb{N}\}.$$

Draw a diagram of your NFA and write down its definition formally.

4.3 Use the subset construction algorithm (cf. Algorithm 3) to build a DFA that is equivalent to the NFA of Exercise 4.1. Draw the diagrams of your DFAs and write down their definitions formally.

4.4 Use the subset construction algorithm to build a DFA that is equivalent to the NFA of Exercise 4.2. Draw the diagrams of your DFAs and write down their definitions formally.

4.5 Model the NFA of Exercise 4.1 in PAT. Check three accepted strings and three unaccepted strings for each of your models.

Instruction. The built-in data types in PAT are integers and Boolean values ("true" and "false"); thus, we need to define new data types or encode other data types into integers. Luckily the languages of Exercises 4.1 and 4.2 only use the alphabet $\{1, 2\}$, so we can conveniently define the input string as an integer. To model an NFA in PAT, we will use the following variables:

```
1  var input = 1212;
2  var bit = 0;
3  var halt = false;
```

The variable `input` is naturally the input string, `bit` is the current bit of the string under examination, and `halt` indicates whether the NFA has processed all the input. Additionally, we define a variable for each state to represent that "we are in this state". There are five states in Exercise 4.1, so we define five variables accordingly.

```
1  var ats0 = 0;
2  var ats1 = 0;
3  var ats2 = 0;
4  var ats3 = 0;
5  var ats4 = 0;
```

For example, if `ats0` is 1, then we are in state s_0.

Next, we need to define some functions for processing the input string. Since the input string is an integer, we will perform integer manipulations to get the first digit of the number and remove the first digit of the number. We define two processes for these operations, respectively, as below. Note: readers of a programming background should code these processes by themselves. Can you write simpler code in the language of PAT (CSP#)?

```
1  getFirstDigit() = get{
2    var tmp = input;
3    while (tmp >= 10) {
4      tmp = tmp / 10;
5    }
6    bit = tmp;
7  } -> Skip;
8
```

```
9   removeFirstDigit() = rm{
10    if (input < 10) {
11      input = 0;
12    }
13    else {
14      var tmp1 = 1;
15      while (tmp1 * 10 <= input) {
16        tmp1 = tmp1 * 10;
17      }
18      var tmp2 = 0;
19      while ((tmp2 + 1) * tmp1 < input) {
20        tmp2 = tmp2 + 1;
21      }
22      input = input - tmp1 * tmp2;
23    }
24  } -> Skip;
```

The process `getFirstDigit()` gets the first digit of the variable `input` and stores it in the variable `bit`. The process `removeFirstDigit()` removes the first digit of `input` and updates this variable. We sequentialise the above two processes into a process called `consume()`, which takes the current input and consumes the first bit.

```
1  consume() = getFirstDigit(); removeFirstDigit();
```

Modelling states and transitions. We encode a state and the transitions from the state into a process. For example, the state s_0 and the two transitions from it can be modelled as follows:

```
1  state0() =
2  s0{ats0 = 1; ats1 = 0; ats2 = 0; ats3 = 0; ats4 = 0;} ->
3  ([input != 0](consume(); ([bit == 1]state1()
4    <> [bit == 2]state2()))
5  [] [input == 0]h0{halt = true;} -> Skip);
```

The process `state0()` first invokes the event `s0` and updates the status of states to say "we are now in the state s_0" (line 2). We only allow the model to be in one state at a time. Do not confuse this modelling method with the statement that "an NFA can be in multiple states at the same time"—that statement is true when we are exploring all the paths at the same time, but PAT takes care of exploring different paths for us, so we only model what happens on a single path. The operation that follows depends on the input string. If the input is not depleted (line 3 and 4), then we will get the first bit of the input and consume it. If the first bit is 1, we go to the state s_1; otherwise, we go to the state s_2. Note that we use a nondeterministic choice `<>` when modelling the transitions. However, since the two transitions from s_0 are activated by different input symbols, the effect for this particular example is the same as using a deterministic choice `[]`. If the input is depleted (line 5), then we halt the execution. Use the above code as an example and model the other states and transitions.

Expressing the reachability property. The final states of the NFA of Exercise 4.1 are s_1 and s_2, so we express a condition accept that means "we have reached a final state when we have processed the entire input string" as follows:

```
#define accept (halt == true && (ats1 == 1 || ats2 == 1));
```

Finally, we can verify whether the input string is accepted by model-checking the reachability property.

```
#assert state0() reaches accept;
```

4.6 Model the NFA of Exercise 4.2 in PAT. Check three accepted strings and three unaccepted strings for each of your models.

4.2 Regular Expressions and Regular Languages

Regular expressions, often shortened as regex or regexp, is a sequence of symbols that define a search pattern. It is a by-product of Kleene's[2] (1909–1994) work on regular languages in the 1950s. Nowadays, regular expressions are widely used in computing. For example, it is used in UNIX-based text processing utilities such as grep; it is built into programming languages such as Perl and Ruby; it is also used in search engines and the lexical analyser component of compilers.

Strictly speaking, a regular expression E itself is *not* a language, but it denotes a language $L(E)$. In other words, the set of strings matched by E form a language $L(E)$. However, in the following, we may loosely equate a regular expression to the language it denotes.

Definition 4.3 (*Regular Expressions*) There are three main operators in regular expressions.

Union, denotes by a vertical bar |, yields the union of two languages. For example, $0|1 = \{0\} \cup \{1\} = \{0, 1\}$. The union operator also represents a choice or a disjunction over strings. That is, $0|1$ can match 0 *or* 1.

Concatenation is simply written as a sequence without spaces. Given two languages $L_1 = \{01, 00\}$ and $L_2 = \{1, 11, 101\}$, their concatenation L_1L_2 contains each string of L_1 concatenated with a string of L_2. That is, $L_1L_2 = \{011, 0111, 01101, 001, 0011, 00101\}$. A concatenation in a regular expression indicates concatenation of sub-strings. For example, 010 is the concatenation of 0 and 1 and 0, in that order.

---

[2] Pronounced "Klay-nee" by himself, although his son noted that this pronunciation was probably invented by his father. The reader should remember Stephen Kleene from a footnote that he gave the name "sequent calculus" in English. He and Alan Turing were both students of Alonzo Church.

Closure [3] of a language L, denoted by a L^*, is the set of strings that is generated by taking any number of strings in L with any repetition and concatenating those strings. We have seen an example of alphabets in the opening of this chapter: Σ^* is the set of all possible strings over the symbols in Σ, and any language over Σ is a subset of Σ^*. If $L = \{000, 11\}$, then L^* is the set of strings over 0 and 1 such that 0s must come in triples and 1s must come in pairs. For example, 1100011, 1111, and 00011000 are in L^*, but 1000 is not. Formally, $L^* = \bigcup_{i \geq 0} L^i$ (see the definition of L^i on Page 119). A closure of a sub-string in regular expressions indicates the repetition of the sub-string for 0 or more times. For example, $(abc)^*$ matches 0 or more repetitions of abc, such as ϵ, abc, $abcabc$, and $abcabcabc$.

The closure operator binds tightest, and the union operator binds loosest. For instance, $01|10^*1$ should be read as $(01)|(1(0^*)1)$.

Example 4.6 The regular expression $0|(1(0|1)^*)$ denotes the set of binary numbers with no leading zeros. This regular expression is often used to match certain number formats such as money.

Practical applications often extend the main operators with other auxiliary ones. For example:

- ? denotes zero or one occurrences of a sub-string.
- $^+$ (also called Kleene plus) denotes one or more occurrences of a sub-string.
- .$\{n\}$ denotes exactly n occurrences of a sub-string.
- .$\{n, \}$ denotes at least n occurrences of a sub-string.
- .$\{n, m\}$ denotes at least n and at most m occurrences of a sub-string.
- ^ represents the beginning of a string.
- \$ represents the end of a string.
- . is a wildcard for any symbol in the alphabet.
- [] matches any symbol that appears in the brackets. That is, $[abc]$ is the same as $a|b|c$. We often write $[a - z]$ for any lowercase English letters and $[A - Z]$ for any uppercase English letters and $[0 - 9]$ for any decimal digit.
- (? = pattern) looks ahead and matches the pattern.

Example 4.7 Passwords that must contain a lowercase letter, an uppercase letter, a number, a special character, and whose length must be between 8 and 30 can be expressed by the regular expression given below.

$$\wedge(? = .^*[0 - 9])(? = .^*[a - z])(? = .^*[A - Z])(? = .^*[@ * \#\$\%\wedge\& - + = ()]).\{8, 30\}\$.$$

We can break this expression down as follows:

---

[3] Also called star or Kleene star or Kleene closure.

- $(? = .*[0 - 9])$ says that there must be a number.
- $(? = .*[a - z])$ says that there must be a lowercase letter.
- $(? = .*[A - Z])$ says that there must be a uppercase letter.
- $(? = .*[@ * \#\$\%^\& - + = ()])$ says that there must be a special character chosen from the set $\{@, *, \#, \$, \%, ^, \&, -, +, =, (,)\}$.
- $.\{8, 30\}$ says that the length must be between 8 and 30.

These extra operators are *not* in the scope of the remainder of this book.

The set of languages that can be denoted by regular expressions are called *regular languages*. Regular expressions are equivalent to finite automata in terms of the languages they denote or accept.

Theorem 4.2 (Kleene's Theorem [2]) *A language can be denoted by some regular expression iff it is accepted by some finite automata.*

Example 4.8 Lexical analysis is the first phase of software program compilation. A lexical analyser, or scanner, checks whether the code matches given regular expressions. Under the hood, a compiler derives an NFA from the regular expression, then converts the NFA to a DFA, e.g., by the subset construction algorithm. The resulting DFA is optimised to a minimal DFA by removing unaccessible states and equivalent states. A standard driver program then takes the DFA as a data structure and decides whether the code has syntactical errors.

In the remainder of this chapter, we will describe languages using grammars because the definition of grammars facilitates the discussion of the classification of languages.

Definition 4.4 (*Grammar*) A *grammar* is a quadruple (V_t, V_n, S, P) where

- V_t is a finite set of *terminal symbols*, i.e., the alphabet.
- V_n is a finite set of *non-terminal symbols*. Further, $V_t \cap V_n = \emptyset$, and we define their union as $V = V_t \cup V_n$.
- $S \in V_n$ is a special non-terminal symbol called the *start* symbol.
- P is a set of *productions*, written as $\alpha \rightarrow \beta$ where $\alpha \in V^* V_n V^*$ and $\beta \in V^*$.

  - α is a string consisting of terminal and non-terminal symbols, and it must include at least one non-terminal symbol.
  - β is a string of zero or more terminal or non-terminal symbols.

Productions are *substitution* (also called rewrite) rules. Given a production $\alpha \rightarrow \beta$ and a string $\gamma\alpha\delta$ that contains α, the result of applying the production to the string is $\gamma\beta\delta$. We write this one-step derivation as $\gamma\alpha\delta \Rightarrow \gamma\beta\delta$. Multiple-step derivations are the reflexive–transitive closure of substitutions, written as $\alpha \overset{*}{\Rightarrow} \beta$, which means that β can be derived from α in zero or more steps.

Definition 4.5 (*Language of Grammar*) The language $L(G)$ generated by a grammar $G = (V_t, V_n, S, P)$ is the set of strings over V_t that can be derived from the start symbol S. Formally,

$$L(G) = \{\alpha \mid S \overset{*}{\Rightarrow} \alpha \wedge \alpha \in V_t^*\}.$$

The strings in $L(G)$ are called *sentences*, which should only contain terminal symbols. The set of strings that can be derived from S, including those that appear in intermediate steps, are called *sentential forms*, which are defined as

$$\{\alpha \mid S \overset{*}{\Rightarrow} \alpha \wedge \alpha \in V^*\}.$$

Sentential forms may contain non-terminal symbols.

Example 4.9 Consider the following grammar:

$$G = (\{0, 1\}, \{A, S\}, S, \{S \rightarrow \epsilon, S \rightarrow 0A1, A1 \rightarrow 0A11, A \rightarrow \epsilon\}).$$

The terminal symbols are $\{0, 1\}$, and they form the alphabet of the language. The non-terminal symbols are $\{A, S\}$, and they include a start symbol S. There are four production rules in this example.

To generate a sentence, we choose a production with S on the left-hand side and try to derive sentential forms using all possible production rules. Sometimes, multiple production rules are available, which result in different sentences. For example, below are three possible derivations:

$$S \Rightarrow \epsilon$$

$$S \Rightarrow 0A1 \Rightarrow 00A11 \Rightarrow 0011$$

$$S \Rightarrow 0A1 \Rightarrow 00A11 \Rightarrow 000A111 \Rightarrow 0000A1111 \Rightarrow 00001111$$

In the above three derivations, only ϵ, 0011, and 00001111 are sentences; the other strings are merely sentential forms.

The above grammar generates the language $\{0^n 1^n \mid n \in \mathbb{N}\}$, which we know cannot be accepted by any finite automaton, and therefore cannot be denoted by any regular expression and is *not* a regular language.

Note that a language can be generated by different grammars, just as it can be accepted by different automata and be denoted by different regular expressions. For example, the following two grammars also generate the above language:

$$G' = (\{0, 1\}, \{A, S\}, S, \{S \rightarrow \epsilon, S \rightarrow 0A1, 0A \rightarrow 00A1, A \rightarrow \epsilon\})$$
$$G'' = (\{0, 1\}, \{S\}, S, \{S \rightarrow \epsilon, S \rightarrow 0S1, S \rightarrow 01\}).$$

We often abbreviate the production rules in a grammar by taking the "disjunction" of the right-hand side of multiple productions which have the same left-hand side. For instance, the productions of G'' in the above example can be written as

$$S \rightarrow \epsilon \mid 0S1 \mid 01.$$

In formal language theory, grammars are classified based on the form of their production rules. The classification is called the Chomsky hierarchy[4] [3], which specifies the below classes of grammars.

Definition 4.6 (*Chomsky Hierarchy*) The Chomsky hierarchy defines the following types of grammars:

- *Unrestricted grammars (Type-0)* have no constraints. Any production of the form $\alpha A \beta \rightarrow \gamma$ is allowed, where α, β, γ are arbitrary strings and A is a non-terminal symbol.
- *Context-sensitive grammars (Type-1)* allow two forms of production rules:

  - $\alpha A \beta \rightarrow \alpha \delta \beta$, where δ is a non-empty string and α and β are strings, are allowed. In this case, $|\alpha A \beta| \leq |\alpha \delta \beta|$.
  - $S \rightarrow \epsilon$, where S is a non-terminal symbol that does not appear on the right-hand side of any productions rule.

- *Context-free grammars (Type-2)* only permit a single non-terminal symbol on the left-hand side. The allowed productions are in the form of $A \rightarrow \alpha$.
- *Regular grammars (Type-3)* can be in either of the below forms where a is a terminal symbol and A and B are non-terminal symbols.

  - *Right-linear grammars* permit the following forms of productions:

    o $A \rightarrow aB$,
    o $A \rightarrow a$,
    o $A \rightarrow \epsilon$.

  - *Left-linear grammars* permit the following forms of productions:

    o $A \rightarrow Ba$,
    o $A \rightarrow a$,
    o $A \rightarrow \epsilon$.

Example 4.10 In Example 4.9, the grammars G and G' are unrestricted grammars; they are not context-sensitive because the left-hand side of $A \rightarrow \epsilon$ is longer than the right-hand side, and A appears on the right-hand side of some production rules. The grammar G'' is context-free.

---

[4] Or Chomsky–Schützenberger hierarchy, the latter also played an important role in the development of formal languages.

Algorithm 4: Convert an NFA to a right-linear grammar.

Data: An NFA $A_N = (\Sigma, \mathbb{S}, s_0, F, R)$
Result: A right-linear grammar $G = (V_t, V_n, S, P)$
$V_t \leftarrow \Sigma$;
$V_n \leftarrow \mathbb{S}$;
$S \leftarrow s_0$;
$P \leftarrow \emptyset$;
foreach *transition relation* $R(s, a, s')$ **do**
 | $P \leftarrow P \cup \{s \to as'\}$;
end
foreach *final state* $s \in F$ **do**
 | $P \leftarrow P \cup \{s \to \epsilon\}$;
end

The Chomsky hierarchy is a containment hierarchy, that is, the set of languages that can be generated by Type-n grammars is a subset of the languages that can be generated by Type-$(n - 1)$ grammars.

Right-linear grammars always expand a sentential form at the right end, one terminal symbol at a time, while left-linear grammars always expand at the left end, and they are two equivalent classes of grammars.

Definition 4.7 (*Regular Languages*) A language L is generated by some right-linear grammar iff L is regular.

Furthermore, the set of regular languages can be described in the following different ways:

- the languages generated by right-linear grammars;
- the languages generated by left-linear grammars;
- the languages accepted by DFAs;
- the languages accepted by NFAs;
- the languages denoted by regular expressions.

We have shown the equivalence of DFAs and NFAs in the last section, and now we demonstrate how to convert an NFA into a right-linear grammar and vice versa. Given an NFA $A = (\Sigma, \mathbb{S}, s_0, F, R)$, where we write $\mathbb{S}$ for the set of states to distinguish from the start symbol S of the grammar, we construct a right-linear grammar $G = (V_t, V_n, S, P)$ as in Algorithm 4.

Example 4.11 Recall the NFA of Example 4.3 given below.

Algorithm 5: Convert a right-linear grammar to an NFA.

Data: A right-linear grammar $G = (V_t, V_n, S, P)$
Result: An NFA $A_N = (\Sigma, \mathbb{S}, s_0, F, R)$
$\Sigma \leftarrow V_t$;
$\mathbb{S} \leftarrow V_n \cup \{S_f\}$;
$s_0 \leftarrow S$;
$F \leftarrow \{S_f\} \cup \{T \in V_n \mid (T \rightarrow \epsilon) \in P\}$;
$R \leftarrow \emptyset$;
foreach *production in P of the form* $A \rightarrow aB$ **do**
  $\mid\ R \leftarrow R \cup \{(A, a, B)\}$;
end
foreach *production in P of the form* $A \rightarrow a$ **do**
  $\mid\ R \leftarrow R \cup \{(A, a, S_f)\}$;
end

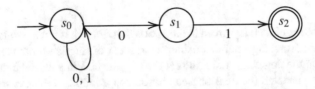

Using Algorithm 4, we convert this NFA to a right-linear grammar $G = (V_t, V_n, S, P)$ where

$$V_t = \{0, 1\}$$
$$V_n = \{s_0, s_1, s_2\}$$
$$S = s_0$$
$$P = \{s_0 \rightarrow 0s_0 \mid 1s_0 \mid 0s_1, s_1 \rightarrow 1s_2, s_2 \rightarrow \epsilon\}.$$

Unsurprisingly, we can slightly modify Algorithm 4 to convert to a left-linear grammar. We leave it as an exercise for the reader.

Conversely, we can convert a right-linear grammar into an NFA using Algorithm 5. In this algorithm, we create a new final state S_f that is not in the grammar. This new final state is used in the second `foreach` loop—for each production $A \rightarrow a$, we create a transition from A to S_f via a. The set of final states in the NFA includes S_f and every non-terminal symbol T such that $T \rightarrow \epsilon$ is a production in P.

Example 4.12 Let $G = (\{a, b\}, \{S, A, B\}, S, \{S \rightarrow aA, A \rightarrow aA, A \rightarrow bB, A \rightarrow b, B \rightarrow bB, B \rightarrow \epsilon\})$ be a right-linear grammar. We convert this grammar to an NFA $A = (\Sigma, \mathbb{S}, S, F, R)$ as follows:

$$\Sigma = \{a, b\}$$
$$\mathbb{S} = \{S, A, B, S_f\}$$

$$F = \{B, S_f\}$$
$$R = \{(S, a, A), (A, a, A), (A, b, B), (A, b, S_f), (B, b, B)\}.$$

Notice that there is no need to create the transition (B, ϵ, S_f) since B is already a final state. This NFA is visualised below. The corresponding language is the set of strings that start with at least one a followed by at least one b.

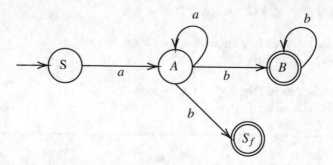

English is not regular. It is proved in the 1950s that English is not a regular language. To see a semi-formal argument, consider a subset A of English sentences: $A = \{$the cat ran, the cat the dog chased ran, the cat the dog the cheetah chased chased ran, the cat the dog the cheetah the tiger chased chased chased ran,...$\}$. These sentences are in the form of

$$(\text{thenoun})^n (\text{transitiveverb})^{n-1} (\text{intransitiveverb}),$$

which is very similar to the non-regular language $\{0^n 1^n \mid n \in \mathbb{N}\}$. By the same token, we can prove that A is not regular.

Let B be the language denoted by the regular expression

$$(\text{thenoun})^* (\text{transitiveverb})^* (\text{intransitiveverb}),$$

then B must be regular.

The set A is equal to $B \cap$ English. A nice property of regular languages is that they are closed under intersections. That is, if B and English are both regular, then their intersection A must also be regular, which is not the case. Since B is regular, we deduce that English is not regular.

Exercises

4.7 Find a regular expression that denotes the language of Example 4.12.

4.8 Find a regular expression that denotes the language of Exercise 4.1 of Sect. 4.1. Convert that NFA into a right-linear grammar.

4.9 Find a regular expression that denotes the language of Exercise 4.2 of Sect. 4.1. Convert that NFA into a right-linear grammar.

4.10 For simplicity, we sometimes denote a grammar by the set of production rules. For instance, it is rather clear what the V_t, V_n and S components are for the following set of production rules:

$$S \to 1A \qquad A \to 2A \mid 1B \mid 2 \qquad B \to 1 \mid \epsilon.$$

Convert the above grammar to an NFA. Draw a diagram of the NFA and write down its definition formally. Write down a regular expression that denotes this language.

4.11 Model the above grammar in PAT. Check three strings that are in the language and three that are not in the language.

Instruction. The way to model a right-linear grammar in PAT is similar to modelling an NFA in PAT. The readers can refer to the modelling method in Exercise 4.5 of Sect. 4.1 and the translation from right-linear grammars to NFAs. A notable tip for this exercise is that the "state" A has two transitions labelled with 2, so we have to use the nondeterministic choice <> between the transitions. For example, this state and its transitions can be modelled as follows:

```
stateA() = a{ats = 0; ata = 1; atb = 0; atsf = 0;} ->
([input != 0](consume();
  (([bit == 2]stateA()) <>
  ([bit == 1]stateB()) <>
  ([bit == 2]stateSf()))) []
[input == 0]ha{halt = true} -> Skip);
```

Also, the "state" S_f does not have any transitions, so we do not consume any input symbols in this state:

```
stateSf() = s{ats = 0; ata = 0; atb = 0; atsf = 1;} ->
  ([input == 0]hsf{halt = true;} -> Skip);
```

4.3 Context-Free Languages

Context-free grammars (CFGs), as introduced in the Chomsky hierarchy (cf. Page 134), allow any production of the form

$$A \to \alpha$$

where A is a non-terminal symbol and α is an arbitrary string over the language. It is context-free because we can replace A by α regardless of what surrounds A. By contrast, productions (except for the start symbol) in context-sensitive grammars are of the form

$$\alpha A \beta \to \alpha \delta \beta.$$

As a result, when we replace A with δ, we have to match the context α and β in the string; hence it is context-sensitive.

Clearly, context-free grammars are special cases of context-sensitive grammars where the contexts are empty strings. Overall, any regular grammar is a context-free grammar, and any context-free grammar is a context-sensitive grammar, and so on, but the converse is not true.

Definition 4.8 (*Context-free Languages*) The set of languages that are generated by context-free grammars is called *context-free languages*.

Parse trees. Recall the CFG G'' of Example 4.9:

$$S \to \epsilon \mid 0S1 \mid 01.$$

We can draw derivations as a *parse tree*. For example, a derivation for 000111 can be drawn as follows:

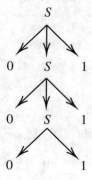

This parse tree has four levels, including the first start symbol S. We can obtain the sentence of this derivation by reading the leaf nodes from left to right as in a depth-first search.

Example 4.13 The second phase of software program compilation is *parsing*, or syntax analysis, which builds the syntactic structure of a program as a parse tree. The structure of parse trees determines how the program is executed, so in a sense, syntax analysis is indirectly related to the semantics of programs.

Consider the following code:

```
if c1 then if c2 then s1 else s2
```

And consider the following CFG, where bexp stands for a Boolean expression and prog for a piece of code:

$$S \to \text{if bexp then } S \mid \text{if bexp then } S \text{ else } S \mid \text{prog}$$

The above piece of code can be derived in different ways, which correspond to different parse trees. We show a possible parse tree below.

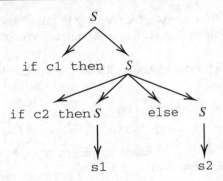

The above parse tree essentially parses the code as follows:

```
if c1 then { if c2 then s1 else s2 }
```

The same grammar permits another derivation which corresponds to the following code:

```
if c1 then { if c2 then s1 } else s2
```

This derivation obviously shows a different way to execute the program and can be visualised by the parse tree as follows:

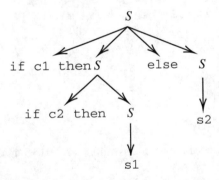

It would be disastrous if a programmer understands the code as the first parse tree and the compiler understands it as the second parse tree! In practice, we would like to have a unique way to parse the code so that the code is executed in the way expected by the programmer. Towards this goal, we define the ambiguity of grammar as follows.

Definition 4.9 (*Ambiguity of Grammars*) A grammar G is *ambiguous* if there exists a sentence $w \in L(G)$ such that w can be derived by more than one parse tree using G. A grammar is *unambiguous* if every string can only be derived by at most one parse tree.

Note that ambiguity is generally[5] a property of grammars, not of languages. A language can have ambiguous grammars and unambiguous grammars.

Example 4.14 The following unambiguous CFG generates the same language as that of Example 4.13:

$$S \to \texttt{if bexp then } S \mid T$$
$$T \to \texttt{if bexp then } T \texttt{ else } S \mid \texttt{prog}$$

The reader can check that the following parse tree represents the only way to generate the code in Example 4.13:

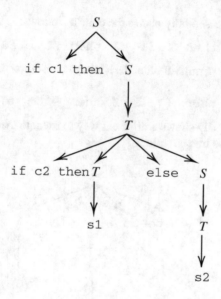

There is a subtle difference between derivations and parse trees. In the above parse tree, the string

$$\texttt{if c2 then } T \texttt{ else } S$$

contains two non-terminal symbols, and we may obtain two different derivations depending on which one we choose to expand first. On the other hand, a parse tree essentially expands all non-terminal symbols "simultaneously", so there is only one parse tree. The fact that there are multiple derivations for a sentence using the above grammar is irrelevant to ambiguity.

Unfortunately, not all context-free languages have unambiguous grammars.

---

[5] We will see a special case of "inherently ambiguous" languages later.

Definition 4.10 (*Inherent Ambiguity*) A language is *inherently ambiguous* if there exists no unambiguous grammar that can generate the language.

Example 4.15 Let L be the following language:

$$L = \{0^i 1^j 2^k \mid i, j, k \in \mathbb{N} \wedge (i = j \vee j = k)\}.$$

Directly finding a CFG for this language may not be straightforward. However, we can split L into two cases:

$$L = \{0^i 1^i 2^j \mid i, j \in \mathbb{N}\} \cup \{0^i 1^j 2^j \mid i, j \in \mathbb{N}\}.$$

Then it is rather easy to find CFGs for each component, as shown below. The left grammar generates an equal number of 0s and 1s and some 2s. The right grammar generates some 0s and an equal number of 1s and 2s.

$$
\begin{array}{ll}
S_1 \rightarrow AB & S_2 \rightarrow CD \\
A \rightarrow 0A1 \mid \epsilon & C \rightarrow C0 \mid \epsilon \\
B \rightarrow B2 \mid \epsilon & D \rightarrow 1D2 \mid \epsilon.
\end{array}
$$

To obtain a grammar for L, we simply take the "disjunction" of the above two grammars:

$$S \rightarrow S_1 \mid S_2.$$

The source of ambiguity in the above grammar is that the "disjunction" is not exclusive. In other words, the intersection of $L(S_1)$ and $L(S_2)$ is not empty, and it is precisely the set given below.[6]

$$L(S_1) \cap L(S_2) = \{0^i 1^i 2^i \mid i \in \mathbb{N}\}.$$

Consequently, if a string is in the intersection, we can either use the left grammar S_1 or the right grammar S_2 to generate it, so there are at least two parse trees for such a string using the above grammar. It is proved that there is no unambiguous CFG for L.

Undecidability of ambiguity. Ideally, we would like to have an algorithm that converts an ambiguous grammar into an equivalent unambiguous grammar. However, such an algorithm does not exist in general, as witnessed by the above example. Even worse, it is proven that there does not exist an algorithm for determining if an arbitrary grammar is ambiguous or not. On the bright side, the above negative statements are general statements. It is still possible to solve some special cases of these problems. Below we demonstrate some techniques that work well for practical applications.

---

[6] Neither S_1 nor S_2 generates exactly the language $L' = \{0^i 1^i 2^i \mid i \in \mathbb{N}\}$. In fact, context-free grammars/languages are *not* closed under intersection, and L' is a well-known example of a non-context-free language.

Example 4.16 The following CFG for generating subtraction over integers is ambiguous:

$$S \to S - S \mid \texttt{int}.$$

For instance, the parse trees below both generate the sentence $7 - 4 - 1$, but the left tree evaluates the sentence to 2, and the right tree evaluates to 4.

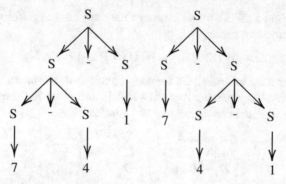

One way to remove the ambiguity of a binary infix operator is by imposing particular associativity of the operator. For example, if we read $7 - 4 - 1$ as $7 - (4 - 1)$, then we are forcing *right-associativity*. If we read the sentence as $(7 - 4) - 1$, which is the custom in algebra, then we are forcing *left-associativity*. To achieve certain associativity via grammars, we need to break the balance of the two sides of the operator. For an example of left-associativity, we force the right-hand side of the operator to be "lower level" symbols. The "lowest level" is for terminal symbols. We modify the grammar as follows:

$$S \to S - \texttt{int} \mid \texttt{int}.$$

The new grammar can only generate the above sentence as $(7 - 4) - 1$, as shown in the parse tree below.

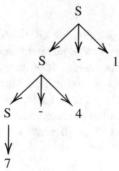

Example 4.17 The following CFG is ambiguous:

$$S \to S + S \mid S \times S \mid \texttt{int}.$$

The reason is similar to the above example. For instance, we can draw two parse trees for the sentence $1 + 3 \times 7$ as follows:

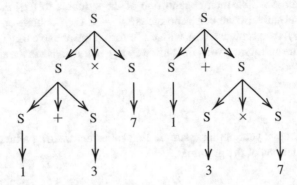

We can use the previous technique to remove ambiguity by making both $+$ and $\times$ left-associative. But in mathematics, we require something stronger: $\times$ should bind tighter than $+$. It turns out that setting a precedence of operators can also remove ambiguity in some cases.

The way to realise precedence in grammars is similar to forcing associativity: we break the balance of the operators and force one side to expand into a lower level of symbols:

$$S \to S + T \mid T$$
$$T \to T \times \texttt{int} \mid \texttt{int}.$$

In the above grammar, we set three levels of symbols. The start symbol S is at the highest level, where we can only generate $+$. If we want to generate $\times$, we have to go to the middle level via T. To obtain terminal symbols, we go to the lowest level.

With the above grammar, the sentence $1+3\times7$ can only be generated as $1+(3\times7)$, as shown below.

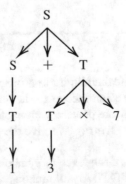

Example 4.18 The CFG below generates sentences with matched brackets.

$$S \to \epsilon \mid (S) \mid SS.$$

The above grammar is much "worse" than the previous ones—there are infinitely many parse trees that produce the sentence () using the above grammar. For instance, we can generate SS first, then expand one of the symbols to (S), then replace all Ss with ϵ. Alternatively, we can generate $SSS \cdots S$, then choose one symbol and expand it as (S), then replace all Ss with ϵ. To forbid the abusive usage of producing ϵ, we modify the grammar so that the only way to generate ϵ is via the start symbol S:

$$S \to \epsilon \mid A$$
$$A \to AB \mid B$$
$$B \to (B) \mid ().$$

This technique is yet another example that relies on creating a hierarchy for the symbols/productions of the grammar.

Exercises

4.12 Find a CFG for the language $\{1^i 2^j 3^{i-j} \mid i \geq j \geq 0\}$.

4.13 Demonstrate that the grammar S given in Example 4.15 is ambiguous.

4.14 Consider the CFG given below.

$$S \to 0S \mid 0S1S \mid \epsilon.$$

1. Describe the language of this grammar.
2. Demonstrate that this grammar is ambiguous.
3. Find an unambiguous grammar that is equivalent to this grammar.

4.15 Find an unambiguous grammar that is equivalent to the grammar as follows:

$$S \to S + S \mid S - S \mid S \times S \mid S / S \mid (S) \mid \texttt{int}.$$

4.4 Pushdown Automata

We have seen finite automata and their limitations in Sect. 4.1, and we have discussed that one of the reasons why they cannot accept the language $\{0^n 1^n \mid n \in \mathbb{N}\}$ is because they do not have a "memory". More powerful automata do allow memory in a linear organisation such as a stack or an array. We give the general structure of automata in Fig. 4.2.

We can think of the input as a sequence of symbols we type from the keyboard. The finite state control is the "CPU". An automaton processes one input bit at a time and performs state transitions accordingly.

Pushdown automata (PDA) have a stack memory that allows us to push and pop symbols in a last-in-first-out (LIFO) order. The state transition is determined by the

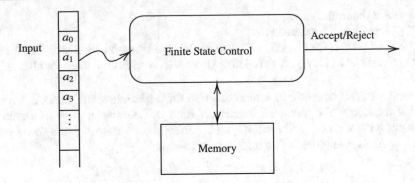

Fig. 4.2 The general structure of automata

current input symbol, the current state, *and the symbol on the top of the stack*. In each transition, a PDA may perform *some* of the following actions:

- consume an input symbol;
- move to a state;
- pop the top symbol of the stack;
- push some symbols into the stack.

After all the input bits are processed, if the finite state control is in a final state, then it outputs "accept"; otherwise, it outputs "reject".

Different ways to accept strings. A PDA can accept a string when it has processed all input symbols and

- the stack is empty, or
- it is in a final state.

The first condition corresponds to a type of PDA called "PDA by empty stack"; the second type is "PDA by final state".

PDAs can also be categorised by their state transitions. Similar to finite automata, a transition function defines deterministic PDAs, while a transition relation defines nondeterministic PDAs.

Definition 4.11 (*DPDA*) A *deterministic pushdown automaton* (DPDA) is defined as a tuple $(\Sigma, \Gamma, Z, S, s_0, F, N)$ where

- Σ, i.e., the alphabet, is the set of input symbols;
- Γ is the set of stack symbols;
- $Z \in \Gamma$ is the initial stack symbol, i.e., the only symbol in the stack when the automaton is initialised;
- S is the set of states;

- $s_0 \in S$ is the initial state;
- $F \subseteq S$ is a set of final states;
- $N : S \times (\Sigma \cup \{\epsilon\}) \times \Gamma \rightharpoonup S \times \Gamma^*$ is a (partial) transition function such that for all $s \in S$ and $t \in \Gamma$, if $N(s, \epsilon, t)$ is defined then $N(s, a, t)$ is undefined for all $a \in \Sigma$.

Unlike DFAs, which have a total function for state transitions, DPDAs have a partial function.[7] The transition function N for a DPDA maps a triple of a state s, an input symbol a or ϵ, and a stack symbol t to a pair of a state s' and a *string* γ of stack symbols. We write such a transition as follows:

$$N(s, a, t) = s'/\gamma \qquad \text{or} \qquad N(s, \epsilon, t) = s'/\gamma.$$

When performing the above-left transition, the DPDA moves from the state s to the state s' while consuming the input symbol a and pops the symbol t from the top of the stack and pushes the string γ into the stack. The above-right transition is similar but does not depend on or consume an input symbol.

In a graphical presentation, we label each arrow (transition) with $a, t/\gamma$ to denote that the input symbol a is consumed, the top of the stack t is popped, and the string γ is pushed into the stack. The notation t/γ can also be read as "t is substituted by γ in the stack".

Example 4.19 Let us design a DPDA that can accept the language $L = \{0^n 1^n \mid n \in \mathbb{N}\}$, which cannot be accepted by finite automata.

The general idea is as follows: First, we use a state s_1 to push all the 0s into the stack. When we finish processing 0s, we move to a state s_2, and pop a 0 from the stack whenever we see a 1 in the input. If the stack is empty when we have finished processing the input, we know that there are the same number of 0s as the number of 1s, so we accept the input.

We can define a DPDA by empty stack as a tuple

$$D = (\{0, 1\}, \{Z, 0, 1\}, Z, \{s_0, s_1, s_2, s_3\}, s_0, \{\}, N)$$

which does not need final states, and the transition function N is defined as below and undefined for all other arguments:

$$N(s_0, 0, Z) = s_1/0Z$$
$$N(s_1, 0, 0) = s_1/00$$
$$N(s_1, 1, 0) = s_2/\epsilon$$
$$N(s_2, 1, 0) = s_2/\epsilon$$
$$N(s_2, \epsilon, Z) = s_3/\epsilon.$$

The transition $N(s_1, 0, 0) = s_1/00$ pops the symbol 0 from the stack and pushes in two 0s, effectively adding one 0 in the stack. The transition $N(s_1, 1, 0) = s_2/\epsilon$

---

[7] A function $f : A \rightarrow B$ is *partial*, in which case we use $\rightharpoonup$ instead of $\rightarrow$, if there exists some $a \in A$ such that $f(a)$ is undefined. On the other hand, if f is total, then $f(a)$, for every $a \in A$, must be mapped to some $b \in B$.

pops a 0 from the stack and pushes in an empty string ϵ, which is equivalent to only popping a 0. We draw this DPDA as follows:

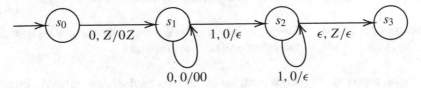

We denote a *PDA configuration* as a triple of (state, remaining input, stack), where the top of the stack is the leftmost bit. A trace of configurations for accepting 000111 can be written as follows:

$$(s_0, 000111, Z) \Rightarrow (s_1, 00111, 0Z) \Rightarrow (s_1, 0111, 00Z) \Rightarrow (s1, 111, 000Z)$$
$$\Rightarrow (s_2, 11, 00Z) \Rightarrow (s_2, 1, 0Z) \Rightarrow (s_2, \epsilon, Z) \Rightarrow (s_3, \epsilon, \epsilon).$$

In the end, we reach a configuration with no input remaining and an empty stack, so we accept the input.

Alternatively, we can define s_3 as the only final state and convert this DPDA to a DPDA by final state.

Input strings such as 00011 and 00111 are not accepted as the automaton gets "stuck" when the transition function is not defined for certain arguments. In such cases, the input is rejected. For instance, a trace of configurations for processing 00111 is given as follows:

$$(s_0, 00111, Z) \Rightarrow (s_1, 0111, 0Z) \Rightarrow (s_1, 111, 00Z)$$
$$\Rightarrow (s_2, 11, 0Z) \Rightarrow (s_2, 1, Z) \Rightarrow ???$$

Since $N(s_2, 1, Z)$ is undefined, this input is rejected.

Similar to the derivation of a grammar, we can define $\overset{*}{\Rightarrow}$ as a reflexive–transitive closure of the "changes of configurations". That is, $(s, \alpha, \gamma) \overset{*}{\Rightarrow} (s', \beta, \delta)$ iff there are zero or more steps of transitions such that we can reach the latter configuration from the former configuration.

The languages of a DPDA. Let $D = (\Sigma, \Gamma, Z, S, s_0, F, N)$ be a DPDA. The language $L(D)$ accepted by the DPDA D *by final state* is

$$L(D) = \{w \mid (s_0, w, Z) \overset{*}{\Rightarrow} (s', \epsilon, \alpha) \wedge s' \in F\}.$$

That is, starting from the initial state s_0 and an initialised stack with only Z, we process the input w and accept it if we reach a final state when w is processed.

We define the language $N(D)^8$ of D by *empty stack* as

$$N(D) = \{w \mid (s_0, w, Z) \overset{*}{\Rightarrow} (s', \epsilon, \epsilon)\}.$$

---

[8] The N in $N(D)$ stands for "null stack".

The class of languages accepted by DPDAs by the final state is strictly a subset of context-free languages, as stated in the theorem below. Consequently, there are context-free languages that are not accepted by any DPDA by the final state.

Theorem 4.3 *The set of languages accepted by deterministic pushdown automata* by final state *is a proper subset[9] of context-free languages.*

Furthermore, the languages accepted by DPDAs *by final state* properly include regular languages. On the other hand, there exist regular languages that are *not* accepted by any DPDA *by empty stack*. It is proved that DPDAs by final state are strictly more powerful than DPDAs by empty stack.

Another interesting result is that, unlike DFAs and NFAs, DPDAs are strictly less powerful than their nondeterministic counterpart.

Example 4.20 The language

$$\{ww^R \mid w \in \{1, 2\}^* \wedge w^R \text{ is } w \text{ reversed}\}$$

of even-length palindromes is context-free but is not accepted by any DPDA.

As with Example 4.19, we can define a state s_1 for pushing w into the stack, and another state s_2 for popping w in reverse order and matching w^R. However, a DPDA cannot determine when it has processed the first half of the input; thus, it does not know when to move from s_1 to s_2.

The languages accepted by DPDA by the final state are called *deterministic context-free languages* (DCFL).

Definition 4.12 (*PDA*) A *nondeterministic pushdown automata* is a tuple $(\Sigma, \Gamma, Z, S, s_0, F, R)$ where R is a *transition relation* defined as

$$R \subseteq S \times (\Sigma \cup \{\epsilon\}) \times \Gamma \times S \times \Gamma^*$$

and the other components are the same as in the definition of DPDA.

Recall that the transition function N of a DPDA has a side condition; in comparison, the transition relation R does not. Since the nondeterministic variant is the most commonly used, we refer to nondeterministic pushdown automata simply as PDA.

Example 4.21 Following Example 4.20, we can design a PDA by empty stack that accepts the language of even-length palindromes by "continuously guessing if we have processed the first half of the string". The PDA can be defined as

$$P = (\{1, 2\}, \{Z, 1, 2\}, Z, \{s_0, s_1, s_2\}, s_0, \{\}, R)$$

---

[9] As a review of algebra basics, $A \subset B$, pronounced "A is a *proper subset* of B", means that $(\forall a.a \in A \rightarrow a \in B) \wedge (\exists b.b \in B \wedge b \notin A)$.

where R is defined as follows:

$$R = \{(s_0, 1, Z, s_0, 1Z), (s_0, 2, Z, s_0, 2Z),$$
$$(s_0, 1, 1, s_0, 11), (s_0, 1, 2, s_0, 12), (s_0, 2, 1, s_0, 21), (s_0, 2, 2, s_0, 22),$$
$$(s_0, \epsilon, 1, s_1, 1), (s_0, \epsilon, 2, s_1, 2), (s_0, \epsilon, Z, s_1, Z)$$
$$(s_1, 1, 1, s_1, \epsilon), (s_1, 2, 2, s_1, \epsilon),$$
$$(s_1, \epsilon, Z, s_2, \epsilon)\}.$$

The first line in the definition of R pushes the first symbol of the input into the stack. The second line stays in the state s_0, i.e., the "push" state, and continuously pushes the input symbol into the stack. The third line nondeterministically moves from the "push" state s_0 to the "pop and match" state s_1 without consuming any input symbol and modifying the stack. The fourth line stays in s_1 and matches the second-half of the input in reverse order by popping the top of the stack. The last line sees that the input has been processed and the stack is empty and accepts the input.

The above PDA is visualised in the below state-transition diagram.

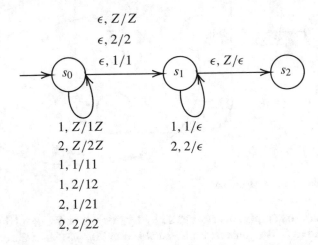

Languages of a PDA. Given a PDA P, we can define the language $L(P)$ of P by final state and the language $N(P)$ of P by empty stack in the same way as those for DPDAs. Interestingly, when nondeterminism is allowed, PDAs by empty stack and PDAs by the final state are equally powerful in general.

Theorem 4.4 *The set of languages accepted by PDAs by the final state is the same as the set of languages accepted by PDAs by an empty stack.*

In other words, for any language accepted by a PDA by final state, we can construct another PDA by the empty stack that accepts the same language; conversely, for any language accepted by a PDA by empty stack, we can construct a PDA by the final state that accepts the same language. We show the constructions without giving a formal proof as follows.

Algorithm 6: Convert a PDA by empty stack to a PDA by final state that accepts the same language.

Data: A PDA $P_N = (\Sigma, \Gamma, Z, S, s_0, \{\}, R_N)$
Result: A PDA $P_F = (\Sigma, \Gamma \cup \{X\}, X, S \cup \{s_0', s_f\}, s_0', \{s_f\}, R_F)$
$R_F \leftarrow \{(s_0', \epsilon, X, s_0, ZX)\}$;
foreach *transition relation* $R_N(s, a, \gamma, s', \delta)$ **do**
  | $R_F \leftarrow R_F \cup \{(s, a, \gamma, s', \delta)\}$;
end
foreach *state* $s \in S$ **do**
  | $R_F \leftarrow R_F \cup \{(s, \epsilon, X, s_f, \epsilon)\}$;
end

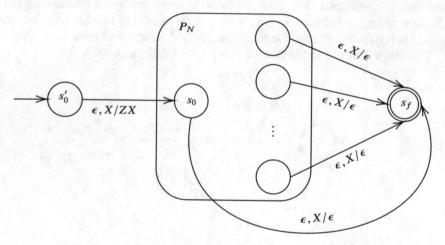

Fig. 4.3 A visualisation of Algorithm 6

From a PDA P_N by empty stack to a PDA P_F by final state. We detail the construction in Algorithm 6. The general idea is visualised in Fig. 4.3. Since the components of P_N and P_F are similar, we implicitly encode parts of the construction in the "Data" and "Result" rows of the algorithm. For example, the alphabet of P_F is the same as the alphabet of P_N, and the set of stack symbols of P_F is the set Γ union with $\{X\}$.

The round-cornered box in the middle of Fig. 4.3 represents the PDA P_N. It has an initial state s_0 and some other states. The new PDA P_F has two new states s_0' and s_f, and a new initial stack symbol X. The states s_0' and s_f are the initial and final states of PDA_F, respectively. The transition relation R_F includes three cases:

1. P_F moves from its initial state s_0' to the initial state s_0 of P_N while pushing the initial stack symbol Z of P_N into the stack of P_F.
2. Once P_F moves "into" P_N, it mimics the transitions of P_N.
3. When the input is processed, and there is only X in the stack, which means that the stack of P_N is empty, P_F moves to the final state s_f and accepts the input.

Algorithm 7: Convert a PDA by final state to a PDA by empty stack that accepts the same language.

Data: A PDA $P_F = (\Sigma, \Gamma, Z, S, s_0, F, R_F)$
Result: A PDA $P_F = (\Sigma, \Gamma \cup \{X\}, X, S \cup \{s_0', s\}, s_0', \{\}, R_N)$
$R_N \leftarrow \{(s_0', \epsilon, X, s_0, ZX)\};$
foreach *transition relation* $R_F(s, a, \gamma, s', \delta)$ **do**
$\quad | \quad R_N \leftarrow R_N \cup \{(s, a, \gamma, s', \delta)\};$
end
foreach *final state* $s_f \in F$ **do**
$\quad$ **foreach** *stack symbol* $t \in \Gamma \cup \{X\}$ **do**
$\quad\quad | \quad R_N \leftarrow R_N \cup \{(s_f, \epsilon, t, s, \epsilon)\};$
$\quad$ **end**
end
foreach *stack symbol* $t \in \Gamma \cup \{X\}$ **do**
$\quad | \quad R_N \leftarrow R_N \cup \{(s, \epsilon, t, s, \epsilon)\};$
end

Example 4.22 The PDA by empty stack in Example 4.21 can be converted to a PDA by final state as follows.

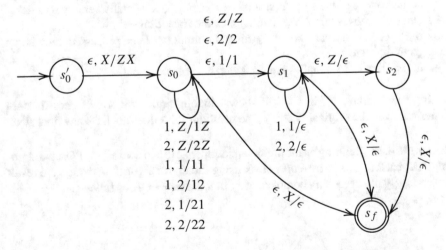

In this example, we add a new initial state s_0' and a new final state s_f. We then add a new stack symbol X, which indicates whether the stack of the PDA in Example 4.21 is empty. When X is the only symbol left in the stack, we add a transition to the final state s_f.

It is immediately clear that Algorithm 6 is not optimised for individual cases—while the above converted PDA by the final state is technically correct, we can find a simpler conversion by just making s_2 a final state.

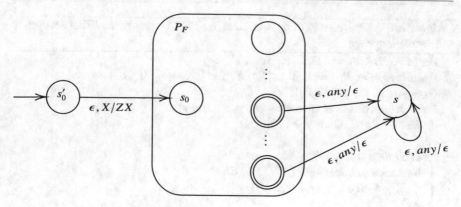

Fig. 4.4 A visualisation of Algorithm 7

From a PDA P_F by final state to a PDA P_N by empty stack. We give the construction in Algorithm 7 and visualise it in Fig. 4.4.

The PDA P_N has two new states s_0' and s and a new initial stack symbol X. The state s_0' is the initial state of P_N. The transition relation R_N of P_N has four cases:

1. P_N moves from its initial state s_0' to the initial state s_0 of P_F while pushing the initial stack symbol Z of P_F into the stack of P_N. Having the extra symbol X at the bottom of the stack is crucial as P_F may "accidentally" empty its stack.
2. Once P_N moves "into" P_F, it simulates the transitions of P_F.
3. If P_N goes to a final state of P_F after the input has been processed, then it can go to the state s.
4. In the state s, P_N empties the stack and accepts the input.

Note that although Fig. 4.4 still shows double circles for some states that are inherited from the original PDA P_F, the resultant PDA does not have any final state.

Example 4.23 Building on the previous examples, we can convert the PDA in Example 4.22 back to a PDA by empty stack using the above algorithm, though the result is obviously unnecessarily complex. We draw the new PDA as follows:

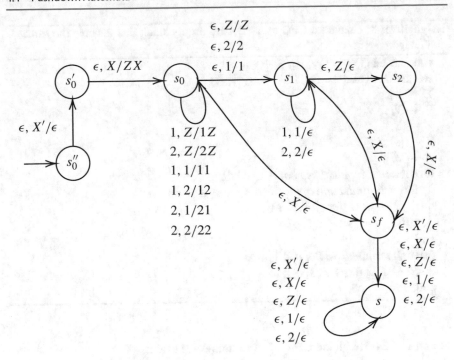

In the new PDA, we add a new initial state s_0'' and a new state s for popping all the symbols out of the stack. We also add a transition from the final state s_f of the previous PDA to the new state s. Obviously, s_f is no longer a final state in the new PDA. The above PDA is equivalent to the much simpler PDA in Example 4.21.

With nondeterminism, PDAs by final state and PDAs by empty stack both correspond to the class of context-free languages. We summarise this result in the theorem given as follows.

Theorem 4.5 *The set of languages accepted by PDAs is exactly the set of context-free languages.*

Again, we give constructions from CFG to PDA by empty stack and vice versa below without formally proving the soundness of the constructions.

From CFG to PDA by empty stack. We give a systematic construction in Algorithm 8 where we denote the set of states by $\mathbb{S}$ to distinguish it from the start symbol S in the grammar.

The constructed PDA only has one state s. For each production of the form $A \to \gamma$, if A is the top of the stack, we replace A by γ in the stack without consuming any input. If the input symbol matches the top of the stack, then we pop the symbol from the stack.

Algorithm 8: Convert a CFG to a PDA by empty stack that accepts the same language.

Data: A CFG $G = (V_t, V_n, S, P)$
Result: A PDA $P = (\Sigma, \Gamma, Z, \mathbb{S}, s, \{\}, R)$
$\Sigma \leftarrow V_t$;
$\Gamma \leftarrow V_t \cup V_n$;
$Z \leftarrow S$;
$\mathbb{S} \leftarrow \{s\}$;
$R \leftarrow \emptyset$;
foreach *non-terminal symbol* $A \in V_n$ **do**
    foreach *production of the form* $A \rightarrow \gamma \in P$ **do**
        | $R \leftarrow R \cup \{(s, \epsilon, A, s, \gamma)\}$;
    end
end
foreach *terminal symbol* $a \in V_t$ **do**
    | $R \leftarrow R \cup \{(s, a, a, s, \epsilon)\}$;
end

Example 4.24 Recall the CFG G'' of Example 4.9 again:

$$S \rightarrow \epsilon \mid 0S1 \mid 01.$$

This CFG can be converted to the PDA as follows.

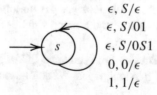

$\epsilon, S/\epsilon$
$\epsilon, S/01$
$\epsilon, S/0S1$
$0, 0/\epsilon$
$1, 1/\epsilon$

This PDA is equivalent to the DPDA in Example 4.19.

From PDA by empty stack to CFG. This direction is a bit tricky. We give the construction in Algorithm 9.

As usual, the terminal symbols are the alphabet Σ. The non-terminal symbols include a special start symbol S and symbols of the form $[sXs']$ where s and s' are states in $\mathbb{S}$ and X is a stack symbol in Γ. Note that $[sXs']$ is *one symbol*, and we reflect this by enclosing it in square brackets. Such a symbol intends to capture an event that the PDA moves from the state s to the state s', and in this process, the "net change" of the stack is that a symbol X is popped. By "net change", we mean that there can be a series of modifications to the stack in the process, but the end result is that only the symbol X is popped compared to the configuration in the state s.

Algorithm 9: Convert a PDA by empty stack to a CFG that generates the same language.

Data: A PDA $P = (\Sigma, \Gamma, Z, \mathbb{S}, s, \{\}, R)$
Result: A CFG $G = (V_t, V_n, S, P)$
$V_t \leftarrow \Sigma$;
$V_n \leftarrow \{S\} \cup \{[sXs'] \mid s, s' \in \mathbb{S} \wedge X \in \Gamma\}$;
$P \leftarrow \emptyset$;
foreach *state* $s \in \mathbb{S}$ **do**
$\quad \mid \quad P \leftarrow P \cup \{S \rightarrow [s_0 Zs]\}$;
end
foreach *transition* $R(s, a, X, s', \gamma)$ *where* $\gamma = Y_1 Y_2 \cdots Y_k, k \in \mathbb{N}$ *and*
$a \in \Sigma \cup \{\epsilon\}$ **do**
$\quad$ **foreach** *possible list of states* $s_1, s_2, \cdots, s_k$ **do**
$\quad \quad \mid \quad P \leftarrow P \cup \{[sXs_k] \rightarrow a[sY_1 s_1][s_1 Y_2 s_2] \cdots [r_{k-1} Y_k s_k]\}$;
$\quad$ **end**
end

The first type of production of the form $S \rightarrow [s_0 Zs]$ generates all the strings that cause the PDA to go from the initial state s_0 to a state s, and pop the initial stack symbol Z as the net stack change. Since Z is the bottom of the stack, such strings are accepted by the PDA.

The second type of production is of the form

$$[sXs_k] \rightarrow a[sY_1 s_1][s_1 Y_2 s_2] \cdots [r_{k-1} Y_k s_k].$$

Note that k can be any natural number, including 0, in which case $\gamma = \epsilon$. Such a production says that the PDA can process the input symbol a (or does not process any input) and move from the state s to the state s_k via k steps; each step i ($1 \leq i \leq k$) pops a symbol Y_i as the net change of the stack and moves from s_{i-1} to s_i (except the first step, which moves from s to s_1). The end result is that the symbol X is popped from the stack. Such productions are intended to capture all possible intermediate transitions that may occur, which pop the symbols in the stack until the stack is empty.

In practice, the PDA to CFG direction is arguably less used than the other direction, so we will not present an example here. Interested readers can see an example in Sect. 6.3 of Hopcroft, Motwani, and Ullman's book [1].

Limitations of pushdown automata. The following language is *not* a context-free language and is not accepted by any PDA:

$$\{0^n 1^n 2^n \mid n \geq 1\}.$$

An informal argument follows: if we were to design a PDA to accept this language, we could use the stack to record the 0s, pop the stack, and match them with the 1s. However, we would then have no idea how many 0s and 1s we have processed. Therefore, we could not match the same number of 2s. Similarly, we could match the 1s with the 2s, but then we could not guarantee that we had processed the same number of 0s. This example shows the limitation of a stack as a form of storage.

Summary. Figure 4.5 summarises important concepts in this chapter in a Venn diagram. We have established the equivalences between DFA, NFA, and Right-Linear Grammars (Algorithms 3, 4, and 5). They correspond to the class of regular languages. We have also shown the conversions between PDA by final state, PDA by empty stack, and context-free grammars (Algorithms 6, 7, 8 and 9). They correspond to the class of context-free languages. The dashed lines represent deterministic context-free languages, a proper subset of context-free languages that correspond to DPDA by final state. The dotted lines represent the languages accepted by DPDA by empty stack.

Exercises

4.16 Find a DPDA for the language

$$\{w3w^R \mid w \in \{1, 2\}^* \land w^R \text{ is } w \text{ reversed}\}.$$

4.17 Convert the following CFG to a PDA by empty stack:

$$S \to S + T \mid T$$
$$T \to T \times U \mid U$$
$$U \to (S) \mid 1 \mid 2.$$

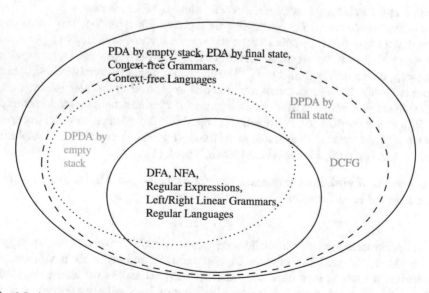

Fig. 4.5 A summary of important concepts in this chapter

4.18 Convert the (ambiguous) CFG of Exercise 4.14 in Sect. 4.3 to a PDA by empty stack.

4.19 Convert the PDA by empty stack obtained in Exercise 4.17 to a PDA by final state.

4.20 Convert the PDA by empty stack obtained in Exercise 4.18 to a PDA by final state.

4.21 Find a PDA by final state for the language L in Example 4.19.

4.22 Convert the PDA by final state obtained in Exercise 4.21 to a PDA by empty stack.

4.23 Model the automaton you devise in Exercise 4.16 in PAT. Check three accepted strings and three unaccepted strings against your model. **Instruction**. To model a

PDA, we first need to model a stack in PAT. We will use an array to encode a stack. We define the following important variables for stack operations:

```
#define STACK_SIZE 10; // The size of the stack.
var stack = [0,-1(STACK_SIZE-1)]; // The stack.
var stackTopIndex = 0; // The index of the stack top.
var stackTop = 0; // The value of stack top.
var stackEmpty = false; // Whether the stack is empty.
var stackOverflow = false; // Flag for stack overflow.
var stackUnderflow = false;   // Flag for stack underflow.
```

In the above code, we initialise the stack with a 0, which represents the special initial stack symbol (usually denoted by Z in this book), and fill the remainder of the stack with -1, which represents an empty cell. We define four common stack operations as follows:

```
// Get the stack top.
peek() = pk{
   if (stackTopIndex < 0) {
      stackUnderflow = true;
   }
   else {
      stackTop = stack[stackTopIndex];
   }
} -> Skip;

// Pop the stack top.
pop() = pp{
   if (stackTopIndex < 0) {
      stackUnderflow = true;
   }
   else {
```

```
17      stackTopIndex = stackTopIndex - 1;
18   }
19 } -> Skip;
20
21 // Push a symbol into the stack.
22 push(symbol) = psh{
23   if (stackTopIndex >= STACK_SIZE) {
24     stackOverflow = true;
25   }
26   else {
27     stackTopIndex = stackTopIndex + 1;
28     stack[stackTopIndex] = symbol;
29   }
30 } -> Skip;
31
32 // Check whether the stack is empty.
33 stackCheckEmpty() = ckepty{
34   if (stackTopIndex < 0) {
35     stackEmpty = true;
36   }
37 } -> Skip;
```

Note that when we pop the top of the stack, we do not actually modify the corresponding value; we simply decrement the index of the stack top.

Modelling states and transitions of a PDA. On top of the operations of an NFA, we need to peek at the stack and perform pop and push appropriately. We can model the "push" state of Exercise 4.16 as follows:

```
1 stateS1() = s1{ats1 = 1; ats2 = 0;} ->
2   ([input != 0](peek(); consume(); (
3        [bit == 1 && stackTop == 0](push(1);stateS1())
4     <> [bit == 2 && stackTop == 0](push(2);stateS1())
5     <> [bit == 1 && stackTop == 1](push(1);stateS1())
6     <> [bit == 1 && stackTop == 2](push(1);stateS1())
7     <> [bit == 2 && stackTop == 1](push(2);stateS1())
8     <> [bit == 2 && stackTop == 2](push(2);stateS1())
9     <> [bit == 3 && stackTop == 1](stateS2())
10    <> [bit == 3 && stackTop == 2](stateS2())
11   ))
12   [] [input == 0]stackCheckEmpty();(hs{halt = true;} -> Skip));
```

The above modelling strictly follows the definition of transitions. If the input is not empty, then we get the stack top and process the current input symbol; these two symbols determine where we go next. In the first transition, we simplify the operation of 0/10 to just pushing 1 into the stack. If the input symbol is 3, we move to the "pop and match" state. These transitions can be simplified further because we basically just push the input symbol into the stack. We give a shorter version as follows:

```
1 stateS1() = s1{ats1 = 1; ats2 = 0;} ->
2   ([input != 0](peek(); consume();
3        ([bit == 1](push(1);stateS1())
```

```
4    <> [bit == 2] (push(2);stateS1())
5    <> [bit == 3] (stateS2())
6    ))
7    [] [input == 0]stackCheckEmpty();(hs{halt = true;} -> Skip));
```

The "pop and match" state should allow a transition that does not process any input symbol. Thus, we structure the code differently and do not consume an input symbol in this case. See the example code given below.

```
1    stateS2() = s2{ats1 = 0; ats2 = 1;} ->
2      ([input != 0] (peek();
3        ((consume(); (
4           [bit == 1 && stackTop == 1] (pop();stateS2())
5         <> [bit == 2 && stackTop == 2] (pop();stateS2()))))
6       <> [stackTop == 0] (pop();stateS2()))
7      )
8      [] [input == 0] (peek();(
9        (stackCheckEmpty();(hs{halt = true;} -> Skip))
10      <> ([stackTop == 0] (pop();stateS2())))))));
```

The transition $\epsilon, 0/\epsilon$ is coded in two places, depending on whether the input is depleted.

Modelling the acceptance condition. We can model the acceptance condition of a PDA by empty stack as below, where halt == true indicates that the input has been completely processed.

```
1    #define accept (halt == true && stackEmpty == true);
```

We can check whether the input can be accepted as follows:

```
1    #assert stateS1() reaches accept;
```

4.24 Model the automaton you devise in Exercise 4.17 in PAT. Check three accepted strings and three unaccepted strings against your model.

Instruction. Follow the same technique discussed in the previous exercise.

Encoding non-numeric symbols. Exercise 4.17 involves the following symbols:

$$V_t = \{1, 2, +, \times, (,)\}$$
$$V_n = \{S, T, U\}$$

Since PAT only deals with integers, we can encode these symbols into integers using the translation given below.

$$1 \mapsto 1 \qquad 2 \mapsto 2 \qquad 3 \mapsto +$$
$$4 \mapsto \times \qquad 5 \mapsto (\qquad 6 \mapsto)$$
$$7 \mapsto S \qquad 8 \mapsto T \qquad 9 \mapsto U$$

The model is an approximation. Recall that the definition of PDAs does not mention the size of the stack; theoretically, the stack can be infinitely large. Since we use STACK_SIZE to constrain the size of the stack, the model is only an approximation of a PDA. This is a common phenomenon in modelling and verification tasks since our computer resources are finite. In fact, the models we built for NFAs are also approximations because NFAs theoretically can process infinitely long strings, but the input variable is finite.[10] Since there are quite a few production rules in Exercise 4.17, you may see errors saying the stack is overflown. In such cases, you can increase the STACK_SIZE to a larger number (e.g., 100).

The state-space explosion problem. Since the model checking technique exhaustively searches all possibilities, the verification can be slow for certain models which have a large number of cases. In Exercise 4.17, a naïve translation to PDA results in transitions that directly encode production rules, and these production rules may yield infinite derivations. Consequently, a depth-first search (the default verification engine) will try all possible productions and quickly overflow the stack. In such cases, you can use the breadth-first search engine (select from "Verification Engine" drop-down list in the "Verification" window) to verify the input. If the input can be accepted, PAT will usually return "VALID" fairly quickly. On the other hand, if the input is not in the language of the PDA, PAT will try all possible ways to accept it, and in the case of a naïve translation of Exercise 4.17, it may take a very long time.

References

1. Hopcroft J, Motwani R, Ullman J (2007) Introduction to automata theory, languages, and computation. Pearson/AddisonWesley. ISBN: 9780321455369
2. Rozenberg G, Salomaa A (1997) Handbook of formal languages: word, language grammar, vol 1. Springer, Berlin. ISBN: 9783540604204
3. Chomsky N (1956) Three models for the description of language. IRE Trans Inf Theory 2:113–124

---

[10] Limited to about 10 digits in PAT.

Turing Machines and Computability

> Before one gets the right answer, one must ask the right question. And the right
> question being asked for the wrong reasons may be an essential part of the
> process of discovery.
>
> —S. Barry Cooper [1]

This is the third time we mention Hilbert's Program, and we will finally discuss
it in more depth. Along with the program, Hilbert posed 23 famous problems, many
of which have been solved today. Those still unsolved mainly have two themes.

The first theme is *provability*. It asks whether we can formalise all mathematical
knowledge via theorems of a certain theory. We can think of a theory as a set of
axioms and deduction rules, e.g., Hilbert's calculus. We would like the theory to be
complete,[1] which means that it can prove or disprove any statement in the language
via a finite deduction. We would also like the theory to be *consistent*, which means
that the theory cannot prove a contradiction. Hilbert's program is in this theme, and
it aims at proving the consistency of common arithmetic *within arithmetic*. For a
counterexample, writing proof of consistency in English does not count.

The other theme is *computability*. It asks whether there are algorithms for solving certain problems. For example, Hilbert's "Entscheidungsproblem" asks whether
there is an algorithm for deciding if a given statement is universally valid or not. In the
context of logic, we call such an algorithm a *proof search procedure*. In the context

---

[1] The definition of completeness in this section is called "syntactic/maximal/negation completeness". By contrast, the definition of completeness in previous sections only requires that all valid
formulae can be derived, and we call it "semantic completeness".

© The Author(s), under exclusive license to Springer Nature Switzerland AG 2021   163
Z. Hou, *Fundamentals of Logic and Computation*, Texts in Computer Science,
https://doi.org/10.1007/978-3-030-87882-5_5

of computation, this problem asks whether there is a type of automata that accepts all the languages. Generally, this theme is concerned with the question of "are there problems that cannot be solved by any algorithm?" Or, in the formal description of Chap. 4, "are there languages that are not accepted by any automaton?".

Here is an interesting account of the story by Cooper [1]. On 8 September 1930, Hilbert delivered an opening address to the Society of German Scientists and Physicians in Königsberg, declaring:

> For the mathematician there is no Ignorabimus[2], and, in my opinion, not at all for natural science either... The true reason why [no one] has succeeded in finding an unsolvable problem is, in my opinion, that there *is no* unsolvable problem. In contrast to the foolish Ignorabimus, our credo avers:
>
> Wir müssen wissen—wir werden wissen.[3]

One day earlier, in the same city, Gödel gave a talk at a philosophical meeting about his now-famous result, known as Gödel's Incompleteness Theorems.

Theorem 5.1 (Gödel's Incompleteness Theorems I and II (informal)) *Any consistent theory containing enough elementary arithmetic is incomplete. Furthermore, any such theory is incapable of proving its own consistency.*

Gödel's result answers the first theme negatively: we now know that a complete and consistent theory that can capture all of the mathematics does not exist and that it is impossible to deduce the consistency of a "large enough" theory within its own language.

In the hope of addressing the second theme, mathematicians attempted to develop computational models for answering what we *can solve*.

> Like buses: you wait two thousand years for a definition of 'effectively calculable', and then three come along at once.
>
> — Philip Wadler [2]

The first computational model in our discussion is *recursive functions*, which was formalised by Gödel and Herbrand in 1933. It is arguably the closest to the form we would use to describe mathematical functions and algorithms. Kleene improved this formalisation and developed the theory of computability as "recursive function/recursion theory". In 1936, Church and his student Kleene developed λ-*calculus*, which is a very simple system for denoting computations. In the same year, Church's other student Turing published another model independently, commonly known as *Turing machines* that mimics how a "machine" performs computations.

---

[2] The Latin phrase "ignoramus et ignorabimus" means that "we do not know and will not know". It represents the idea that scientific knowledge is limited.

[3] Means "We must know, we shall know." in English. Perhaps ironically, these are the words engraved on Hilbert's tombstone.

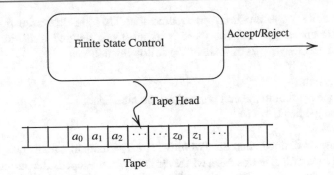

Fig. 5.1 The architecture of a Turing machine

Church and Turing proved that the above three computational models are equivalent to each other, and they argue that these models capture what *can be solved*. The second theme is also answered negatively, as evidenced by Turing's construction of the Halting Problem. The end of 1936 saw the world change as we began to understand what "computers" cannot compute, however powerful.

5.1 Turing Machines

In 1936, Turing published a 36-page paper entitled "On computable numbers, with an application to the Entscheidungsproblem" [3], which claimed to solve a long-standing problem of Hilbert.[4] The paper proposed a remarkably simple abstract machine which Turing argued can perform any possible computation. Young readers should note that Turing's work was in an era when modern computers did not exist. A "computer" in the 1930s refers to a human performing computation with pencil and paper.

Turing machines as language acceptors. Turing machines (TMs) generalise pushdown automata by using a tape memory for the storage instead of a stack. We can access any position of the tape by moving the "tape head" accordingly. We can think of the tape as an unlimited array and the tape head as the index for accessing the array. Since the tape is infinite and unbounded at both ends, we will never run out of space. Therefore, unlike realistic machines, we can unify all sorts of memory into one tape. For example, instead of having a tape for input and another tape for the memory, we can simply write the input onto the tape as a part of initialisation and put the tape head at the beginning of the input. We visualise a TM in Fig. 5.1. In this figure, $a_0, a_1, \cdots$ represent input data and $z_0, z_1, \cdots$ represent scratch space for computation.

---

[4] At that time, Turing was only 23 and had not obtained his PhD degree yet.

Without further specification, we assume that TMs are deterministic[5]; that is, given a state and a tape symbol, there is at most one defined transition. In each transition, a TM may perform *some* of the following actions:

- move to a state;
- write a tape symbol in the cell pointed by the tape head;
- move the tape head.

If no action is defined, then the TM *halts*. If a TM halts in a final state, it accepts the original input; also, in this case, whatever is left on the tape is the output (besides the accept/reject answer). The set of strings accepted by a TM is its language. If a TM halts in a non-final state, then it rejects the input. A TM may never halt.

We give the formal definition of TM as follows.

Definition 5.1 (*TM*) A TM is a seven-tuple $(\Sigma, \Gamma, B, S, s_0, F, N)$ where

- Σ is the set of input symbols;
- Γ is the set of tape symbols;
- $B \in \Gamma$ is the blank symbol, which represents an empty cell;
- S is the set of states;
- $s_0 \in S$ is the initial state;
- $F \subseteq S$ is a set of final states;
- $N : S \times \Gamma \rightharpoonup S \times \Gamma \times \{L, R, -\}$ is a (partial) transition function, where L, R, and $-$ are tape head movements for left, right, and stay, respectively.

We can assume that a TM halts when it enters a final state, and only one final state suffices for any such TM. Therefore, we can simplify the above definition to only allowing a single final state. The above assumption and simplification do not affect the computational power of TMs.

In a graphical presentation, we write a transition as follows:

$$a/b, D$$

where a and b are tape symbols and $D \in \{L, R, -\}$ is a direction. This transition means that the current tape cell shows a, and we write b in the place of a, then move the tape head in the direction D for one cell (or stay put).

Example 5.1 Consider the language $\{0^n 1^n 2^n \mid n \geq 1\}$ which is not accepted by any PDA. With a TM, we assume that the input is written on the tape and the tape head points to the leftmost digit of the input initially. A TM that accepts the above language performs the following "algorithm":

---

[5] By contrast, we assume that PDAs are nondeterministic.

1. In state s_0,

   a. if read a 0, replace it by X and move right, and go to state s_1;
   b. if read a Y, skip it and move right, and go to state s_4.

2. In state s_1, move right to skip the remaining 0s (and Ys), and find the first 1. Replace the 1 by Y and move right. Go to state s_2.
3. In state s_2, move right to skip the remaining 1s (and Zs), and find the first 2. Replace the 2 by Z and move left. Go to state s_3.
4. In state s_3, skip all the Zs, 1s, Ys, and 0s and move all the way left to find an X, then move right. Go to state s_0.
5. In state s_4, move right to skip all the Ys and Zs. If the first symbol that is not a Y nor a Z is an empty cell B, then go to state s_5 and accept the input. Otherwise, reject the input.

We draw the state transitions of this TM in Fig. 5.2.

If the transition for a pair of state and tape symbol is not defined, the TM goes to an "error state", which is not shown in the state-transition diagram. In such cases, the TM halts and rejects the input.

In what follows, we establish the relation between Turing machines and their corresponding class of languages and grammars.

Definition 5.2 (*Recursively Enumerable Languages*) The set of languages generated by unrestricted grammars are *recursively enumerable (RE) languages*.

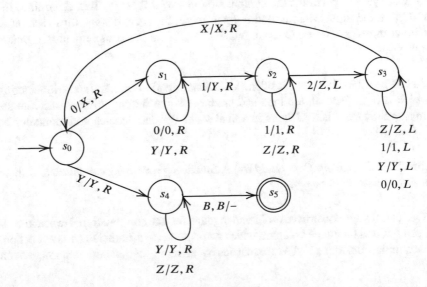

Fig. 5.2 A Turing machine that accepts the language $\{0^n 1^n 2^n \mid n \geq 1\}$

It is proved that TMs correspond to recursively enumerable languages, which in turn correspond to unrestricted grammars. This result is stated as follows.

Theorem 5.2 *If a language can be generated by an unrestricted grammar, then there is a TM that accepts this language. If a language is accepted by a TM, then there is an unrestricted grammar that produces this language.*

Turing machines as functions. We have accustomed ourselves to automata that accept languages. However, Turing's original view of his machine was a computational model for performing integer calculations. He used unary numbers[6] to represent integers and performed computations by adding or removing digits of numbers. In such cases, we are interested in the output left on the tape after the Turing machine halts in a final state.

Example 5.2 We give an example of TM as a function in binary numbers, which are used in almost all modern computers.

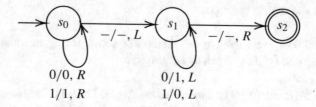

The above TM performs the computation in two stages: the first stage finds the last digit of the input without modifying the tape, the second stage flips each bit of the input in reverse order. Overall, this TM computes the complement of a binary number.

Let M be a TM. We can consider M as a function f_M that takes some input string i which is initialised on the tape and produces some output string o which is the string on the tape when M halts in a final state. We denote such a computation as $f_M(i) = o$.

Definition 5.3 (*Turing Computability*) A function f is *Turing-computable* if there is a TM M such that $f = f_M$.

One can always construct a problem/language for any computational task and construct a TM as a language acceptor, which corresponds to a(nother) TM as a function. For example, consider a TM M that carries out an input–output computation, we can

---

[6] For example, 2 is written as 11 and 5 as 11111.

find a TM M' that accepts the language of strings of the form "input#output", where # is a tape symbol that separates input and output. The new TM M' may include M as a component that transforms an input into an output, then M' checks whether the left-hand side of # matches the right-hand side. In this case, the TM M as a function is essentially the "indicator function" (cf. Page 47) of the relation captured by the other TM M' as a language acceptor. However, it may be easier to undertake a task in one way than the other.

Programming with TMs. Although the definition of TMs is reasonably simple, performing computational tasks with TMs is by no means trivial. The representation of data often involves certain encodings. For example, integers are often encoded by unary or binary numbers. As long as appropriate tape symbols are used, one can also encode variables, arrays, and even files in general.

In terms of program control, common TM operations include finding, inserting, overwriting, and deleting symbols on the tape.

A particularly useful technique is using states to record information. For example, in Fig. 5.2, we use s_0 to represent that we have found and overwritten a 0 with an X, s_1 for overwriting 1 and s_3 for overwriting 2, and so on. In this way, we can use a finite set of states to store a finite amount of data.

Another widely used technique is the composition of TMs. For example, if we have a TM M_1 that increments a number, we can compose two M_1s sequentially to add 2 to a number. This composition is visualised as follows:

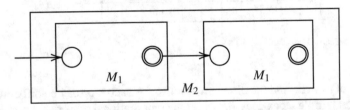

The TM M_1 in the above case is a "subroutine" of a larger TM M_2. The subroutine should have an initial state and a final state. A function call is represented as a transition to the initial state of the subroutine. The final state "returns" the control to M_2.

Branches and loops are easy to realise with state transitions, as shown in numerous previous examples.

Extensions to TMs. A *multitape* TM has a finite state control and a finite number of tapes and tape heads, as illustrated in Fig. 5.3. As a convention for initialisation, the input is written on the first tape, and the head of the first tape points to the leftmost bit of the input. All other cells are initially blank, i.e., hold the symbol B. The heads of other tapes point at arbitrary cells.

In each transition, a multitape TM may perform some of the following:

- move to a state;
- *for each tape*, write a tape symbol in the cell pointed by the tape head;
- move *each* tape head.

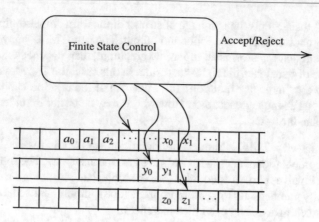

Fig. 5.3 An example of multitape TM

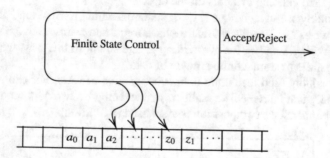

Fig. 5.4 An example of multihead TM

The symbol to write and the direction to move for each tape can be different.
   Having multiple tapes does *not* increase computational power.

Lemma 5.1 *Every language accepted by a multitape TM is recursively enumerable and is accepted by some TM.*

A *multihead* TM has one tape but multiple tape heads which can access multiple symbols at the same time. Such a machine is visualised in Fig. 5.4.
   In each transition, a multihead TM may perform some of the following:

• move to a state;
• *for each tape head*, write a tape symbol in the cell pointed by the head;
• move *each* tape head.

The symbol to write and the direction to move for each head can be different.
   Having multiple tape heaps does *not* increase computational power, either.

Lemma 5.2 *Every language accepted by a multihead TM is recursively enumerable and is accepted by some TM.*

A *nondeterministic* TM (NTM) has a transition relation R instead of a transition function.

$$R \subseteq S \times \Gamma \times S \times \Gamma \times \{L, R, -\}.$$

The computation carried out by an NTM may have multiple "possibilities". We can think of NTM as having the ability to always guess the right choice of state transitions. In other words, an NTM M_N accepts an input w if there exists any sequence of transitions that leads to a final state where M_N halts. The existence of other sequences that do not lead to acceptance is irrelevant.

Adding nondeterminism also does not increase computational power. However, we will see in Sect. 5.4 that NTMs *may* make the computation faster.

Lemma 5.3 *If a language is accepted by an NTM, then there is a TM that accepts the same language.*

TMs versus modern computers. The architecture of modern computers evolves from the von Neumann architecture [4], which was published in 1945 and shown in Fig. 5.5.

The central processing unit (CPU) contains a control unit (CU), some arithmetic logic units (ALU), and some registers. Nowadays, the ALU often includes an integer unit (IU), a floating-point unit (FPU), and some co-processor units. The CPU performs computation by executing instructions. Registers are used to hold state variables and the input and output of instructions.

The input and output (I/O) of a computer allow transmission of data to devices such as mouse, keyboard, and monitor.

Two commonly used types of memories are random-access memory (RAM, or just memory) and read-only memory (ROM). RAM stores data and programs that

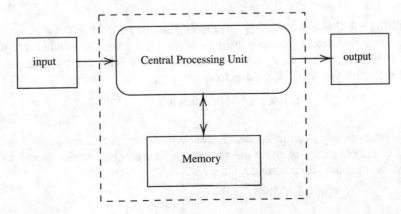

Fig. 5.5 An illustration of the von Neumann architecture

the computer executes. RAM is *temporary*—its content is erased when the computer is turned off. ROM is permanent and is used to store the boot instructions of the computer. Modern computers also have secondary memories, i.e., hard drives or storage for mass data, which are also permanent and allow read and write. On some devices, the hard drive replaces ROM as the storage for boot instructions.

The CPU accesses the memory and I/O devices via *buses*. This leads to the *von Neumann bottleneck*, which refers to the computation inefficiency caused by different read/write speeds of different memories. For example, RAM is usually small but fast, and hard drives are large but slow. When the CPU needs to access data that is not in RAM, it has to wait for the data to be loaded from the hard drive to RAM. Similarly, accessing registers is much faster than accessing memory. Modern computers employ many mitigations, such as having multiple levels of cache between the CPU and the memory as intermediary storage.

Let us first consider how a computer can simulate a TM. The finite state control of a TM has a finite number of states and transitions. Similarly, the set of tape symbols is finite. Therefore, we can write a program that encodes the state-transition diagram of a TM. However, the tape of a TM is infinitely long, but the cache, memory (RAM), and storage of a computer are finite. Consequently, a physical computer can only approximate a TM. The approximation can be very precise if we allow swapping storages (e.g., removable hard drives) during computation, however inefficient, and assuming we have all available hard drives (which are still finite) in the world at hand.

On the other hand, we can use a multitape TM to simulate a computer by using a tape as the hard drive, a tape as the memory, a tape as registers, a tape for input and output, a tape as scratch, and so on. The simulation also applies to a normal TM since multitape TMs have the same computational power as TMs, though maybe more efficient for certain tasks.

The speed in terms of seconds used for computation is not comparable since the definition of TMs does not limit how fast the tape head moves and how fast the state transition happens. So theoretically, a TM computes as "fast" as one wishes. However, we can measure the time complexity of computation by how many operations a machine performs.

Definition 5.4 (*Time Complexity*) The running time of a TM M on input w, denoted by $t_M(w)$, is the number of state transitions M performs when processing w before it halts. If M does not halt on w, then the running time is infinite. The time complexity of M is the function $T(n)$ defined as follows:

$$T(n) = \max_x t_M(x) \text{ such that } |x| = |n|.$$

Time complexity is parametric to a value n that returns the maximum running time for all input strings of size n. In other words, time complexity denotes the worst case of running time for a certain sized input.

Lemma 5.4 *Given a program that is executed by a computer in n instruction cycles, there is a TM M that can perform the same computation with time complexity of n^c where c is a constant.*

A detailed argument for the above lemma can be found in Hopcroft et al.'s book [5]. Here, the reader only needs to understand that n^c, where c is a constant, denotes a *polynomial* time complexity, which means that a machine can perform such a computation *efficiently*. Problems that can be solved in polynomial time are called *tractable* problems; otherwise called *intractable* problems. The above lemma implies that if a problem can be solved by a computer in polynomial time, then it can be solved by a TM in polynomial time. The converse is also true if we assume that the computer does not run out of memory.

We close this section with Turing's major claim in his paper, nowadays referred to as *Turing's thesis*, which is an unprovable assumption that is widely accepted by computer scientists.

Hypothesis (Turing's Thesis) Every effectively computable function is Turing-computable.

What we mean for a function f being "effectively computable" is that there exists an algorithm that systematically computes any value $f(x)$ for which $f(x)$ is defined. Or in Turing's own words [6]:

> It was stated ... that a function is effectively calculable if its values can be found by some purely mechanical process. We may take this literally, understanding that by a purely mechanical process one which could be carried out by a machine. The development ... leads to ... an identification of computability with effective calculability.

Exercises

5.1 Find a TM that increments a binary number. Draw the state-transition diagram of the TM.

5.2 Find a TM that decrements a binary number. Draw the state-transition diagram of the TM. Decrementing 0 is not allowed; the TM rejects 0 as an input.

5.3 Find a TM that adds two binary numbers. Draw the state-transition diagram of the TM. **Hint:** You are allowed to use the TMs of Exercises 5.1 and 5.2 as "subroutines".

5.4 Find a TM that multiplies two binary numbers. Draw the state-transition diagram of the TM. **Hint:** You are allowed to use the TMs of Exercises 5.1 ∼ 5.3 as "subroutines". You may need to modify them slightly.

5.5 Model the TM you find in Exercise 5.1 in PAT. Verify the output of three accepted input strings.

Instruction. Modelling a Turing machine in PAT is actually simpler than modelling PDAs and NFAs, as we can just use an array to realise the tape. Again, our model is only an approximation, as infinite arrays are not allowed. See the code given below.

```
1  // The size of the tape.
2  #define N 20;
3  // The input and the tape is realised by an array.
4  // -1 stands for the blank symbol B.
5  var tape = [-1(5),1,0,0,0,1,0,1,1,-1(7)];
6  // The tape head is simply an index of the array.
7  var head:{0..(N-1)} = 5;
8  var halt = false;
```

We use `:{0..(N-1)}` to constrain the range of the index to $[0, (N-1)]$.

The following auxiliary functions are not really necessary; we just define them for readability.

```
1  // Write a symbol on the tape.
2  write(x) = w{
3      tape[head] = x;
4  } -> Skip;
5
6  // Move the tape head.
7  // d = -1 -> move left.
8  // d = 0 -> stay.
9  // d = 1 -> move right.
10 move(d:{-1..1}) = mv{
11     head = head + d;
12 } -> Skip;
```

For Exercise 5.1, we only need three states. The definition of the states and transitions are given below, where `state2` is the final state.

```
1  var ats0 = 0;
2  var ats1 = 0;
3  var ats2 = 0;
4
5  state0() = s0{ats0 = 1; ats1 = 0; ats2 = 0;} ->
6      (if (tape[head] == 0) {
7          move(1);state0()
8          } else if (tape[head] == 1) {
9              move(1);state0()
10         } else if (tape[head] == -1) {
11             move(-1);state1()
12         }
13         else { // undefined transition, halt.
14             h0{halt = true;} -> Skip
15      });
16
17 state1() = s1{ats0 = 0; ats1 = 1; ats2 = 0;} ->
```

```
18    (if (tape[head] == 0) {
19       write(1);state2()
20       } else if (tape[head] == 1) {
21          write(0);move(-1);state1()
22       } else if (tape[head] == -1) {
23          write(1);state2()
24       }
25       else { // undefined transition, halt.
26          h1{halt = true;} -> Skip
27    });
28
29 state2() = s2{ats0 = 0; ats1 = 0; ats2 = 1;} ->
30    h2{halt = true;} -> Skip;
```

The halting condition can be coded as follows:

```
1 #define accept (halt == true && ats2 == 1);
2 #assert state0() reaches accept;
```

The modelled TM accepts any binary number as long as it is within the range of the array. What we are really interested in is whether the output of the computation is correct. To see the output, click "Verification" and verify that the input is accepted. Then in the verification window, click "Simulate Witness Trace" to bring up the simulation window. From there, you can locate the trace of executed events that leads to the final state in the bottom-right component called "Event Trace". Click on the last item in "Event Trace", and the output of the TM should be displayed as the variable tape in the "State Info" on the left-hand side.

5.6 Model the TM you find in Exercise 5.2 in PAT. Verify the output of three accepted input strings.

5.2 Recursive Functions and λ-calculus

This section introduces two other computational models that also aim to capture all effectively computable functions. We then discuss their relation with Turing's work. Hopefully, branching out and studying other models and finally seeing that these models collapse into one notion of computability will strengthen our view that Turing's thesis is plausible.

We focus on functions over *natural numbers* in this section, as other sets of numbers, such as integers and rational numbers, can be represented by naturals. On the other hand, we do not consider real numbers, complex numbers, etc., as they exceed the scope of computability.

Gödel's recursive functions emerge from logic, which we have extensively discussed in Part I of this book. Recursive functions are defined inductively, and by now, the reader should be able to see the analogy between inductive definitions and recursions.

We begin with a proper subset of recursive functions called *primitive recursive functions*.

Definition 5.5 (*Primitive Recursive Functions*)

Base cases: the below functions are primitive recursive.

- The *zero function* defined as

$$0(n) = n, \forall n \in \mathbb{N}.$$

- The *successor function* defined as

$$suc(n) = n + 1, \forall n \in \mathbb{N}.$$

- The *projection function* P_i^k defined as

$$P_i^k(\overrightarrow{n}) = n_i, \text{ where } k \geq 1 \wedge 1 \leq i \leq k \wedge \overrightarrow{n} = n_1, n_2, \cdots, n_k.$$

Inductive cases: if $g, h, h_0, \cdots, h_j$ where $j \geq 0$ are primitive recursive functions, so is f formed by the rules given below.

- *Substitution*, formed by

$$f(\overrightarrow{n}) = g(h_0(\overrightarrow{n}), \cdots, h_j(\overrightarrow{n})), \text{ where } k \geq 1 \wedge \overrightarrow{n} = n_1, n_2, \cdots, n_k.$$

- *Primitive recursion*, formed by

$$f(\overrightarrow{m}, 0) = g(\overrightarrow{m}), \text{ and}$$

$$f(\overrightarrow{m}, suc(n)) = h(\overrightarrow{m}, n, f(\overrightarrow{m}, n)), \text{ where } k \geq 1 \wedge \overrightarrow{m} = m_1, m_2, \cdots, m_k.$$

The three base cases are straightforward. The zero function just returns the input. The successor function gives the successor of a natural number. Recall that we have used this function to define natural numbers on Page 71. The projection function essentially selects the ith element of the list $n_1, \cdots, n_k$. We can think of it as accessing an element of an array. Note that we write "$n + 1$" as another way to express "the successor of a natural number n" since the general reader should understand it. We will define the addition function $+$ later.

The substitution rule allows us to apply a function g by substituting each argument with another function application $h_i(\overrightarrow{n})$, where $1 \leq i \leq j$.

The primitive recursion rule allows us to define a function inductively on natural numbers. The base case, for the natural 0, is that $f(\overrightarrow{m}, 0)$ is defined by some function g. The inductive case defines f for $n + 1$ in terms of $f(\overrightarrow{m}, n)$ using a function h which is also parametric to $\overrightarrow{m}$ and n—nothing we do not already know inductively.

Example 5.3 The addition function $+$ over natural numbers is primitive recursive. We can define $+$ using the primitive recursion rule as below, where we write $+(x, y)$ as $x + y$.

$$m + 0 = 0(m),$$
$$m + suc(n) = suc(P_3^3(m, n, m + n)) = suc(m + n).$$

In the above definition, the base case is defined by the zero function, i.e., we can match $0()$ with $g()$ in the primitive recursion rule. The inductive case is defined by a composition of the successor function and the projection function. That is, we can match $suc(P_3^3())$ with $h()$ in the primitive recursion rule.

Example 5.4 The multiplication function $\times$ is primitive recursive, as defined below, where we write $\times(x, y)$ as $x \times y$.

$$m \times 0 = 0(0),$$
$$m \times suc(n) = m + P_3^3(m, n, m \times n) = m + (m \times n).$$

In this example, we use the fact that $+$ is primitive recursive. We can match $+(m, P_3^3())$ with $h()$ in the primitive recursion rule. Indeed, the projection function can be used to expand the number of arguments, and we will make this step implicit from now on.

We can build up many useful functions from the definition of primitive recursive functions, but these are strictly a subset of all computable functions. Ackermann defined a famous function in 1928 that is computable but not primitive recursive. We give the definition simplified by Péter as follows.

Definition 5.6 (*The Ackermann-Péter Function*)

$$A(m, 0) = m + 1$$
$$A(0, n + 1) = A(1, n)$$
$$A(m + 1, n + 1) = A(A(m, n + 1), n).$$

Ackermann used *nested recursion*, which is shown in the last equation, where there are two nested applications of $A()$. Consequently, the Ackermann function grows faster than any primitive recursive function. See some examples below for how fast it grows.

$$A(0, 0) = 1, \quad A(1, 1) = 3, \quad A(1, 2) = 4, \quad A(2, 2) = 7,$$
$$A(3, 3) = 61, \quad A(3, 4) = 125, \quad A(4, 3) = 2^{2^{65536}} - 3, \quad A(4, 4) = 2^{2^{2^{65536}}}.$$

Primitive recursive functions are naturally total functions. That is, for any given input, there is a defined output. In the following, we extend primitive recursive functions with a rule that may result in undefined output.

Definition 5.7 (*Partial Recursive Functions*) A function f is partial recursive (p.r.) if it can be defined from the base cases of primitive recursive functions using a finite number of applications of the rules in inductive cases and of the below rule.

μ-operator/minimalisation: if $g(\vec{n}, m)$ is partial recursive, then so is f, which is defined as

$$f(\vec{n}) = \mu(g(\vec{n}, m) = 0), \text{where}$$

$$\mu(g(\vec{n}, m) = 0) = m' \text{ iff } g(\vec{n}, m') = 0 \wedge (\forall m'' < m'.g(\vec{n}, m'') \downarrow \neq 0).$$

Although the μ-operator has a rather involved definition, it corresponds to a very common and well-understood operation—*search*. The application $\mu(g(\vec{n}, m) = 0)$ iterates through each value from 0 to m' and finds the first value m'' such that $g(\vec{n}, m'') = 0$. The downarrow $\downarrow$ means that an object is defined. Programmers might be more familiar with the below pseudocode.

```
1 μ(g(n⃗,m) = 0) = {
2    foreach m from 0 to infinity {
3        if (g(n⃗,m) == 0) {
4            return m;
5        }
6    }
7 }
```

Clearly, the search may loop forever if such an m does not exist, in which case $f(\vec{n})$ is undefined. In computability, we are often interested in total functions, so we call a *total* p.r. function simply a *recursive function*.

Definition 5.8 (*Recursive Functions*) A function is *recursive* if it is partial recursive and it is a total function.

Lemma 5.5 *The Ackermann function is recursive.*

Church made an important hypothesis in the early 1930s,[7] called *Church's thesis*, which equates p.r. functions to effectively computable functions.

Hypothesis (*Church's Thesis*) A function f is recursive iff f is total and effectively computable. A function f is partial recursive iff f is effectively computable.

Let us rewind and see how the story unfolded. Evidence suggests Gödel proposed a similar conjecture in 1934. At that time, he was visiting Princeton University, where Church and Kleene were, and the latter two had been working on a different formulation called λ-calculus. However, Gödel himself was not convinced that such conjecture was true. When Church introduced Gödel with λ-calculus and claimed that it cap-

---

[7] Most say in 1934.

tured all "effectively computable" functions,[8] Gödel was unpersuaded, and "regarded [Church's arguments for λ-calculus] as thoroughly unsatisfactory". Church then challenged Gödel to present a different definition for "effectively computable" functions and promised to prove that whatever Gödel came up with was equivalent to λ-calculus. Then Gödel presented partial recursive functions, and Church did the proof. However, not only was Gödel unsatisfied, he started to doubt that his own definition was correct. Kleene recalled that Gödel was only convinced after he saw Turing's thesis, combined with which we have the now-famous *Church–Turing thesis*.

Hypothesis (The Church–Turing Thesis) A function f is partial recursive iff f is Turing-computable iff f is effectively computable.

Let us take the path of Church and Kleene and have a brief look at their λ-calculus, which later became the basis of many functional programming languages such as Lisp, ML, and Haskell.

The syntax of λ-calculus is extremely simple; it contains three rules for defining well-formed λ-terms.

Definition 5.9 (λ-*terms*) A λ-term is inductively defined as follows:

- A *variable* x is a λ-term.
- An *abstraction* $\lambda x.E$, where x is a variable and E is a λ-term, is a λ-term.
- An *application* $E_1 E_2$, where E_1 and E_2 are λ-terms, is a λ-term.

Alternatively, in BNF format, we can define the syntax as

$$E:: = x \mid \lambda x.E \mid EE.$$

An *abstraction* is essentially a way of defining a function. The λ-term $\lambda x.E$ can be understood as a function that has an argument x and a function body E, which may contain x. For instance, we can understand $\lambda x.E$ as a function $f(x)$ in the pseudocode given below.

```
1  f(x) = {
2      E
3  }
```

Since an abstraction does not involve the name of the function, programming languages such as Lisp use λ-terms as *anonymous functions*.

An *application* naturally corresponds to a function application, which is realised by β-reduction given below.

To improve readability, we assume that λ-terms are *left-associative*. For instance, xyz means $(xy)z$. We also allow multiple arguments for a function. For instance, $\lambda xy.E$ means $\lambda x.(\lambda y.E)$.

---

[8] This is an equivalent statement of Church's thesis.

A familiar concept arises on how the symbol λ *binds* variables. Consider the λ-term $(\lambda xy.fxy)y$; the variable x is bound, and the variable f is free. The variable y occurs both bound and free for the first and the second occurrence, respectively. The binding of variables in λ-terms is similar to quantified variables in first-order logic. If a λ-term has no free variables, then it is a *closed* term.

The semantics of a λ-term is defined by how the term can be *reduced*. There are three reduction rules, which are defined as follows.

Definition 5.10 (*Reduction Rules of λ-calculus*)

α-reduction: $\lambda x.E = \lambda y.E[y/x]$ if y is not free in E.
β-reduction: $(\lambda x.E_1)E_2 = E_1[E_2/x]$ if the free variables in E_2 have no bound occurrences in E_1.
η-reduction: $(\lambda x.E)x = E$ if x is not free in E.

Intuitively, α-reduction allows renaming of bound variables, provided that the new name does not clash with existing free variables in the term. β-reduction realises function application via substitution. We can understand E_1 as the function body, x as the function argument, and E_2 as the input parameter passed into the function. The function application replaces every occurrence of x in E_1 with E_2—this is exactly how we apply functions in daily computation. The condition of β-reduction is known as *capture-avoiding substitution*. η-reduction removes redundant abstractions.

Definition 5.11 (*Normal Form of λ-terms*) If a λ-term cannot be further reduced by β-reduction and η-reduction, then it is in normal form.

Lemma 5.6 $(\lambda x.((\lambda z.zx)(\lambda x.x)))y$ *has normal form* y.

Proof See the reduction given below.

$$
\begin{aligned}
&(\lambda x.((\lambda z.zx)(\lambda x.x)))y \\
&= ((\lambda z.zx)(\lambda x.x))[y/x] && (\beta\text{-reduction}) \\
&= (\lambda z.zy)(\lambda y.y) \\
&= zy[\lambda y.y/z] && (\beta\text{-reduction}) \\
&= (\lambda y.y)y \\
&= y && (\eta\text{-reduction}).
\end{aligned}
$$

Note that we cannot directly apply β-reduction in the last step, as the last y is free, but it has a bound occurrence in the "function body". Alternatively, we can use α-reduction to rename the first two ys and obtain $(\lambda x.x)y$, then apply β-reduction to obtain $x[y/x] = y$.

There is no rule that can be applied on y, so it is in normal form.   □

Computation with natural numbers. To define useful computations on natural numbers, we first need to encode natural numbers in λ-terms. Church defined an encoding, later referred to as *Church numerals*, as follows.

Definition 5.12 (*Church Numerals*)

$$0 :: = \lambda sz.z$$
$$1 :: = \lambda sz.s(z)$$
$$2 :: = \lambda sz.s(s(z))$$
$$\cdots$$

$$n :: = \lambda sz.\overbrace{s(s\cdots(s(z)))}^{n \text{ times}}.$$

Informally, we can view the z in Church numerals as "0" and s as the "successor function" suc. As a result, $suc(0)$ is 1 and $suc(suc(suc(0)))$ is 3. Formally, we can define the successor function in the following example.

Example 5.5 The successor function suc over natural numbers can be defined as follows:

$$suc :: = \lambda wyx.y(wyx).$$

For example, we can compute $suc(0)$ as follows:

$$
\begin{aligned}
suc(0) &= (\lambda wyx.y(wyx))(\lambda sz.z) \\
&= (\lambda yx.y(wyx))[\lambda sz.z/w] && (\beta\text{-reduction}) \\
&= \lambda yx.y((\lambda sz.z)yx) \\
&= \lambda yx.y((\lambda z.z)[y/s]x) && (\beta\text{-reduction}) \\
&= \lambda yx.y((\lambda z.z)x) \\
&= \lambda yx.y(z[x/z]) && (\beta\text{-reduction}) \\
&= \lambda yx.y(x) \\
&= \lambda sz.s(z) && (\alpha\text{-reduction}) \\
&= 1.
\end{aligned}
$$

Example 5.6 The addition function $+$ over natural numbers can be defined as follows:

$$+ :: = \lambda xy.(\lambda wu.((xw)(ywu))).$$

For example, we can compute $1 + 2$ as $+12$ as follows:

$$
\begin{aligned}
+12 &= (\lambda xy.(\lambda wu.((xw)(ywu))))(\lambda sz.s(z))(\lambda sz.s(s(z))) \\
&= (\lambda y.(\lambda wu.((xw)(ywu))))[(\lambda sz.s(z))/x](\lambda sz.s(s(z))) && (\beta\text{-reduction}) \\
&= (\lambda y.(\lambda wu.(((\lambda sz.s(z))w)(ywu))))(\lambda sz.s(s(z))) \\
&= (\lambda y.(\lambda wu.((\lambda z.(s(z))[w/s])(ywu))))(\lambda sz.s(s(z))) && (\beta\text{-reduction}) \\
&= (\lambda y.(\lambda wu.((\lambda z.w(z))(ywu))))(\lambda sz.s(s(z)))
\end{aligned}
$$

$$= (\lambda y.(\lambda wu.((w(z))[ywu/z])))(\lambda sz.s(s(z))) \qquad (\beta\text{-reduction})$$
$$= (\lambda y.(\lambda wu.w(ywu)))(\lambda sz.s(s(z)))$$
$$= (\lambda wu.w(ywu))[(\lambda sz.s(s(z)))/y] \qquad (\beta\text{-reduction})$$
$$= \lambda wu.w((\lambda sz.s(s(z)))wu)$$
$$= \lambda wu.w((\lambda z.(s(s(z))))[w/s]u) \qquad (\beta\text{-reduction})$$
$$= \lambda wu.w((\lambda z.w(w(z)))u)$$
$$= \lambda wu.w((w(w(z)))[u/z]) \qquad (\beta\text{-reduction})$$
$$= \lambda wu.w(w(w(u)))$$
$$= \lambda sz.s(s(s(z))) \qquad (\alpha\text{-reduction})$$
$$= 3$$

Definition 5.13 (λ-*computability*) An n-ary function f is λ-computable if there exists a λ-term E such that for all $x_1, \cdots, x_n \in \mathbb{N}$, $f(x_1, \cdots, x_n) = y$ iff $Ex_1, \cdots, x_n$ has normal form y.

Unlike the Church–Turing thesis which relates two formally defined computational models with an informal concept of "effectively computable" functions, thus unprovable, Church did prove that λ-calculus and partial recursive functions are indeed equivalent, as told previously.

Theorem 5.3 *A function is partial recursive iff it is λ-computable.*

By the above equivalence and that λ-computability is defined by normal forms, it is not surprising that normal forms do not always exist.

Example 5.7 The λ-term $(\lambda x.xx)(\lambda x.xx)$ does not have normal form. See an example reduction given below.

$$(\lambda x.xx)(\lambda x.xx) = xx[(\lambda x.xx)/x] \qquad (\beta\text{-reduction})$$
$$= (\lambda x.xx)(\lambda x.xx)$$
$$= xx[(\lambda x.xx)/x] \qquad (\beta\text{-reduction})$$
$$= (\lambda x.xx)(\lambda x.xx)$$
$$= \cdots$$

Combinators. A closed λ-term, i.e., one that does not have free variables, is also called a *combinator*—it represents "completely specified" functions. For example, the combinator I is the identity function defined as follows:

$$I ::= \lambda x.x.$$

It is easy to see that $Iy = y$. That is, I simply returns its argument.

The combinator S is defined as follows:

$$S:: = \lambda xyz.xz(yz).$$

The S combinator can be understood as a "substitute-and-apply" function—it first substitutes z into both x and y, then applies x to y. In other words, x is applied to y inside the environment z.

The K combinator is defined as follows:

$$K:: = \lambda xy.x.$$

If we apply K to a term M, which we assume does not contain x and y, we have the following via β-reduction:

$$(\lambda xy.x)M = \lambda y.x[M/x]$$
$$= \lambda y.M$$

which is a constant function whose value for any argument is M.

Theorem 5.4 *Every λ-term can be composed by S and K.*

By the Church–Turing thesis, the combinators S and K capture all effectively computable functions.

Turing showed the equivalence between Turing machines and λ-calculus.

Theorem 5.5 *A function is Turing-computable iff it is λ-computable.*

Thus, the three computational models we have discussed so far are equivalent to each other, and if the Church–Turing thesis is indeed true, they are equivalent to the class of effectively computable functions. The fact that *all attempts*[9] to define a formal model of "effectively computable" functions have turned out to be equivalent to each other is often considered a very strong argument to accept the Church–Turing thesis.

Since Turing's thesis is widely accepted, people often compare other equivalent computational models with Turing machines.

Definition 5.14 (*(Turing completeness)*) A computational model is *Turing-complete* if it can compute every Turing-computable function.

Obviously, partial recursive functions, λ-calculus, and the S-K combinators are Turing-complete. There are many other Turing-complete models. We give some examples as follows:

---

[9] Not just the above three computational models, but all the models for capturing "effectively computable" functions that people have developed since the 1930s, and many of them are of drastically different forms. See examples given below.

- unrestricted grammars;
- most modern programming languages such as C, Python, and OCaml;
- communicating sequential processes (CSP) used in PAT;
- hardware description languages such as VHDL;
- software such as Microsoft PowerPoint;
- games such as Minecraft and Minesweeper.

Turing machines versus p.r. functions versus λ-calculus. λ-calculus has a simple and elegant definition, so simple that many mathematicians in that era could not believe it captures all effectively computable functions. However, carrying out computation in λ-calculus is as cumbersome, if not more, as via Turing machines. Partial recursive functions are arguably the closest way to which one would define algorithms, and we have seen how easy it is to define basic arithmetic via primitive recursion. Turing machines are deemed as the "most intuitive" of the three, as one does not need much mathematics to understand how they operate.

We end this section with some comparisons on the three models from the creators themselves.

Gödel described Turing's formulation as "most satisfactory":

...the concept of mechanical by the sharp concept of 'performable by a Turing machine' is both correct and unique... Moreover it is absolutely impossible that anybody who understands the question and knows Turing's definition should decide for a different concept.

Church acknowledged the superiority of Turing machines:

Computability by a Turing machine ... has the advantage of making the identification with effectiveness in the ordinary (not explicitly defined) sense evident immediately.

Turing agreed that his analysis was "possibly more convincing" than Church's. Kleene compared the three computational models in an interview, and he reaffirmed the importance of Turing's thesis in support of the other computational models:

Turing's definition of computability was intrinsically plausible, whereas with the other two (partial recursive functions and lambda calculus), a person became convinced only after he investigated and found, much by surprise, how much could be done with the definition.

Exercises

5.7 Show that the exponential function m^n is primitive recursive.

5.8 Show that the *predecessor* function

$$pred(n) = \begin{cases} n - 1 & \text{if } n > 0, \\ 0 & \text{if } n = 0 \end{cases}$$

is primitive recursive.

5.9 Show that the *recursive difference* function

$$m \dot{-} n = \begin{cases} m - n & \text{if } m \geq n, \\ 0 & \text{otherwise} \end{cases}$$

is primitive recursive.

5.10 Show that the *absolute difference* function

$$|m - n| = \begin{cases} m - n & \text{if } m \geq n, \\ n - m & \text{otherwise} \end{cases}$$

is primitive recursive.

5.11 Find the normal form of $(\lambda f x. f(f x))(\lambda y. y)x$.

5.12 Find the normal form of $(\lambda f x. f(f x))(\lambda y. xy)$.

5.13 Let the multiplication function $\times$ over natural numbers be

$$\times :: = \lambda x y.(\lambda w u.((x(yw))u)).$$

Show the computation of 1×2 in λ-calculus.

5.14 Show the computation of $1 + 2 \times 2$ in λ-calculus.

5.15 At this point, the reader should have seen how to define and perform basic arithmetic operations such as addition and multiplication using Turing machines, partial recursive functions, and λ-calculus. Write a 100-word review for each of the three computational models.

5.3 Computability

As we have established convincing arguments that the Church–Turing thesis is very likely true via a detour to partial recursive functions and λ-calculus, we now return to Turing machines and study computability.

We talk of functions being computable and problems being decidable. These two forms of expression are equivalent to each other. A function is *totally computable* if it is recursive (cf. Definition 5.8). A function is *partially computable* if it is partial recursive, i.e., some input values may lead to undefined results.

A problem is *totally decidable*, or just *decidable*, if there is an automaton that can decide whether each string is in the corresponding language *or not*; otherwise, the problem is *undecidable*. An automaton for a decidable problem corresponds to an algorithm that is a *decision procedure*. A problem is *partially decidable* if we can only find an automaton that can answer "yes" to every string in the language but may

Table 5.1 A summary of jargons of computability

	(Informal) functions	(Formal) functions	Automata	Languages	Problems	Algorithms
Total	Totally computable	Recursive/ λ-terms with normal form	Turing machines that halt	Recursive	(Totally) decidable	Decision procedure
Partial	Partially/ effectively computable	Partial recursive/ λ-terms	Turing machines	Recursively enumerable	Partially/ semi-decidable	Semi-decision procedure

never halt for some strings not in the language. Clearly, some undecidable problems are partially decidable. An automaton for a partially decidable problem corresponds to an algorithm that is a *semi-decision procedure*. We summarise the above technical jargon and its equivalences in Table 5.1.

Limitations of Turing machines. We have discussed the limitations of finite automata and pushdown automata in their respective sections. Turing machines, too, have their limitations. That is, the bottom row of Table 5.1 are not the hardest problems; many problems are harder than semi-decidable, and no automaton nor algorithm can give any answer whatsoever. To demonstrate this, we need to describe a language that is not recursively enumerable, or in other words, is not accepted by any TM.

We begin by encoding TMs into binary numbers, assuming that the TMs in discussion only use the alphabet $\{0, 1\}$.[10] Then we focus on the problem "does a TM accept its own binary encoding as input?". If there is no TM that can solve this problem, then surely the more general problem, which allows arbitrary alphabet, is not recursively enumerable, either. In fact, there is always a way to encode a language over an arbitrary alphabet into a language over a binary alphabet, so we are not concerned with other alphabets in this section.

Given a TM $M = (\{0, 1\}, \Gamma, B, S, s_1, F, N)$, where F only has one final state,[11] we map it to a binary number as follows:

- The states in S are ordered as $s_1, s_2, \cdots$, where s_1 is the initial state and s_2 is the final state. Each state is mapped to an integer via $s_i \mapsto i$.
- The tape symbols in Γ are $X_1, X_2, X_3, \cdots$, where X_1 is 0, X_2 is 1, and X_3 is the blank symbol B. Each tape symbol is mapped to an integer via $X_i \mapsto i$.
- The tape head movement directions $\{L, R, -\}$ are mapped as follows: $L \mapsto 1$, $R \mapsto 2$, and $- \mapsto 3$.

---

[10] The process of encoding components of functions into natural numbers is called *Gödelisation*, which is a technique Gödel used to prove his incompleteness theorems.

[11] Recall in Sect. 5.1 that this assumption does not reduce computational power.

- A transition $N(s_i, X_j) = (s_k, X_l, D_m)$ is mapped to the binary string

$$0^i 10^j 10^k 10^l 10^m.$$

That is, 1s are separators, and 0s encode the information.
- Let $C_1, C_2, \cdots, C_n$ be the list of transitions (encoded in binary) of the TM M. We encode M as

$$C_1 11 C_2 11 \cdots 11 C_n.$$

Not every binary string corresponds to a valid TM. For example, every binary string that starts with 1 is an invalid encoding in the above scheme. Nonetheless, we can think of an invalid encoding as a TM that only has one state and no transitions, i.e., it rejects everything. This interpretation gives us a bijection between binary strings and TMs. As a result, we can now refer to the ith binary number w_i as the ith TM M_i. That is, $M_1 = w_1 = 1$, $M_2 = w_2 = 10$, $M_3 = w_3 = 11$, and so on. We denote the language of the ith TM as $L(M_i)$. Naturally, if i is not a valid encoding of TM, then $L(M_i) = \emptyset$.

Definition 5.15 (*The Diagonalisation Language*) The *diagonalisation language L_d* is the following set of strings:

$$L_d = \{w_i \mid w_i \notin L(M_i)\}.$$

Every string $w \in L_d$ represents a TM that does not accept its own encoding as input. We draw a table that represents whether M_i accepts w_i in Fig. 5.6, in which the binary numbers are filled randomly. The bottom row is for M_1, whereas the leftmost column is for the first binary string w_1. A 0 means that the string is rejected, whereas a 1 means that the string is accepted. For example, the bottom-left corner is 0, which means that M_1 rejects w_1. Also, M_2 rejects w_1, M_3 accepts w_2, etc. The ith row is called the *characteristic vector* for the language $L(M_i)$—each 1 in the vector corresponds a string in the language.

The language L_d contains exactly those strings that have a 0 in the diagonal line. In the example of Fig. 5.6, L_d contains $\{w_1, w_3, w_6, \cdots\}$. The operation of *diagonalisation* complements the digits in the diagonal line, and the result is exactly

Fig. 5.6 A table for the acceptance of M_i for the string w_i

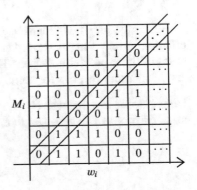

the characteristic vector of L_d, hence the name diagonalisation language. Since the characteristic vector of L_d disagrees with every row in the complemented digit, there does not exist any $L(M_i)$ that has the same characteristic vector as that of L_d, which means that L_d is not accepted by any TM. Let us formally prove this result as follows.

Theorem 5.6 *There exists no Turing machine that accepts L_d.*

Proof Proof by contradiction. Assume that there is a TM M that accepts L_d. Since L_d is over binary strings, M must be one of the TMs in our encoding scheme. Therefore, there must be a number i that corresponds to M, i.e., $M = M_i$. We do a case analysis of whether $w_i \in L_d$.

- If $w_i \in L_d$, then M_i accepts w_i. But L_d is defined as the set of strings *not* accepted by the encoded TM, so we have a contradiction.
- If $w_i \notin L_d$, then M_i does not accept w_i. By the definition of L_d, w_i must be in L_d, again we have a contradiction.

Since we derive contradictions either way, we conclude that the assumption must be wrong, and such a TM does not exist.   □

Corollary 5.1 *L_d is not recursively enumerable.*

There are *many* other non-recursively enumerable problems. We give an example in the logic given below.

Theorem 5.7 *Validity of second-order logic formulae is not recursively enumerable.*

Similarly, the validity problem (i.e., theorem proving) for any higher order logic (third-order, fourth-order, etc.) is not recursively enumerable. Consequently, we also have the following negative result:

Corollary 5.2 *There does not exist a sound and complete proof theory for second-order logic.*

Generally, for a non-recursively enumerable problem, no algorithm can give any effective answer whatsoever. Nevertheless, this does not stop us from solving special cases of those problems. Isabelle/HOL, for example, is based on higher order logic and has various theories for useful applications.

Undecidable but recursively enumerable problems. We now move to an easier class of problems/languages: those that are not recursive but are still within the recursively enumerable class. We call these problems *undecidable* problems.[12] These problems correspond to effectively computable functions that are not total and TMs or algorithms that can give partial answers. That is, given such a language L, there exists a TM M such that $L(M) = L$ and

- if $w \in L$, then M eventually halts and accepts w;
- if $w \notin L$, then M may never halt.

In the above case, the TM M still accepts the language L—it accepts every string in L and nothing else. The issue is that we cannot use such a TM to effectively test an arbitrary input string, as we may wait forever without getting an answer.

We shall study the above class with its subset *recursive languages*, which are those accepted by TMs that eventually halt. Such TMs correspond to total functions.

Definition 5.16 (*Recursive Languages*) A language L is *recursive* if there is a TM M such that $L(M) = L$ and

- if $w \in L$, then M eventually halts and accepts w;
- if $w \notin L$, then M eventually halts and rejects w.

Recursive languages are closed under complementation, which means that if a language L is recursive, then its complement $\overline{L}$ is also recursive, where $\overline{L}$ is defined as follows:

$$\overline{L} = \{w \mid w \notin L\}.$$

Lemma 5.7 *If L is a recursive language, so is $\overline{L}$.*

Proof Let M be a TM that accepts L and always halts. We construct a TM $\overline{M}$ for the language $\overline{L}$ as follows.

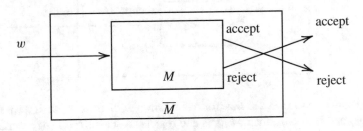

---

[12] Clearly, if a problem is not recursively enumerable, it is (even harder than) undecidable. But in this case, we will be explicit and call it non-recursively enumerable (non-RE). The literature often refers to non-recursive but recursively enumerable problems as undecidable/semi-decidable problems.

If M accepts a string, then $\overline{M}$ rejects it, and if M rejects a string, then $\overline{M}$ accepts it. More specifically, $\overline{T}$ is a modification of M defined as follows:

- Make the final state of M a non-final state with no transitions. Consequently, if M accepts a string, $\overline{M}$ halts in a non-final state and rejects the string.
- Create a new final state s_f which has no transitions.
- Modify the transition function N of M such that for each pair (s, X) of a non-final state s and a tape symbol X where $N(s, X)$ is undefined, add the following transition:

$$N(s, X) = (s_f, X, -).$$

As a result, whenever M halts and rejects a string, $\overline{M}$ moves to the final state s_f and accepts the string.

Therefore, $\overline{M}$ accepts the language $\overline{L}$.   □

Lemma 5.8 *If a language and its complement are both recursively enumerable, then they are both recursive.*

Proof Let L and $\overline{L}$ be the languages in the discussion. Since they are both recursively enumerable, there must exist two TMs M_1 and M_2 such that

- For any $w \in L$, M_1 halts and accepts w.
- For any $w' \in \overline{L}$, i.e., $w' \notin L$, M_2 halts and accepts w'.

We construct a TM M as follows:

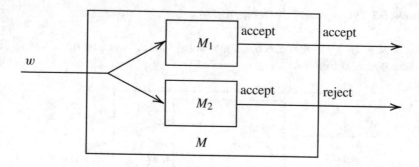

It is straightforward to see that for each string w, if $w \in L$, then M halts and accepts w, and if $w \notin L$, then M halts and rejects w. Therefore $L(M) = L$, and L is recursive. By Lemma 5.7, we can also construct a symmetric TM $\overline{M}$ that always halts and accepts $\overline{L}$. Therefore, both L and $\overline{L}$ are recursive.   □

We then obtain a corollary for the class of languages we are interested in.

Corollary 5.3 *If a language L is recursively enumerable but is not recursive, then $\overline{L}$ is not recursively enumerable.*

Equipped with the above results, we now introduce a recursively enumerable language that is not recursive. We use 111 to separate the encoding of a TM M, whose alphabet is $\{0, 1\}$, and a binary input string w. The pair (M, w) can be represented as the binary string

$$T111w.$$

Definition 5.17 (*The Universal Language*) The *universal language L_u* is defined as follows:
$$L_u = \{(M, w) \mid w \in L(M)\}.$$

Theorem 5.8 (Universal Turing Machine) *There exists a Turing machine U, called the* universal Turing machine, *such that $L(U) = L_u$.*

Proof (*Sketch*) We can construct a multitape TM and simulate the operations of a given TM M on an input w. For example, the first tape contains the input $M111w$; the second tape is exactly the tape of M; the third tape records the state of M, and we can have another tape for scratch. In modern terms, this multitape TM is a "virtual machine" that simulates other TMs. Since multitape TMs have the same computational power as TMs (cf. Lemma 5.1), we obtain that a (single-tape) universal Turing machine U must also exist.   □

Corollary 5.4 *L_u is recursively enumerable.*

Theorem 5.9 *L_u is not recursive.*

Proof Proof by contradiction. Assume that L_u is recursive, then by Lemma 5.7, its complement $\overline{L_u}$ is also recursive. It follows that there is a TM $\overline{U}$ that accepts $\overline{L_u}$ and always halts. Note that the language $\overline{L_u}$ consists of strings of the form $M111w$ such that w is rejected by M. We then construct a TM D as follows:

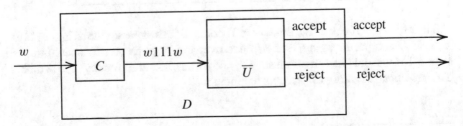

The TM D has two components: the first sub-TM C preprocesses the input w and yields $w111w$. Clearly, such a TM is plausible. The second sub-TM, the hypothetical $\overline{U}$, checks whether a TM encoded as w, here denoted as M_w, accepts its own code as input. $\overline{U}$ outputs "accept" if w is rejected by M_w, and outputs "reject" if w is accepted by M_w. Our TM D directly takes $\overline{U}$'s output.

As a result, the TM D accepts exactly the language L_d, which we know is impossible by Theorem 5.6, so we have a contradiction. We conclude that L_u is not recursive.
                                                                                                          □

Let us consider another famous undecidable problem: *the halting problem*.[13]

Definition 5.18 (*The Halting Problem*) Given a Turing machine M and an input w, does M halt on w?

The halting problem is analogous to the problem "does my code loop forever?", which a programmer may face quite often.

Theorem 5.10 *The halting problem is undecidable.*

Proof Proof by contradiction. Assume that the halting problem is decidable, which means that there is a TM, here called H, such that for any TM encoding M and any input w:

- if M halts on w, then H halts and accepts $M111w$;
- if M does not halt on w, then H halts and rejects $M111w$.

We construct another TM P as follows:

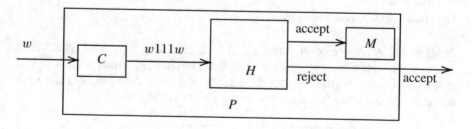

The TM C preprocesses the input as in Theorem 5.9, then passes the string $w111w$ to H. If H accepts the string, then M takes over and loops forever. We can think of M as a TM that only has an initial state s_0 and a transition to s_0 for any tape symbol. If H rejects $w111w$, then P accepts the input w.

---

[13] Theorem 5.5 indicates that the halting problem of TMs corresponds to the question "does a λ-term have normal form?".

We now do a case analysis of whether P halts on its own encoded string P as input, i.e., what happens if $w = P$?

- If P halts on P, then H accepts $P111P$, then M loops forever, therefore P does not halt on P.
- If P does not halt on P, then H rejects $P111P$, then P accepts P as input, therefore P halts on P.

Either way, we obtain a contradiction. We conclude that the halting problem must be undecidable.   □

Consequently, mathematics cannot effectively capture the class of automata that accept recursive languages (i.e., TMs that halt).

On the other hand, we can construct a TM M', much like the universal TM, such that given any pair (M, w), if M halts on w, then M' accepts w. Clearly, M' accepts the language of the halting problem, although it may not halt on some input. Hence, the halting problem is recursively enumerable.[14]

There are *many* undecidable problems. We give some examples below. Note that these problems are still recursively enumerable. In particular, we have discussed a semi-decision procedure for the validity problem of first-order logic on Page 67.

Theorem 5.11 *Validity of first-order logic formulae is undecidable.*

Theorem 5.12 *Whether a λ-term has normal form is undecidable.*

Theorem 5.13 *Determining the ambiguity of CFGs is undecidable.*

The above list is non-exhaustive, as indicated by *Rice's theorem* [7]. We denote *a set of* recursively enumerable languages as a *property*. A property is *trivial* if it is either the empty set $\emptyset$ or is the set of *all* recursively enumerable languages; otherwise, it is *non-trivial*.

Theorem 5.14 (Rice's Theorem) *Every non-trivial property of recursively enumerable languages is undecidable.*

Example 5.8 For example, the set of context-free languages is a non-empty proper subset of all recursively enumerable languages—it is non-empty because we have seen numerous examples of context-free languages in Sect. 4.3, and it is a proper subset of all recursively enumerable languages because we have seen languages that

---

[14] It is called "recursively enumerable" because we can go through the input in the order of natural numbers and *enumerate* each input that is in the language. But given an arbitrary input, we may not be able to give an answer.

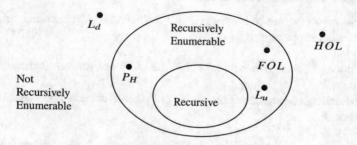

Fig. 5.7 A summary of the languages/problems discussed in this section

are RE but not context-free (e.g., the universal language L_u). On the other hand, every context-free language is clearly recursively enumerable. Therefore, context-free is a non-trivial property of recursively enumerable languages, and according to Rice's theorem, determining whether a language is context-free is undecidable.

We illustrate the important languages and problems discussed in this section in Fig. 5.7, where P_H stands for the halting problem, FOL is first-order logic, and HOL is higher order logic.

Exercises

5.16 Let L_e be the language

$$L_e = \{M \mid L(M) = \emptyset\}.$$

And L_{ne} be the language

$$L_{ne} = \{M \mid L(M) \neq \emptyset\}.$$

1. Prove that L_{ne} is recursively enumerable.
2. Prove that L_{ne} is not recursive.
3. Prove that L_e is not recursively enumerable.

5.17 Construct a TM for the proof of Rice's theorem.

5.18 Prove that whether a language is regular is undecidable.

5.19 Prove that the satisfiability of first-order logic formulae is undecidable.

Hint: you can use the lemmas and theorems in this book when proving the above problems.

5.4 Complexity

This section zooms in Fig. 5.7 and focuses on the recursive "ring", i.e., decidable problems. Since these problems are solvable, we are mainly concerned with the question "can we solve them efficiently?"

Time complexity. Recall in Definition 5.4 that we say a TM has time complexity $T(n)$ if when given an input of length n, the TM halts after *at most* $T(n)$ transitions regardless of whether it accepts the input or not.

Definition 5.19 (*The $\mathcal{P}$ Class*) A problem is in class $\mathcal{P}$ if there is a TM with a *polynomial* time complexity that solves the problem.

Example 5.9 (*Linear Search*) Given an array a, search for a symbol s in a is a $\mathcal{P}$ problem. We can initialise the array as the input of a TM, and check each symbol in the array until we find s. Obviously, the TM needs to move at most n transitions for this search task, thus $T(n) = n$, which is a polynomial.

Big-O notation. We often use big-O notation to describe the time complexity of an algorithm.

Definition 5.20 (*Big-O Notation*) Let f be a function over real or complex numbers and g be a function over real numbers.

$$f(x) = O(g(x))$$

if there exists a positive real number c and a real number x_0 such that

$$|f(x)| \leq c \cdot g(x) \text{ for all } x \geq x_0.$$

Example 5.10 Big-O notation describes the upper bound of the growth rate of functions. In Example 5.9, $T(n) \leq 1 \cdot g(n)$ where $g(n) = n$. Therefore, the time complexity is $O(n)$.

We list some common time complexities in big-O notation in Table 5.2 in ascending order with respect to the hardness. That is, constant time is the easiest and double exponential time is the hardest in the table. Of course, there are harder decidable problems that are not shown in the table. In Table 5.2, n is a variable for the size of the input, and c is a constant.

In big-O notation, all the sub-classes that are easier than or equal to polynomial time belong to the class $\mathcal{P}$. However, exponential time, factorial time, etc., are not in $\mathcal{P}$. We say a problem/algorithm is *tractable* or feasible if it is in $\mathcal{P}$, which means that there is an *efficient* algorithm that solves the problem; otherwise, the problem/algorithm is *intractable* or infeasible. Note that there may be multiple algorithms for solving a problem, and the time complexity of those algorithms may vary. We usually define the hardness of a problem as the hardness of the most efficient algorithm that solves the problem.

Table 5.2 Examples of time complexities in big-O notation

Notation	Name	Example
$O(1)$	Constant	Popping on stack
$O(log\ n)$	Logarithmic	Binary search
$O(n)$	Linear	Linear search
$O(n\ log\ n)$	Linearithmic	Merge sort
$O(n^2)$	Quadratic	Bubble sort
$O(n^3)$	Cubic	Naïve matrix multiplication
$O(n^c)$	Polynomial	Linear programming
$O(c^n)$	Exponential	Solving the TSP via dynamic programming
$O(n!)$	Factorial	Solving the TSP via brute force
$O(2^{2^n})$	Double Exponential	Truth in Presburger arithmetic

Nondeterministic polynomial time. There is an interesting case between polynomial time and beyond. We define it as the class $\mathcal{NP}$ as follows.

Definition 5.21 (*The $\mathcal{NP}$ Class*) A problem is in the class $\mathcal{NP}$ if there is a *nondeterministic* TM with a polynomial time complexity that solves the problem.

Lemma 5.9 $\mathcal{P} \subseteq \mathcal{NP}$.

The proof for the above lemma is trivial because every deterministic TM is a nondeterministic TM. The other direction ($\mathcal{NP} \subseteq \mathcal{P}$), however, is one of the deepest open problems of mathematics and computer science, as it (in conjunction with Lemma 5.9) implies $\mathcal{P} = \mathcal{NP}$.[15]

Polynomial-time reduction. We often compare two problems using *reduction* techniques. In the context of $\mathcal{NP}$ problems, we are interested in polynomial-time reductions.

Definition 5.22 (*Polynomial-time Reduction.*) Given two problems p_1 and p_2, a *polynomial-time reduction* is an algorithm that converts every instance of p_1 into an instance of p_2 in time that is some polynomial in the length of the p_1 instance.

The above definition also implies that the converted p_2 instance will be of a length that is polynomial in the length of the p_1 instance. Essentially, if we can find a polynomial reduction from p_1 to p_2, then p_1 is "not harder than" p_2, or "p_2 is at least as hard as p_1", because an algorithm for p_2 can be used to solve p_1 as well.

A problem is *NP-hard* if it is at least as hard as any other problem in $\mathcal{NP}$.

---

[15] $\mathcal{P}$ versus $\mathcal{NP}$ has a million-dollar prize funded by the Clay Mathematics Institute.

Definition 5.23 (*NP-Hardness*) A problem p is *NP-hard* if for every problem $p' \in \mathcal{NP}$, there exists a polynomial-time reduction from p' to p.

A problem is *NP-complete* if it is in $\mathcal{NP}$ and is NP-hard.

Definition 5.24 (*NP-completeness*) A problem p is *NP-complete* if

- $p \in \mathcal{NP}$, and
- p is NP-hard.

Example 5.11 The halting problem is NP-hard but not NP-complete because it is not in $\mathcal{NP}$—it is much harder than $\mathcal{NP}$-complete problems. Linear search is not NP-complete because it is not NP-hard.

Instead of finding a reduction for every problem in $\mathcal{NP}$, we can build up the set of NP-complete problems using known NP-complete problems, as described in the lemma given below.

Lemma 5.10 *If p_1 is NP-complete, and $p_2 \in \mathcal{NP}$, and there is a polynomial-time reduction from p_1 to p_2, then p_2 is NP-complete.*

Since all NP-complete problems are as hard as any problem in $\mathcal{NP}$, we have the following result:

Lemma 5.11 *If any NP-complete problem is in $\mathcal{P}$, then $\mathcal{P} = \mathcal{NP}$.*

Unfortunately, all efforts for finding polynomial-time algorithms for any of the thousands of NP-complete problems known so far have been unsuccessful; this has led many people to lean towards $\mathcal{P} \neq \mathcal{NP}$.[16]

Nowadays, a standard technique for proving that a problem is NP-complete is by using Lemma 5.10. However, before we can do so, we need to introduce at least one NP-complete problem first. Hence, it is worth mentioning *Cook's theorem* [8], which bootstraps the theory of NP-completeness.

---

[16] Some may ask, can quantum computers solve NP-complete problems efficiently? If we go with our definition of "solving a problem efficiently" means solving it in polynomial time, then to the best of our knowledge, the answer is no. For example, with Grover's search algorithm, a quantum computer can provide a worse-case quadratic speed-up than the best-known classical algorithm. However, $O(\sqrt{c^n})$ is still exponential time. Confusions arise when the integer factorisation problem is involved. Shor's algorithm, the best-known quantum algorithm for this problem, does run in polynomial time, and there is no known efficient classical algorithm for this problem. However, integer factorisation is *not known* to be NP-complete, although it is in $\mathcal{NP}$.

Theorem 5.15 (Cook's Theorem) *Satisfiability (SAT) of propositional logic formulae is NP-complete.*

Unlike other NP-completeness proofs, the proof of Cook's theorem follows Definition 5.24. That is, it first shows that SAT is in $\mathcal{NP}$, then it shows that absolutely every problem in $\mathcal{NP}$ can be reduced to SAT. The general idea is to construct a nondeterministic TM M for an arbitrary problem in $\mathcal{NP}$. For each input w to M, build a propositional logic formula F which expresses the following:

- M is initialised correctly,
- the next transition of M is performed correctly,
- M halts in a final state correctly.

As a result, M accepts w iff F is satisfiable. Interested readers can see a detailed treatment in Hopcroft et al.'s book [5].

In fact, satisfiability of a restricted form of propositional logic formulae is also NP-complete. We say a formula is a *literal* if it is either an atomic formula p or a negated atomic formula $\neg p$. A *clause* is the disjunction of a set of literals. A formula is in *conjunctive normal form* (CNF) if it is the conjunction of a set of clauses.

Example 5.12 The following are examples of clauses:

- p,
- $p \vee q$,
- $p \vee q \vee \neg r$.

The following are examples of CNF formulae:

- $(p \vee q) \wedge (q \vee \neg r)$,
- $(p \vee \neg q) \wedge (q \vee q) \wedge (\neg q \vee r)$.

We say a formula is in k-CNF if every clause has exactly k distinct literals. For example, the CNF formulae in the above example are both in 2-CNF.

Theorem 5.16 *Satisfiability of propositional logic formulae in CNF (CSAT) is NP-complete.*

Generally, any propositional logic formula can be converted to an equivalent formula in CNF using the laws given below.

- De Morgan's laws:

    - $\neg(A \wedge B) \rightarrow \neg A \vee \neg B$,
    - $\neg(A \vee B) \rightarrow \neg A \wedge \neg B$.

- Double negation elimination: $\neg(\neg A) \rightarrow A$.
- Distributive law: $A \vee (B \wedge C) \rightarrow (A \vee B) \wedge (A \vee C)$.

However, the distributive law may result in a CNF formula that is exponentially longer than the original formula, which is not permitted in a polynomial-time reduction. Instead, the proof Theorem 5.16 reduces SAT to CSAT via a polynomial-time formula transformation that only preserves satisfiability but not logical equivalence.

Assuming the above results, let us see a reduction proof in full.

Theorem 5.17 *Satisfiability of propositional logic formulae in 3-CNF (3SAT) is NP-complete.*

Proof As the first part of the proof, we show that 3SAT is in $\mathcal{NP}$. This part is trivial because SAT is in $\mathcal{NP}$, and 3SAT is a special case of SAT, so 3SAT must also be in $\mathcal{NP}$. From an algorithmic point of view, we can construct a nondeterministic TM and nondeterministically guess the values of all propositional variables and then evaluate the formula. We can think of this process as assigning all possible combinations of values to propositional variables in parallel, and if any branch of the computation returns true for the formula, then we accept the input. Clearly, this computation can be carried out in nondeterministic polynomial time, as each "parallel branch" of the computation only scans through the formula once.

In the second part of the proof, we show that 3SAT is NP-hard by giving a polynomial-time reduction from CSAT to 3SAT. Given an arbitrary CNF formula $F = c_1 \wedge c_2 \wedge \cdots \wedge c_k$ where each c_i ($1 \leq i \leq k$) is a clause, we give a polynomial-time algorithm below, which transforms F into a 3-CNF formula F' such that F is satisfiable iff F' is satisfiable. The algorithm transforms each clause c_i according to the following four cases:

1. If c_i is a single literal, say x (which may be a negated proposition), we create two new propositional variables p and q and replace c_i with the following sub-formula:

$$(x \vee p \vee q) \wedge (x \vee p \vee \neg q) \wedge (x \vee \neg p \vee q) \wedge (x \vee \neg p \vee \neg q).$$

   Since p and q appear in all combinations of positive and negative literals, the only way to satisfy the above sub-formula is to satisfy x.

2. If c_i has two literals x and y, i.e., $c_i = x \vee y$, we introduce a new propositional variable p and replace c_i with the following sub-formula:

$$(x \vee y \vee p) \wedge (x \vee y \vee \neg p).$$

   Similarly, since p appears in all combinations, the only way to satisfy the above sub-formula is to satisfy $x \vee y$.

3. If c_i has three literals, we keep it as it is.

4. If c_i has at least four literals, i.e., $c_i = x_1 \vee x_2 \vee \cdots \vee x_m$ where $m \geq 4$, we introduce $m - 3$ new propositional variables $p_1, p_2, \cdots, p_{m-3}$ and replace c_i

with c_i' as follows:

$$c_i' = (x_1 \lor x_2 \lor p_1) \land (x_3 \lor \neg p_1 \lor p_2) \land (x_4 \lor \neg p_2 \lor p_3) \land \cdots$$
$$\land (x_{m-2} \lor \neg p_{m-4} \lor p_{m-3}) \land (x_{m-1} \lor x_m \lor \neg p_{m-3}).$$

If there is a truth assignment v that satisfies c_i, then at least one of $x_1, \cdots, x_m$ is true. Assume that x_j, where $4 \le j \le m-3$, is true, which is shown in the following sub-formula relevant to x_j:

$$\cdots (x_{j-1} \lor \neg p_{j-3} \lor p_{j-2}) \land (x_j \lor \neg p_{j-2} \lor p_{j-1}) \land (x_{j+1} \lor \neg p_{j-1} \lor p_j) \cdots$$

We extend v to make $p_1, \cdots, p_{j-2}$ true and make $p_{j-1}, \cdots, p_{m-3}$ false, then the extended truth assignment satisfies c_i'. The corner cases of x_1, x_2, x_3, x_{m-2}, x_{m-1}, and x_m also hold. We leave them to the reader to check.

If v makes c_i false (by making each of $x_1, \cdots, x_m$ false), then it is not possible to extend v to satisfy c_i'. We can follow a chain of reasoning to see why it is the case. Since x_1 and x_2 are false, p_1 must be true to keep c_i' "alive". But then x_3 is false and $\neg p_1$ is also false, so p_2 must be true. Similarly, x_4 and $\neg p_2$ is false, so p_3 must be true, and so on. In the end, we reach that p_{m-3} must be true. But x_{m-1} and x_m are false, and $\neg p_{m-3}$ is also false, so the last clause is false after all, and thus c_i' must be false. Therefore, c_i is satisfiable iff c_i' is satisfiable.

The above formula transformation converts a CNF formula of size n to a 3-CNF formula of size at most $(32/3) \times n$, which implies that the transformation can be done in polynomial time. Furthermore, the transformed formula is satisfiable iff the original formula is satisfiable. Since CSAT is NP-complete, it follows that 3SAT is also NP-complete.   □

Karp followed Cook's theorem and further proved the NP-completeness for 21 problems in his landmark paper "Reducibility among combinatorial problems" [9]. Cook and Karp received a Turing Award for their fundamental contributions to the theory of complexity. We show a partial map of common NP-complete problems in Fig. 5.8. The arrows indicate the direction of reduction. The abbreviations are explained as follows:

   IS: independent set.
  NC: node cover.
3DM: 3-dimensional matching.
   IP: integer programming.
DHC: directed Hamilton circuit.
  HC: (undirected) Hamilton circuit.
 TSP: travelling salesman problem.

Note that there are many ways to choose from which problem to reduce, so the flow of Fig. 5.8 is not unique.

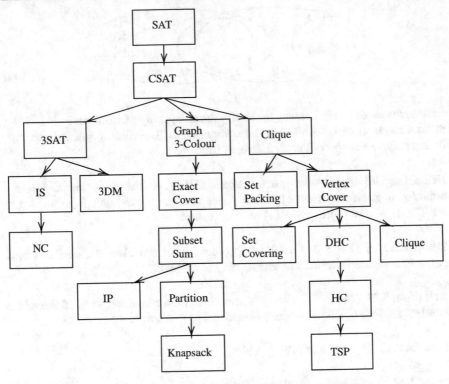

Fig. 5.8 Reductions among some common NP-complete problems

Co-$\mathcal{P}$ and Co-$\mathcal{NP}$ The class $\mathcal{P}$ is closed under complement, as stated in the lemma given below.

Lemma 5.12 *If a language L is in $\mathcal{P}$, then its complement $\overline{L}$ is also in $\mathcal{P}$.*

We define the class Co-$\mathcal{P}$ as the set of languages whose complements are in $\mathcal{P}$. By the above lemma, Co-$\mathcal{P} = \mathcal{P}$. Similarly, the class Co-$\mathcal{NP}$ is the set of languages whose complements are in $\mathcal{NP}$. However, it is *not known* whether Co-$\mathcal{NP} = \mathcal{NP}$. Interestingly, it has not been proved for any NP-complete problem that its complement is in $\mathcal{NP}$, which strongly indicates that Co-$\mathcal{NP} \neq \mathcal{NP}$. To summarise, we have two cases:

- If $\mathcal{P} = \mathcal{NP}$, then $\mathcal{P} = \mathcal{NP} = $ Co-$\mathcal{P} = $ Co-$\mathcal{NP}$ and NP-complete = Co-NP-complete.
- If $\mathcal{P} \neq \mathcal{NP}$, then we suspect that the relationship between the above classes is *very likely* the following:

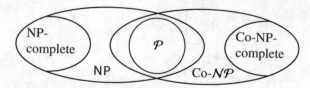

Space complexity. Another way to classify the complexity of problems is by looking at how much space is required in the computation. To formalise this concept, we define polynomial-space-bounded TMs as follows.

Definition 5.25 (*Polynomial-space-bounded TMs*) A TM is *polynomial-space-bounded* if given any input of size n, there is some polynomial $P(n)$ such that the TM never uses more than $P(n)$ cells of its tape.

Definition 5.26 (*The $\mathcal{PS}$ Class*) A problem is in the class $\mathcal{PS}$ if there is a polynomial-space-bounded TM that solves the problem.

Definition 5.27 (*The $\mathcal{NPS}$ Class*) A problem is in the class $\mathcal{NPS}$ if there is a *nondeterministic* polynomial-space-bounded TM that solves the problem.

Lemma 5.13 $\mathcal{P} \subseteq \mathcal{PS}$ *and* $\mathcal{NP} \subseteq \mathcal{NPS}$.

Proof The proof is trivial: if a TM makes n transitions, then it can use at most $n + 1$ cells. If a TM only makes a polynomial number of transitions, then it can only use a polynomial number of cells.   □

The following theorem, however, requires a non-trivial proof and is due to Savitch in 1970 [10].

Theorem 5.18 (Savitch's Theorem) $\mathcal{PS} = \mathcal{NPS}$.

Since the above theorem holds, the literature often unifies $\mathcal{PS}$ and $\mathcal{NPS}$ and refers to both as *PSPACE*.

Definition 5.28 (*PSPACE-completeness*) A problem p is PSPACE-complete if

- p is in PSPACE, and
- every problem in PSPACE is polynomial-time reducible to p.

Example 5.13 Let us look at an extension of propositional logic with quantifiers (but not quite first-order logic), called *quantified Boolean formula* (QBF). The syntax of QBF is defined as follows:

- any propositional logic formula is a QBF;
- if F is a QBF that *does not include a quantification over* x, then $\forall x.F$ and $\exists x.F$ are QBFs.

Moreover, the literature often refers to *fully* quantified Boolean formulae as QBF. That is, each propositional variable is quantified exactly once. A QBF in this form is usually written in *prenex normal form*, which puts quantifications before the remainder of the formula, as follows:

$$Q_1 x_1 Q_2 x_2 \cdots Q_n x_n . \phi(x_1, x_2, \cdots, x_n)$$

where $Q_1, \cdots Q_2$ are quantifiers (i.e., either $\forall$ or $\exists$) and ϕ is a propositional formula over $x_1, \cdots, x_n$.

The semantics for quantifications is as follows:

- $\forall x.F$ is true iff all Boolean values (i.e., $\top$ or $\bot$) of x make F true.
- $\exists x.F$ is true iff there exists a Boolean value of x that makes F true.

Definition 5.29 (*The QBF Problem*) Given a QBF with no free variables, is it true?

We state the following theorem as an example of a PSPACE-complete problem without proof.

Theorem 5.19 *The QBF problem is PSPACE-complete.*

We summarise the important concepts of this chapter in Fig. 5.9. If $\mathcal{P} = \mathcal{NP}$, then the dashed lines collapse (i.e., $\mathcal{P} = \mathcal{NP} = \text{Co-}\mathcal{NP} = \text{PSPACE}$) and the dotted lines collapse (i.e., NPC = Co-NPC, where NPC means NP-complete). As with most figures that illustrate the solar system (which often draw the planets next to each other), Fig. 5.9 may seem deceptive as the recursive "ring" in reality is *much* bigger than PSPACE, and there are many other classes in between, such as EXPTIME and EXPSPACE, which are not covered in this chapter. Similarly, the recursively enumerable ring is *much* bigger than the recursive ring (cf. Theorem 5.14). Finally, the set of non-RE problems is *much* larger than the set of problems in RE.

Exercises

5.20 Prove Lemma 5.10.

5.21 The 1-IN-3SAT problem is defined as follows:

> Given a set of clauses $\{c_1, \cdots, c_m\}$ where $m \geq 1$ and each c_i is a disjunction of *exactly three* literals. Is there a truth assignment that makes exactly one literal true in each clause?

Prove that 1-IN-3SAT is NP-complete.

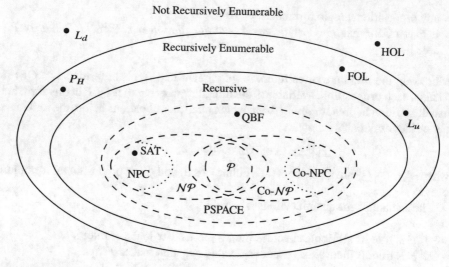

Fig. 5.9 Important concepts of Chap. 5

5.22 The MAX 2SAT problem is defined as follows:

Given a set of clauses $\{c_1, \cdots, c_m\}$ where $m \geq 1$ and each c_i is a disjunction of *at most two* literals. Let k be an integer such that $1 \leq k \leq m$. Is there a truth assignment that satisfies k or more clauses?

Prove that MAX 2SAT is NP-complete.

5.23 The travelling salesman problem (TSP) is defined as follows:

Given an undirected graph G with integer weights on the edges, and an integer k. Is there a cycle that passes through each node of G exactly once such that the sum of the weights on the edges is less than or equal to k?

Prove that TSP is NP-complete.

Hint: You can assume that the Hamilton circuit (HC) problem is NP-complete and reduce it to TSP. HC is defined as follows:

Given an undirected graph G, is there a cycle that passes through each node of G exactly once?

5.24 Prove Lemma 5.12.

5.25 Prove the following lemmas:

1. If a PSPACE-complete problem is in $\mathcal{P}$, then $\mathcal{P} = $ PSPACE.
2. If a PSPACE-complete problem is in $\mathcal{NP}$, then $\mathcal{NP} = $ PSPACE.

References

1. Cooper S (2003) Computability theory. Taylor & Francis. ISBN: 9781584882374
2. Wadler P (2015) Propositions as types. Commun ACM 58, 75–84. ISBN: 0001-0782
3. Turing AM (1937) On computable numbers, with an application to the Entscheidungsproblem. Proc Lond Math Soc s2-42, 230–265. ISBN: 0024-6115
4. Von Neumann J (1982) The origins of digital computers: selected papers. Randell B (ed). Springer Berlin Heidelberg, Berlin, Heidelberg, pp 383–392. ISBN: 978-3-642-61812-3
5. Hopcroft J, Motwani R, Ullman J (2007) Introduction to automata theory, languages, and computation. Pearson/AddisonWesley. ISBN: 9780321455369
6. Turing AM (1939) Systems of logic based on ordinals. Proc Lond Math Soc s2-45, 161–228
7. Rice HG (1953) Classes of recursively enumerable sets and their decision problems. Trans Amer Math Soc 74:358–366
8. Cook SA (1971) The complexity of theorem-proving procedures in proceedings of the third annual acm symposium on theory of computing. Association for Computing Machinery, Shaker Heights, Ohio, USA. pp 151–158. ISBN: 9781450374644
9. Karp RM (1972) Reducibility, among combinatorial problems in proceedings of a symposium on the complexity of computer computations, held March 20–22, 1972, at the IBM Thomas J. Watson research center, Yorktown Heights, New York, USA. Miller RE, Thatcher JW (eds). Plenum Press, New York, pp 85–103
10. Savitch WJ (1970) Relationships between nondeterministic and deterministic tape complexities. J Comput Syst Sci 4, 177–192. ISBN: 0022-0000

Part III
Logic and Computation

Logic Is Computation

6

Powerful insights arise from linking two fields of study previously thought separate. Examples include Descartes's coordinates, which links geometry to algebra, Planck's Quantum Theory, which links particles to waves, and Shannon's Information Theory, which links thermodynamics to communication. Such a synthesis is offered by the principle of Propositions as Types, which links logic to computation.

—Philip Wadler [1]

We have seen many correspondences previously: Turing machines correspond to λ-calculus, which corresponds to partial recursive functions; pushdown automata correspond to context-free languages; regular expressions correspond to finite automata; sequent calculus for FOL correspond to natural deduction for the same logic, and so on. This chapter concludes the book with a discussion on the Curry-Howard Correspondence. For those who have been wondering why we put logic and computation in one book, the short answer is—logic *is* computation and vice versa.

To see this correspondence, we have gone through various logics and their proof theories, the purpose of which is to determine the truth of logical formulae. On another path, we have studied the theory of computation, which aims at capturing computable functions of various difficulties. The reader should have seen that logic and reasoning play an important role in the theory of computation. Many proof techniques in Part I, such as proof by induction, contradiction, and contraposition, are essential in understanding Part II. Moreover, logical problems, such as SAT solving, are central in complexity theory. We now unify the notion of logic and computation and provide a concrete example of how one is mapped to the other.

© The Author(s), under exclusive license to Springer Nature Switzerland AG 2021
Z. Hou, *Fundamentals of Logic and Computation*, Texts in Computer Science,
https://doi.org/10.1007/978-3-030-87882-5_6

6.1   The Curry-Howard Correspondence

In 1934, Curry observed a correspondence between logic and computation, which is closely related to the intuitionistic interpretation (cf. Sect. 3.1) developed by Brouwer, Heyting, and Kolmogorov. The correspondence is refined by Howard in 1969 and published in 1980. As an overview, the Curry-Howard Correspondence establishes isomorphisms (cf. Sect. 3.2) of different depths:

- propositions as types;
- proofs as programs;
- simplification of proofs as evaluation of programs.

The foundation of Howard's observation, under the intuitionistic reading, is as follows:

- Conjunction $A \wedge B$ corresponds to product type $A \times B$. In programming languages, this type is often implemented as a pair or a record with two fields. A proof of $A \wedge B$ requires a proof of A *and* a proof of B. A value of type $A \times B$ consists of a value of type A and a value of type B.
- Disjunction $A \vee B$ corresponds to sum type $A + B$, which is also called tagged union or variant in some programming languages. A proof of $A \vee B$ requires a proof of A *or* a proof of B. A value of type $A + B$ is either a value of type A or a value of type B.
- Implication $A \rightarrow B$ corresponds to function type $A \rightarrow B$. A proof of $A \rightarrow B$ is essentially a procedure that transforms a proof of A to a proof of B. A value of type $A \rightarrow B$ is a function that takes a value of type A as input and returns a value of type B as output.

The above notions naturally extend to other formulae and types. For example

- $\top$ corresponds to the unit type, which only allows one value. For example, in Python it is written as `NoneType`; in C++(17) it is `std::monostate`; in Swift it is `Void`; in Haskell it is `()`.
- $\bot$ corresponds to the bottom type, which has no value. For example, in Python it is `typing.NoReturn`; in Common Lisp it is `NIL`; in Haskell it is `Empty`.

To illustrate concrete examples of the correspondence, let us first backtrack to Church's work on λ-calculus. An untold story of Sect. 5.2 is that Church initially developed λ-calculus for encoding logical formulae. However, this attempt failed because self-application of λ-terms (e.g., Example 5.7) leads to inconsistency analogous to Russell's paradox[1] and the halting problem. This failure is unavoidable:

---

[1] Let $R = \{x \mid x \notin x\}$, then $R \in R$ if $R \notin R$.

if a computational model is powerful enough to be Turing complete, then it cannot solve its own halting problem.

To resolve this issue, Church proposed another system called *simply-typed λ-calculus*, which forbids self-applications and consequently yields a consistent logical formulation through the fact that every term in simply-typed λ-calculus has normal form. The halting problem for this restricted system is trivial: every program halts. Let us see the formal definition of this system given below.

Let B be a set of *base types*, which can be understood as basic built-in types such as integers and Booleans in a programming language.

Definition 6.1 (*Types*) The syntax of types is defined as follows, where $T \in B$

$$\tau ::= T \mid \tau \to \tau.$$

The clause $\tau \to \tau$ is called a *type constructor*, i.e., it constructs a (function) type. Note that the function type associates to the right, that is, $\tau_1 \to \tau_2 \to \tau_3$ should be read as $\tau_1 \to (\tau_2 \to \tau_3)$. The subtlety of right associativity of the function type is that if f is a function of type $\tau_1 \to \tau_2 \to \tau_3$ and x is a term of type τ_1, then the application fx, which corresponds to only providing partial arguments to f, results in a *function* of type $\tau_2 \to \tau_3$. This way of thinking prevails in functional programming.

Definition 6.2 (*Syntax of Simply-typed λ-calculus*) The syntax of simply-typed λ-terms is given as follows:

$$E ::= x \mid \lambda x : \tau.E \mid EE \mid c,$$

where $x : \tau$ means that the variable x is of type τ, and c is a term constant.

The above syntax only associates types to variables. In general, λ-terms are related to types via *typing rules*. A typed λ-term has the form

$$E : \tau$$

where E is a λ-term and τ is its type. A *typing environment*, written as Γ, is a set of *typing assumptions* of the form $x : \tau$ where x is a variable and τ is a type. Simply-typed λ-calculus has four typing rules as shown below

Definition 6.3 (*Typing Rules of Simply-typed λ-calculus*)

$$\frac{x : \tau \in \Gamma}{\Gamma \vdash x : \tau} \; var \qquad\qquad \frac{c \text{ is a constant of type } T}{\Gamma \vdash c : T} \; cons$$

$$\frac{\Gamma, x : \sigma \vdash E : \tau}{\Gamma \vdash (\lambda x : \sigma.E) : (\sigma \to \tau)} \; abs \qquad \frac{\Gamma \vdash E_1 : \sigma \to \tau \qquad \Gamma \vdash E_2 : \sigma}{\Gamma \vdash E_1 E_2 : \tau} \; app$$

We explain the typing rules as follows:

- The rule *var* gives the type of the variable x from the environment Γ.
- The rule *cons* says that term constants have appropriate base types.
- The rule *abs* deduces the type for abstractions. If the typing environment has $x : \sigma$, and the function body E has type τ, then the function $\lambda x : \sigma.E$ has type $\sigma \to \tau$.
- The rule *app* gives the type for function application. If E_1 is a function of type $\sigma \to \tau$ and E_2 has type σ, i.e., it is of the input type of E_1. Then the application of $E_1 E_2$ results in the return type τ.

Reduction rules in simply-typed λ-calculus is the same as those in untyped λ-calculus (cf. Definition 5.10), subject to additional type restrictions.

Definition 6.4 (*Reduction Rules of Simply-typed λ-calculus*)

α-reduction:　$\lambda x : \tau.E = \lambda y.E[y/x]$ if y is not free in E and $\Gamma \vdash y : \tau$.

β-reduction:　$(\lambda x : \sigma.E_1)E_2 = E_1[E_2/x]$ if the free variables in E_2 have no bound occurrences in E_1. Also, $\Gamma, x : \sigma \vdash E_1 : \tau$ and $\Gamma \vdash E_2 : \sigma$ for some τ.

η-reduction:　$(\lambda x : \sigma.E)x = E$ if x is not free in E and $\Gamma \vdash E : \sigma \to \tau$ for some τ.

Lemma 6.1 *Every term in simply-typed λ-calculus has normal form.*

Lemma 6.2 *Simply-typed λ-calculus is not Turing-complete.*

Definition 6.5 The *type inhabitation problem* is defined as follows: given a type τ and a typing environment Γ, is there a λ-term E such that $\Gamma \vdash E : \tau$?

In a type inhabitation problem, if the environment Γ is empty, i.e., $\vdash E : \tau$ holds, then E is an *inhabitant* of τ, and τ is an *inhabited type*. Think the analogy with $\vdash F$ in theorem proving.

We now have the basic ingredients to present an example of the Curry-Howard Correspondence that relates the natural deduction system NJ for intuitionistic logic (cf. Sect. 3.2) to simply-typed λ-calculus. Howard observed the following correspondences for these two systems:

NJ/Logic	Simply-typed λ-calculus/Program
Axiom	Variable
Introduction rule	Constructor
Elimination rule	Destructor
Normal reduction	Normal form
Normalisation	Normalisation
Provability	Type inhabitation problem
Theorem	Inhabited type

An axiom in a proof is a variable in a program. Every introduction rule in natural deduction constructs a term of a given type, and every elimination rule destructs a term of a given type. A proof in normal deduction (cf. Definition 1.14) is a λ-term in normal form. The normalisation of proofs is thus mapped to the normalisation of terms. A logical formula is provable if a type has an inhabitant, and a theorem corresponds to an inhabited type.

Example 6.1 In this example (given by Walder [1]), we shall focus on a function over pairs. The relevant natural deduction rules are given as follows:

$$
\begin{array}{cc}
\begin{array}{c}
[a : A] \\
\vdots \\
\dfrac{B}{A \to B} \to I, \text{discharge } a
\end{array}
&
\dfrac{A \to B \quad A}{B} \to E
\end{array}
$$

$$
\dfrac{A \quad B}{A \wedge B} \wedge I
\qquad
\dfrac{A \wedge B}{A} \wedge E_l
\qquad
\dfrac{A \wedge B}{B} \wedge E_r
$$

We extend the simply-typed λ-calculus with product types, which is a derived construction from the original syntax. The typing rules in Definition 6.3 are presented in a sequent calculus style. We transform the relevant rules into natural deduction style for comparison and show them below, where we use A and B to denote types and E to denote a λ-term.

$$
\begin{array}{cc}
\begin{array}{c}
[x : A] \\
\vdots \\
\dfrac{E : B}{(\lambda x : A.E) : A \to B} \to I, \text{discharge } x
\end{array}
&
\dfrac{E_1 : A \to B \quad E_2 : A}{E_1 E_2 : B} \to E
\end{array}
$$

$$
\dfrac{E_1 : A \quad E_2 : B}{(E_1, E_2) : A \times B} \times I
\qquad
\dfrac{E : A \times B}{\pi_l E : A} \times E_l
\qquad
\dfrac{E : A \times B}{\pi_r E : B} \times E_r
$$

The term $\pi_l E$ selects the left (first) element of the pair E, and the term $\pi_r E$ selects the right (second) element of the pair E.

Let us consider the following proof in NJ:

$$
\dfrac{\dfrac{[a : B \wedge A]}{A} \wedge E_r \quad \dfrac{[a : B \wedge A]}{B} \wedge E_l}{\dfrac{A \wedge B}{(B \wedge A) \to (A \wedge B)} \to I, \text{discharge } a} \wedge I
$$

The above proof is quite trivial—it simply shows the commutativity of conjunction. More interestingly, it corresponds to the following program in simply-typed λ-calculus:

$$\cfrac{\cfrac{[x : B \times A]}{\pi_r x : A} \times E_r \quad \cfrac{[x : B \times A]}{\pi_l x : B} \times E_l}{\cfrac{(\pi_r x, \pi_l x) : A \times B}{(\lambda x : (B \times A).(\pi_r x, \pi_l x)) : (B \times A) \to (A \times B)} \to I, \text{discharge } x} \times I$$

The above program is of type $(B \times A) \to (A \times B)$; it is indeed a program that swaps the elements of a pair. We can write the above program in a more familiar format (C++) to the programmers given below.

```cpp
std::par<A,B> swap(std::pair<B,A> x) = {
    A x1 = std{:}{:}get<1>(x);
    B x0 = std{:}{:}get<0>(x);
    std::pair<A,B> y(x1,x0);
    return y;
}
```

But the Curry-Howard Correspondence goes deeper still. Let us look at how we can simplify/normalise proofs with $\wedge$ and $\to$. If a proof introduces $\wedge$ and then eliminates it, we can simplify the proof as below. The case for $\wedge E_r$ is symmetric.

$$\cfrac{\cfrac{\vdots \qquad \vdots}{\cfrac{A \qquad B}{A \wedge B} \wedge I}}{A} \wedge E_l \qquad \rightsquigarrow \qquad \begin{array}{c} \vdots \\ A \end{array}$$

If a proof introduces $\to$ and then eliminates it, we simplify the proof as follows:

$$\cfrac{\cfrac{[a : A]}{\vdots}}{\cfrac{\cfrac{B}{A \to B} \to I, \text{discharge } a \qquad \begin{array}{c} \vdots \\ A \end{array}}{B}} \to E \qquad \rightsquigarrow \qquad \begin{array}{c} \vdots \\ A \\ \vdots \\ B \end{array}$$

Now let us consider a (partial) proof below, which has some redundant steps.

$$\cfrac{\cfrac{\cfrac{[a : B \wedge A]}{A} \wedge E_r \quad \cfrac{[a : B \wedge A]}{B} \wedge E_l}{\cfrac{A \wedge B}{(B \wedge A) \to (A \wedge B)} \to I, \text{discharge } a} \wedge I \qquad \cfrac{B \qquad A}{B \wedge A} \wedge I}{A \wedge B} \to E$$

According to the simplification scheme for $\to$, we should remove the grey part of the proof and reconstruct a proof for $A \wedge B$ as follows:

$$\cfrac{\cfrac{\cfrac{A \qquad B}{A \wedge B} \wedge I}{A} \wedge E_l \quad \cfrac{\cfrac{B \qquad A}{B \wedge A} \wedge I}{B} \wedge E_l}{A \wedge B} \wedge I$$

Again, we can simplify the grey part using the scheme for $\wedge$, and finally obtain the following proof:

$$\frac{A \qquad B}{A \wedge B} \, {\scriptstyle \wedge I}$$

On the other hand, below is a reduction scheme for λ-programs with unnecessary $\times$ constructor and destructor.

$$\frac{\dfrac{E_1 : A \qquad E_2 : B}{(E_1, E_2) : A \times B} \, {\scriptstyle \times I}}{\pi_l(E_1, E_2) : A} \, {\scriptstyle \times E_l} \qquad \rightsquigarrow \qquad E_1 : A$$

The reader can see the strong analogy with the simplification of proofs with $\wedge$. Similarly, the reduction for function type $\rightarrow$ is similar to simplification for implication. We give the reduction scheme below. These reduction schemes correspond to the β-reduction rule and η-reduction rule of simply-typed λ-calculus. We write "dis" for "discharge" to save space.

$$\frac{\dfrac{\begin{array}{c}[x : A]\\ \vdots \\ E_1 : B\end{array}}{(\lambda x : A.E_1) : A \rightarrow B} \, {\scriptstyle \rightarrow I, \text{dis } x} \qquad \begin{array}{c} \vdots \\ E_2 : A \end{array}}{((\lambda x : A.E_1)E_2) : B} \, {\scriptstyle \rightarrow E} \qquad \rightsquigarrow \qquad \begin{array}{c} \vdots \\ E_2 : A \\ \vdots \\ E_1[E_2/x] : B \end{array}$$

Below we construct a (partial) program in simply-typed λ-calculus that corresponds to the original (partial) proof with redundant steps.

$$\frac{\dfrac{\dfrac{[z : B \times A]}{\pi_r z : A} {\scriptstyle \times E_r} \qquad \dfrac{[z : B \times A]}{\pi_l z : B} {\scriptstyle \times E_l}}{(\pi_r z, \pi_l z) : A \times B} {\scriptstyle \times I}}{(\lambda z : (B \times A).(\pi_r z, \pi_l z)) : (B \times A) \rightarrow (A \times B)} {\scriptstyle \rightarrow I, \text{dis } a} \qquad \dfrac{y : B \qquad x : A}{(y, x) : B \times A} {\scriptstyle \times I}}{(\lambda z : (B \times A).(\pi_r z, \pi_l z))(y, x) : A \times B} {\scriptstyle \rightarrow E}$$

The grey part can be reduced by β-reduction, which corresponds to the evaluation of a function application. Alternatively, the above program can be written in C++ as follows:

```
1  std::par<A,B> swap(std::pair<B,A> z) = {
2      A z1 = std::get<1>(z);
3      B z0 = std::get<0>(z);
4      std::pair<A,B> z3(z1,z0);
5      return z3;
6  }
7  B y;
8  A x;
9  std::pair<B,A> z4(y,x);
10 swap(z4);
```

We apply the reduction scheme for function type $\rightarrow$ and reconstruct an intermediate program as follows:

$$\frac{\dfrac{\dfrac{x:A \qquad y:B}{(x,y):A \times B}\times I}{\pi_l(x,y):A}\times E_l \qquad \dfrac{\dfrac{y:B \qquad x:A}{(y,x):B \times A}\times I}{\pi_l(y,x):B}\times E_l}{(\pi_l(x,y),\pi_l(y,x)):A \times B}\times I$$

Finally, we apply the reduction scheme for $\times$ and obtain the following:

$$\frac{x:A \qquad y:B}{(x,y):A \times B}\times I$$

The above program can be written as a pair (x,y) of the C++ type `std::pair <A,B>`, which is the expected outcome of the evaluation of the program.

Other correspondences. The Curry-Howard Correspondence is much more than the above example—it applies to many logics and many computational models. For example, the S-K combinator system (cf. Sect. 5.2), which is Turing complete, corresponds to the following axioms of intuitionistic logic:

$K: A \rightarrow (B \rightarrow A),$
$S: (A \rightarrow (B \rightarrow C)) \rightarrow ((A \rightarrow B) \rightarrow (A \rightarrow C)).$

A non-exhaustive list follows: quantifiers in first-order logic correspond to *dependent types*. The existential quantifier in second-order logic corresponds to *data abstraction*, which inspires the design of *generic types* in Java and C#. Peirce's Law (cf. Sect. 3.1) in classical logic corresponds to a type for the *call-with-current-continuation* (call/cc) scheme. Double negation embedding of classical logic into intuitionistic logic, due to Kolmogorov and Gödel, corresponds to *continuation-passing style*. Cut-elimination (cf. Sect. 2.4) corresponds to reduction in a form of abstract machine, and priority to right-hand side cut-elimination is *call-by-name* reduction, whereas priority to left-hand side corresponds to *call-by-value* reduction.

Computational interpretations in temporal logics include *partial evaluation* and *reactive programming*. Linear logic relates to *session types*.

The Curry-Howard Correspondence remains an active research area.

Reference

1. Wadler P (2015) Propositions as types. Commun ACM 58, 75–84. ISSN: 0001-0782

Index

Printed in the United States
by Baker & Taylor Publisher Services